# RELATE
# STARTING AGAIN

By the same author

*Working Mother*
*Better Relationships*
*Sex In Loving Relationships*

# relate

# STARTING AGAIN

How to learn from the past for a better future

# SARAH LITVINOFF

**Vermilion**
LONDON

*With love and thanks and great respect to my parents,*
*Cherry Marshall ad Emanuel Litvinoff, who showed by their own example*
*that divorce can be managed with the minimum of pain for the children.*

11 13 15 17 16 14 12 10

First published in 1993 by Vermilion, an imprint of Ebury Publishing
This revised edition published in 2001 by Vermilion

Ebury Publishing is a Random House Group company

Copyright text © Sarah Litvinoff and Relate 1993

Sarah Litvinoff and Relate have asserted their right to be identified
as the authors of this Work in accordance with the Copyright,
Designs and Patents Act 1988.

Address ... ...e found at

A CIP ... ...n Library

The R... ...rdship
Council ... ...nisation.
All our t... ...ed paper
carry... ...paper procurement policy can be found at
www.rbooks.co.uk/environment

Printed and bound in Great Britain by
CPI Cox & Wyman, Reading, RG1 8EX.

ISBN 9780091856670

Copies are available at special rates for bulk orders. Contact the sales
development team on 020 7840 8487 or visit www.booksforpromotions.co.uk
or more information.

To buy books by your favourite authors and register for offers, visit
www.rbooks.co.uk

# CONTENTS

# ACKNOWLEDGEMENTS

Grateful thanks to Ann Leck, the Chair of RELATE, and a counsellor and sex therapist herself. She read and commented on the book while it was being written and was helpful, wise and encouraging throughout. Zelda West-Meads, RELATE's Press Officer, was, as always, a constant support, offering valuable advice and encouragement.

The following counsellors helped by talking about their experiences with many clients: Rosemary Ackroyd, Julian Barnard, Liz Bircham, Irene Bridge, Sara Clarke, John Fisher, Penny Haigh, Jennifer Halmshaw, Rachel Harrison, Sue Henderson, Jean Hollis, Barbara Lippitt, Mel Mackay, Cindy Mann, Eileen Miller, Mary Miller, Julia Pedley, Jenna Plewes, Vivienne Serpell, Eleanor Somerset, Felicity Stretton, Adriana Summers, Margaret Ward, Sue Willock. The experience of many other counsellors and sex therapists have also contributed to the book, through the interviews they gave for *The RELATE Guide to Better Relationships* and *The RELATE Guide to Sex in Loving Relationships*. Thanks also to Peter McCabe, the Director of Fundraising for RELATE.

# CASE HISTORIES

All the case histories in this book are based on real people. However, all names and distinguishing details have been changed so that the couples are unrecognisable.

# INTRODUCTION

No one falls in love thinking that the relationship will end. Yet relatively few people find that their first love is their last. This simple truth conceals much pain. When a relationship breaks down – be it a love affair that lasts a few months, or a marriage that has survived many years – unhappiness is mixed with the turbulent emotions of anger, self-doubt, jealousy and the grief that accompanies any major loss.

Yet through it all there is the urge to start again – to get it right, do it better next time – to find a love that lasts. Some people have a series of major relationships, perhaps marrying the new love each time. In some of these cases each relationship is a learning experience and finally they attain what they have been seeking – a happy and harmonious partnership. But it is just as common to find that that the problems that crippled the first relationship recur. The failure rate for second marriages, for instance, is higher than for first – and they usually break down more quickly.

There are many reasons for this. A typical one is that time and again the partner you choose, superficially so different from partners in the past, turns out, underneath, to have many of the same characteristics that made the relationships so difficult for you before. With hindsight it is a possible to see a repeating pattern in all your relationships; and if you look further back it is possible to see that the very same pattern was operating in the first relationship you experienced – the one between your parents.

But it is not just that you continue to choose the 'wrong' partner. A relationship is steered by two people, and if your relationships continue to follow a destructive pattern, it is also because of the way *you* behave. One of the purposes of this book is to help you become aware of the patterns you are unconsciously repeating, and to recognise your own contribution to what is happening. Counsellors have found that when people are aware of these issues, they finally are able to change – developing new, healthy relationships with a better chance of success.

This is not the only way the book can help. Some second or subsequent relationships are doomed because of timing. In your haste to turn misery into happiness you might jump too quickly into a new relationship. But a relationship that starts before the old one is properly laid to rest has the odds stacked against it. Unfinished business with your ex-partner gets in the way. If you are still emotionally connected to a past relationship – even if those emotions are ones of anger, hatred or revenge – you have less emotional energy for the positive feelings of love and joy. When your thoughts are still engaged by what once was, you can't give the appropriate attention to future happiness. This book helps you deal with getting over a relationship that has finished, and also helps you discover whether you are yet ready for another serious relationship.

There is one particularly good reason for waiting. While you are on the rebound, you are only partially 'you'. When you are still hurting, or still missing the togetherness of a relationship, you make decisions out of need and fear. This is a poor start. The relationships with the best chance are those formed by two people who are happy and confident in themselves. When you choose to be together because you want to be – not because you *need* someone – you start with a good and healthy attitude. If you can make yourself happy, you have the ability to make someone else happy. If you know that you can manage independently, you can approach any of the normal problems that arise in a relationship positively, rather than fearfully.

This is why the central section of the book concentrates on you alone. Whether your relationship broke down, or was ended by the death of your partner, the issues are the same. The aim is to help you build your confidence, become complete in yourself, and 'whole'. Then forming a new relationship becomes a matter of choice. Some people who build self-esteem successfully find that they do not have an urgent need to find another partner. Others, although they might want to meet a new love, feel that they have it within themselves to lead a fulfilling and rewarding life, even if they do not find another partner. Paradoxically, the better you feel about yourself, and the less you feel you need someone to 'complete' you, the more you are likely to find that others are attracted to you.

The book also deals with the other issues that can arise in subsequent relationships. The chief of these is dealing with children – your own children after the break-up of a marriage, step-children in future relationships, and any children you and your next partner have between you. All of this needs to be handled with sensitivity and maturity. In a society where more and more relationships are breaking down, there is a complex web of relationships in the new family networks that result. You might be dealing with more than one set of in-laws, many grandparents and the issue of divided loyalites. None of these is impossible to handle, but they create difficulties which need to be faced.

If you are going to start again successfully, you need more than love and romance to see you through. Your experiences to date can give you the skills you need to tackle all these issues with strength and delicacy, if you allow them. For great emotional pain can increase your compassion and your wisdom. Learning from what went wrong in the past, accepting your own responsibility, developing your inner resources – these are things that increase your capacity to create happiness and help you negotiate your way through any of the problems that you might meet.

## Part One

# THE END OF A RELATIONSHIP

# 1

# DO YOU REALLY WANT TO BREAK UP?

Sometimes you have no choice in the ending of a relationship. Your partner leaves you, or dies, and you have to struggle to come to terms with what has happened. But in many cases the ending is more drawn out. It can take years of uncertainty, a see-saw time during which sometimes you feel that everything will be all right, followed by times of despair. Although it is usually one of you who takes the initiative to leave the relationship, in most cases both of you have suffered the disappointments and misery of living in a partnership that is not working.

This chapter is for people who are thinking of ending a relationship, but who haven't done so yet. It might be the right thing to do – but it might not. Surveys of people who have gone on to marry more than once show that many of them wish that they were still with their original partners, and some of these were the people who made the decision to leave. How can this be – when they must have been very unhappy to have left their partners in the first place?

The main reason is that many people have an unrealistic idea of what to expect in a relationship. They believe that love will create happiness and banish problems. But however much you love someone, you will still meet difficulties in your life together. The relationship will change, and both of you will change too, which means that at times there will be difficulties as you adjust to each other. As the romantic stage passes, your feelings towards each other, and your sexual feelings, also change – not necessarily becoming bad, but different. Even without this, the mere fact of building a life together – perhaps having children, dealing with outside problems, such as money difficulties, bereavements, work issues, and many other matters – creates stress. In a healthy relationship these difficulties are negotiated and dealt with, so that the relationship becomes stronger and more rewarding. Love changes, but in these cases it deepens.

If you believe, however, that you should always be happy in a relationship, then when problems arise you are likely to feel that something is badly wrong between you. Some people leave a relationship when the first major problem arises – sometimes for someone else. Others continue in the relationship, but allow each problem to drive them further apart, rather than tackling it in a way that brings them closer. Years later something happens that is the final straw, and then they leave. A new relationship, they believe, will succeed where the other failed – to bring problem-free happiness.

Of course, it doesn't. After a honeymoon period problems arise in the new relationship, too – as they always will, in any relationship. Sometimes this is what leads people to reassess the first relationship. They can see that the problems that caused them to part were not so dramatically terrible, that they had ignored what was good in the relationship because of temporary unhappiness or misunderstanding. The recognition that no relationship guarantees perfect, unblemished happiness is often discovered the hard way – by a series of relationships, each of which becomes unhappy in its own way, if lessons have not been learnt.

But there is another reason why some people regret ending an early, major relationship, especially one that continued for many years. Sometimes they under-estimate the unhappiness that will result from breaking up a shared home – the distress of their children, the disruption of friends and family, and, often, the reduced financial circumstances of both partners. The long-term misery this can create is sometimes more painful than the original problems between the couple – more difficult to resolve, perhaps, than it would have been to try to tackle the problems in the first place. Certainly, where children are involved, the problems – and the responsibilities – are magnified. Breaking up without children is more straightforward. It is easier to accommodate the needs of two people, far harder to do so when more are involved.

For instance, Penny walked out on her husband, Roger, after twenty-two years of marriage. They had two adult children who were still living at home. The marriage had been bad for a long time. Roger put Penny down, and Penny, who had been put down all her life, let him. She felt drained by the marriage, and drained by the demands of her adult children, who still expected her to wait on them hand and foot. Three years previously she had taken a part-time job – against Roger's wishes. There she had met another man, who treated her much better than Roger had ever done. One day she just left Roger and moved in with him.

Penny had tried for years to make Roger and her children happy at the expense of her own happiness. She hoped that her gesture would would make them realise what they were missing – and that from her children, at least, she would get sympathy and support.

Instead, they all turned against her. Roger said the stress had made him ill, and the children took his side. Penny tried to show her children that she was still their mother and still loved them, but they didn't want to know.

One problem was that although Penny was now free of the daily pressures that had made her feel so tired and unappreciated, and had a man who treated her kindly, she felt that she had given up more than she gained. She told her counsellor that if she could turn the clock back, she would. She now lived in a small flat and her future was uncertain. She said she felt as if she were living in an unreal nightmare, having left behind a dream – the life she once had – nice house, lovely children and stability.

What could Penny have done differently? The counsellor says, 'In many ways she tried *too* hard. She never asserted herself as a person. She took on all the responsibility in the home, and didn't try to make them help, or respect herself enough to make sure she got the appreciation she deserved. She tried and tried in her marriage till her heart broke.'

It is not the purpose of this book to suggest that couples who are better off apart should stay together. It is also true that the difficulties of splitting up can be handled in such a way as to minimise distress for all concerned. In Penny's case, she hurt her children and set them against her by fleeing straight into the arms of another man.

Where a relationship still exists, however, it is worth taking time to see if matters can be put right between you, rather than making a hasty decision to part. Penny's husband Roger was, in fact, a stern and autocratic man. He joined the counselling for a few sessions, but he was unable and unwilling to look at his contribution to the breakdown of the marriage. There is no way of knowing whether he would have changed if Penny had asserted herself early enough – but she didn't try. Waiting until she could take no more was no solution. She felt she had lost all that she had worked for, and because of her misery the relationship with the new man started to go wrong, too.

## Why problems are ignored

It is ignoring problems, rather than dealing with them, that causes the trouble. People ignore problems for many reasons. One is that they hope the problems will go away of their own accord. Some people believe that talking about a problem gives it reality, whereas pretending it doesn't exist might make it vanish. Another reason is that they are frightened of dealing with problems or talking about them, in case it makes everything worse. You might feel that you would be burning your boats if you admit to being unhappy or angry – that your partner might admit to similar feelings, which means you would not be able to trundle along pretending that everything is all right. Problems also arise when one of you is unhappy for some reason, and the other just doesn't want to know or become involved.

Some people are made very angry by problems – and they show their anger by cutting themselves off emotionally from their partners, rather than trying to find a solution. Other people apparently face problems – in the sense that they have rows and express open hostility. But in this case they are only dealing with the emotions raised by the problems, not trying to find a solution to the underlying causes.

People also avoid talking to their partners about issues that are disturbing them in their relationships for fear of confrontation or of hurting each other. If you have children you might feel it is better not to admit to problems or face the possibility of parting because of what it might do to them. Although the motives might be good, the result is damaging to the relationship. The feelings remain, even if the words are unspoken, and sometimes an atmosphere of resentment builds up that can't be tackled directly because the reasons for it are not understood. If you don't talk about things that are important to you, closeness goes. As in Penny's case, sometimes the unhappy feelings, left to fester for years, increase to a point where one of you can't take it any more, and 'suddenly' leaves. As far as children are concerned it is debatable which is worse – to live with the parents' hostility or to cope with the parents' divorce. Better by far, for the children's sake, is to deal with the problems.

## DEALING WITH PROBLEMS

The best way to stop problems undermining your relationship is to deal with them as they arise. This does not mean that you have to make a drama out of every incident, but it does mean recognising when irritation, sadness, fear or anger is becoming a feature of your relationship. The cause might be an outside problem – to do with money difficulties or problems at work or with your children. It might be more intimate – to do with the way you and your partner are getting on, or with your sexual relationship. It could also be changes in yourself, to do with wanting and needing different things in life, or coming to terms with a family bereavement, or ill-health or ageing.

In a healthy relationship, where problems and issues such as these are dealt with in the course of everyday life, it is usually the case that the couple routinely talk to each other. They don't let weeks go by without a proper conversation. At least once or twice a week they spend time talking about whatever is important to them – the good things as well as the bad. Nothing is pent up for long, and both partners feel able to say what they think and feel. When one of them is upset or angry the other offers support, knowing that support will be there when he or she needs it in the future.

It is sometimes only with hindsight that people can see how different their relationship was from this. Stuart saw a counsellor after his wife, Dee, left him. They had been married for fifteen years and had two teenage children. Stuart, a thirty-five-year-old businessman, was devastated.

During counselling Stuart recognised that although there had apparently been a lot of 'talk' in their marriage, it all came from him. He liked being the knowledgeable and articulate one, and he had needed Dee to be the listener. He had been in charge of the relationship and had 'looked after' Dee, whom he saw as another child. When the counsellor asked him how Dee had felt at various points in the marriage, he realised that he could only guess – he had never encouraged her to talk about her feelings. He literally had no idea why she had left him.

Then Stuart remembered that two years previously Dee's mother had died. She had been very depressed and had seen a bereavement counsellor. Stuart had been relieved, at the time, that 'someone else was taking care of the problem'. They had scarcely talked about what Dee was going through. He began to see that this was the point at which their relationship had changed. Dee had become more distant, had found a job, starting seeing friends without him. He understood that at the very time she really needed 'looking after', he had ignored her. She had had to find resources in herself, grow up – and eventually grow out of the relationship. If he had offered support at that time she would still have matured and changed – but the balance of their relationship might have changed too, becoming more equal, a marriage between two adults. The chance to make a better relationship, with a renewed but different closeness had gone. He had continued to treat her in the old way, and she had resented it and felt the need to get away.

It was not all Stuart's fault, of course. Dee reacted by turning away from him emotionally, rather than using her new confidence to demonstrate how different she was, or to try to get through to him, so that the relationship could change for the better.

Again, this example shows the lost opportunity when problems are ignored. It might well have been difficult and painful for Stuart and Dee to have confronted Dee's misery and grief, and to have made changes in their relationship, but other couples have done so – and have gone on to be happier because of it. That option was no longer open to them.

It is unlikely that you will be reading this book if the problems between you are trivial. If you are thinking of ending your relationship and starting again you are likely to be struggling with feelings of great anger, sadness and disappointment. But while you are still together you have everything to gain from looking at the problems and seeing if you can resolve them. At best, you might be able to come up with solutions that change your relationship for the better. Even if you can't, and you do decide to part, you will still have a better understanding of why you can no longer live together. You will also have taken an important step – recognising that problems can and should be talked about. In the future you are likely to take this step earlier – before the problems become entrenched.

RELATE know that dealing with these matters on your own is hard. Sometimes counselling can help when your good intentions fail. Talking about emotional issues with a trained third-party present is often the best way to deal with them effectively. Certainly, counsellors see many couples with relationships that have deteriorated almost to the point of no return, who, with help, are able to rebuild good feelings and decide they want to stay together.

Clare and Howard sought help when their marriage was in ruins. They had met and married when Clare was sixteen and Howard was twenty-five. She had been a pretty, bubbly girl with the flirtatious mannerisms of a child. In contrast, Howard had felt very sophisticated and mature. He had come from a strict family, and he was now strict with Clare. When she talked to him, she would lapse into a baby voice and girlish ways, despite the fact that she was now in her late twenties and had two children of her own. Howard behaved like her father at all times: 'Because I say so!' was one of his favourite phrases.

Despite this, Clare had a lot of spirit. Their marriage had gone through rocky patches from the very beginning. When things were bad, Clare would throw Howard out. Although it might seem strange, Howard would always go. It was repeating the pattern from his childhood, when his mother would blow up at his father and his father would leave. When things were very bad between his parents, Howard would be sent to stay with his grandparents. He had no experience of staying around when things were difficult.

They were in counselling for five months. They originally came because they had separated once again. This time Clare had left – because she felt even more desperate about their marriage than on the occasions when she had thrown Howard out. But she had no money of her own and felt she had no choice but to return. She had suggested counselling as a last resort.

Clare was back, but they were still rowing all the time. Howard thought Clare was incompetent. She thought everything was his fault. She ran him down constantly (just as his mother had run his father down – and just as *her* mother had run *her* father down). But Howard managed to feel superior because he still thought of Clare as a little girl, albeit a disagreeable one.

After a number of stormy sessions they were beginning to come to terms with each other. Clare, who had previously just 'known' she was unhappy without giving thought to what would improve matters for her, now started to examine what she really wanted. She decided to train in computer skills, to ready herself to find a good job in the future. Her little-girl ways were inappropriate in this context, and for the first time she saw an advantage in behaving with maturity. Her self-esteem increased and at last she started to grow up.

This set them back. Whereas before Clare had attacked Howard's behaviour, now she wondered whether she liked him at all. Howard could not cope with Clare wanting to be anything other than a little girl. Their relationship seemed to be at its lowest point.

The counselling sessions mirrored the pattern of the marriage. Sometimes they saw the counsellor together. Then one of them would become angry, say it was useless, and stop coming. He or she would eventually rejoin counselling for a while – then the other would become angry and storm off.

But at least they never stopped seeing the counsellor completely. Gradually the rows died down and they started to sort things out between them. It took a lot of adjustment. Howard had to learn about the new Clare, and relate to her as a woman. He had to come down from his 'pedestal of superiority', and discover a side of himself that was more emotional and less controlling. Clare had to learn to stop repeating her mother's pattern of running men down – a defence that hid feelings of inferiority. She had to lose the habit of complaining at Howard, and use her new maturity to see him as a person who could also be hurt – and someone worthy of tact and respect – not as a bad 'daddy' but as a partner.

The counsellor says, 'At the end of counselling they were very aware of all these issues and the difference in them was absolutely astounding. They were a man and woman sharing and working *together*. They learned to discuss. They managed to share feelings, which is something Howard had never done before. Neither of them had previously thought that men *had* feelings, and neither had thought that women had any real worth. All that had changed.'

The process had its ups and downs, and was tempestuous and painful. But a marriage that had seemed to stand no chance was now better than it had ever been.

This story shows the three ingredients necessary for a relationship to emerge *improved* from a crisis: the willingness to understand yourself; the willingness to listen to your partner; and the willingness to make necessary changes. Because these are so important, we will look at them in more detail.

● **The willingness to understand yourself.** Many people are aware of feelings of anger and misery, but don't examine what it is in themselves that makes them react so. Understanding your needs as a person is important to discover what would make you feel good about yourself – and about your life and your relationship. It can show you why something has gone wrong.

This understanding also confers a responsibility – it shows that you have to make changes to bring about the possibility of happiness. When aspects of your relationship are making you unhappy you need to look at your own contribution to the pattern you have fallen into. If you are always rowing, for instance, how do your reactions and behaviour make this possible? If your partner ignores or belittles you, have you ever demonstrated your own value – or really felt it yourself? If your partner is unsupportive, have you only asked for support in a way that creates friction? Or have you never even asked – expecting your partner to know instinctively what you need?

Knowing how to ask and, indeed, recognising that it is necessary to ask, is an important issue. If your partner regularly disappoints you in any area (to do with sex, bringing up children, handling finances, discussing issues, sharing housework, having fun together – or anything else), how do you ask? Do you state your feelings angrily, sulkily, demandingly – or never mention them, expecting them to be understood?

The point of this process of self-examination is not to assume all responsibility for what has gone wrong, but to recognise where any partial responsibility lies. A relationship is the interaction between two people and there is never a saint and sinner – even if one carries more of the burden of guilt. Indeed, saintliness is not a healthy contribution to a relationship. 'Saints' either deny their own needs, so are not happy (therefore their relationships aren't happy), or they are 'holier than thou', too rigorously concerned with doing the right thing to allow for human error and feelings in themselves or their partners.

It is just as important to look at your own feelings and needs when you are quite clear in your mind that your partner is at fault. This might be the case if your partner is violent towards you or your children, or sexually abuses the children, or perhaps is in the grip of an addiction – to drink, drugs or gambling. In this category you might place a partner's affair. Sometimes, if you are honest, you can see that you have had a part to play. For instance, you knew about the violence or the addiction before. Or, if your partner has an affair, in retrospect you can see that there were difficulties in your relationship before it started, or signs of restlessness or unhappiness in your partner.

Exploring your feelings, deciding what you need, and working out in what way you have contributed to your own unhappiness is not easy. It is also painful. Emotionally it seems more satisfying to blame someone else. But self-examination is a necessary process – not just because it might help you sort out what has gone wrong in your relationship, but also because it can help you find happiness in the future, even if this relationship ends. The following tasks can help.

**!**
—————————————— *Task* ——————————————

## What went wrong?

Make a list of what makes you unhappy. Be specific: not 'I hate my partner', but which aspects make you feel like this. There might be one major issue, or many. If there is more than one, transfer each to a separate sheet of paper. Then make a series of headings:

● **When did it start?** Pinpoint when you noticed it making you unhappy, even if it was present from the beginning.

● **Was there ever a good side to this?** Sometimes an issue wasn't always disturbing. See if you remember it having the reverse effect, and why. For instance, a woman whose husband was sexually demanding remembered when it made her feel desired. A man whose wife was indecisive and fearful remembered it making him feel tender and loving.

● **Were there signs that this could happen?** Sometimes you remember signs you once ignored. For instance, a woman whose husband got into debt remembered justifying times when he spent unwisely. A man whose wife was obsessively jealous remembered early episodes he had discounted.

● **Have attempts to improve matters failed?** Have you tried to tackle the problem? What did you do? What was the outcome of your efforts? Why do you think they didn't work?

● **How I contributed.** This is hard – but think honestly about whether any of your actions have made it worse.

**!**

This task can give you a clearer picture of the progress of unhappiness in your relationship than if you just concentrate on the here and now. It can help you see in what way, if any, you have made the problem worse – either by ignoring it, or by actively contributing by behaviour of your own. It is important for you to know these things, because it helps in understanding. It is also useful for when you talk to your partner about the issue. A better understanding means you are less likely to attack or blame.

The next task is about what you feel and what you want.

---

**!** ═══════════════ *Task* ═══════════════

**I feel . . .**

● **What it makes me feel.** List everything the problems make you feel. Not just 'sad' or 'angry', but as many words as you can. For example, 'neglected', 'frustrated', 'worthless', 'helpless'.

● **Other times I have felt like this.** Cast your mind back to childhood, or later, when you had similar feelings. When events remind you of childhood misery they can affect you even more painfully.

● **The outcome I want.** What would you like to happen? If you find it difficult to think about this logically, award yourself 'three wishes' that would make you feel happy, even if one of them is to part.

● **What my partner could do to make it better.** List changes your partner could make that would improve matters for you, even if you have to admit to 'nothing'.

● **What I could do to make it better.** List changes you could make to improve matters yourself. This can include asking your partner for the changes you have listed. But it should also include any steps you could take to make yourself feel happier. This can include leaving.

**!**

---

When you have sorted out your ideas and looked at your true feelings, the next step is to talk to your partner about the way you both feel. Even if you have come to the conclusion that the only solution is to leave your partner, it is still essential, if possible, to explain why you feel like this. Hearing your partner's side can help fill in the missing gaps in your understanding. Sometimes you gain realisations that make a solution possible. Even if this does not happen, anything you learn will show you more about what went wrong, which can help in future relationships.

● **The willingness to listen to your partner.** It is easy to become immersed in your own feelings when things are going wrong and to forget that your partner has feelings too. When you are very angry about aspects of your partner's behaviour, you can ignore the fact that his or her actions might be motivated by strong feelings, too.

For instance, if your partner has been having an affair it is human nature to concentrate on the way that this has hurt you. But what motivates people to start affairs is not only sexual gratification or the search for pleasure. Sometimes that person has been unhappy, lonely, insecure – or frightened about such things as ageing or professional failure. Similarly, a person who feels ignored or put down by a partner might escape into an affair. These might not be things you wish to know but, ultimately, understanding them is an important part of the process of healing the wounds that the affair opens.

It is best to arrange to talk with your partner about the issues that distress you. Fix a date and a time this week for this conversation. It is unhelpful if it arises in the heat of the moment, when one of you is very angry or upset. Planning allows you to sort out what you want to say and how you are going to say it.

Sometimes your partner is not prepared to do this. If things are very bad between you, or your partner is very frightened of the truth, he or she might not want to co-operate. You can't force such a conversation, but you should clearly state that without it you find it difficult to see a future together. The only circumstance that make this unrealistic is if your partner is physically violent. Then, your best option might be to put your energies into finding somewhere to go, and only attempt reconciliation if your partner receives help, and when you have other people present to see that you come to no harm.

If you both agree to talk, bear in mind that the aim is for you both to be truthful about what you feel and what you want. There is nothing to be gained by avoiding the truth. Careful listening is also essential. Sometimes, understanding your partner's feelings and motives can make difficulties easier to bear.

A successful outcome for these talks is for you to have a better idea of where each other stands, even if what you hear is not pleasant to you.

You should also agree some ground rules before you start:

● **Rule 1: This is not an argument.** If feelings run high and you start to argue, shout or interrupt then you will stop.

● **Rule 2: You should talk about yourself and your own feelings, not criticise each other.** Your aim is to help your partner understand why you are so distressed and what you need to feel better, not to score points. If you attack each other you will learn nothing useful.

● **Rule 3: Both should have an equal chance to speak.** Agree on a time limit of half an hour or one hour. Divide the time equally – for instance, one of you speaks for half the time and then the other has a turn. Or one of you speaks for ten minutes and the other speaks for a further ten minutes. Then the first partner speaks again, and so on. Use a clock to time yourselves. You can toss a coin to see who starts. Stop at the agreed time. If it was too short, agree a longer period next time.

● **Rule 4: The one listening should give full attention.** While one of you speaks the other should listen without interrupting. During this time, the listener should look at the speaker and try to understand the feelings expressed.

! ——————————————— *Task* ———————————————

### Saying your piece

When it is your turn to talk, aim to explain your feelings, why you are unhappy and what would make you happier. These should not be demands, but statements. Do not dwell on your partner's behaviour, but on your own reactions.

If you bring up specific issues, use the notes you made for the task WHAT WENT WRONG, explaining your own changing feelings and, where relevant, how you think you have contributed to the problem. The point of this talk is to give your partner a clear idea of what it feels to be you – not necessarily to find solutions yet.

!

The more calmly and objectively you are able to explain your position, the easier it will be for your partner to listen to what you say. Nevertheless, some of what you say is likely to be shocking or painful to hear. Even with the best intentions, your partner might become too upset or angry to continue the conversation. Do not despair, but try to fix a time another day, when some of what you say has sunk in. After the initial shock, these conversations can become easier to handle.

It is just as important for you to hear what your partner has to say, and this can be difficult too. The truth is often painful. Compare it to the pain of a boil being lanced to release the poison. This is far better than leaving the poison inside to do more damage.

!

=== *Task* ===

## Listening effectively

When it is your turn to listen, try to concentrate on what your partner is saying, rather than explore your own feelings and reactions. Resist the attempt to make any comments, however distressed or angry you become. Silence is even better than reassuring comments.

!

After this conversation you will need time to consider what you both have said. If all has gone well, and you now have a better idea of what the problems are, you are likely to want to repeat this – making more time to talk about the issues raised, using the same ground rules.

Ideally you should talk intensively over a short period until you both have a good grasp of how each other is feeling, and are starting to come to terms with it. An hour every evening, or every other evening would be ideal. Couples who are able to do this can find that however difficult or unpleasant the truth is, it is easier to cope with than the bad atmosphere and suspicions within a relationship where the problems are not addressed. Growing to understand each other, even when this causes you to feel sad, can sometimes help you see a way forward.

If what you discover makes you feel that the relationship has a chance, then you will have to agree changes that will make it better for both of you.

● **The willingness to make necessary changes.** When you have a good understanding of each other's position you will know whether you want to try to make the relationship work. This almost always involves both of you adapting your ways to reach a new way of living together that is more harmonious. Sometimes small changes make a lot of difference. Some couples find that the very act of making more time together to discuss things changes their relationships radically for the better.

If more far-reaching changes are necessary it helps to come to an agreement about what each of you will do. In *The RELATE Guide to Better Relationships* there is the example of a couple who, on the point of separation, negotiated every aspect of daily living in detail. In their case, they concentrated on the small but explosive issues, such as who would get what items out for breakfast, and when each would do the washing up. This rather stilted and awkward arrangement worked so well that it became second nature to them. They developed the habit of discussing any issue that arose and agreeing how they would handle it.

Although this detailed negotiation wouldn't suit many people, the principle is good. For changes to work, both must make them and they must be agreeable to both of you. You can reach your agreement informally, but sometimes it helps to have it written down, as the following task suggests.

! ================= *Task* =================

## Agreement to change

Fix a time to discuss what changes you need to make to improve your relationship. You can agree as many changes as you like, but it is usually best to restrict yourself to one or two at the beginning.

The idea is for both of you to ask the other to do something that will make you happier. If what you ask is too demanding, it should be discussed and negotiated until you agree on a possible alternative. When you are satisfied with the arrangement, write down what you have agreed and date it.

*[date]*

*What [you] have agreed to do:*

*What [your partner] has agreed to do:*

!

The intention is not to make drawing up an agreement sound easy. Of course it is hard – and the longer you have had problems the harder it is. Standing by an agreement is also difficult, and you will only know how difficult it is when you put it into practice. However, now that you have begun to talk, you should continue to do so, and regularly review what you have agreed. Is it working? Were some of the things you agreed too difficult to put into practice? Are there any modifications or changes you want to make?

If your relationship is actively improving because of what you have agreed, you should also build on this. Continue to make time together – but not just to discuss problems and solutions. Try to find things to do together that you both enjoy. Talk about other matters, and try to rebuild positive feelings for each other. If the relationship is looking promising again, you will find further help in the companion book, *The RELATE Guide to Better Relationships*, which examines in detail ways you can continue to improve your relationship.

All three of these steps are essential for both partners if the relationship is to survive healthily. Some people stay together without doing any of them, but they remain unhappy. Others only do one or two – or only one partner is prepared to make any effort. These relationships either stumble on or fail.

For instance, some people become mature in themselves and understand themselves and their needs better. But they are not prepared to listen to their partners or make changes. These people are likely to take the initiative to end the relationship. Others will participate in the talks that increase self-understanding and understanding of their partners, but when it comes to it they feel that the changes necessary to improve the relationship ask too much of them. Or through their talks and increased understanding, they both realise that parting would be the healthiest solution.

Some people, however, make every effort to listen to their partners and make changes to accommodate their partners' needs. But they do this without self-understanding, deny their own needs, and are therefore likely to make themselves unhappy, even if the relationship survives.

When only one of you is prepared to put in the work and do the changing, the relationship might feel calmer and happier for a while, but it is unbalanced. When both of you recognise that both must change, the relationship has developed the flexibility that gives it the best chance when you meet problems in the future.

## WHEN THE BREAK HAS TO COME

It is sometimes inevitable that a relationship must end. Either you have tried your very best to make it work to no avail, or you have left it too late for any effort to make a difference, or fundamental differences between you have been exposed by your talks. Sometimes, unfortunately, your attempts to find a solution actually increase the distance between you – usually when the decisions you have made have not addressed the real problem. For instance, some people marry after having lived together for years because they are *not* getting on well. They hope that by making it legal they will solve the problem, whereas it can often highlight the issues that have been causing distress. Other people, more sadly, believe that having a baby will bring them together, when, in reality, a relationship has to be in very good shape to manage the changes becoming parents makes.

An example is Laura and Adam, who came for counselling when they had been married for eighteen months. They were having great difficulties. Laura's harsh and deprived background made it difficult for her to trust anyone close to her, although she yearned for an intimate relationship. She was a neglected child, shown little affection by her divorced mother, who concentrated instead on her series of feckless lovers. Adam was a mother's boy, who was spoilt by his mother but ignored by his father. As a result he felt insecure about himself. But he was also selfish – he thought women were there to look after his needs, as his mother always had.

They married because they were very attracted to each other, and Laura thought it was wrong to have sex outside marriage. But sex was disappointing, and Laura soon went off it. She also kept Adam at arm's length emotionally. Intimacy made her feel uncomfortable because she had never known any before. She had no experience of a balanced, close relationship – and feared that closeness meant loss of identity.

Counselling went some way towards helping them, and they were very cheered by it. Although the counsellor felt that they were not ready, they decided to set the seal on their success by having a baby. During the pregnancy they were very happy. Adam became less selfish and more concerned about Laura. They stopped coming for counselling.

Just over a year later they were back in counselling, and this time things looked bleak. As soon as the baby was born, Adam's gentleness evaporated. Neither of them had expected a child to take up so much time and energy. Adam was now back to his old ways. Laura didn't feel he valued her.

Laura maintained that it was Adam's selfishness that was the problem, but it was clear to the counsellor that the issues in her unloving childhood were just as relevant. They stopped her wanting to love and be loved. Now that she had the baby she couldn't find the will or the energy to do anything about her relationship with Adam.

The counsellor says, 'Adam was equally to blame. He couldn't understand that Laura was not like his mother. He wanted everything to be all right without him having to do anything to make it so. He wanted Laura to look after him and the baby, and be sexually available to him whenever he wanted her.'

Because Laura and Adam had not resolved the real problems between them in the first round of counselling, having a baby actually drove them further apart. They dropped out of counselling again because Laura saw no further point. Enough was enough: she wanted the marriage to be over.

The counsellor was sorry that they did not continue with counselling – not because she saw any future for them as a couple, but because she could have helped them deal with the parting in order to minimise the pain.

People are sometimes surprised to find that RELATE counsel a couple through separation and beyond. But this is an important part of RELATE's work. The end of a relationship can be acrimonious and cause bitterness that lasts for many years. A counsellor can help to reduce the bad feeling, so that the couple are more able to move on healthily to the next phase in their lives. When they can do this, any children they might have between them will also cope better with the separation. While RELATE cannot help with the legal issues in a divorce (and neither does this book) the emotional and practical issues still need sorting out.

Counselling can also help when a couple dither about ending a relationship. If there are children, and there is some way through the difficulties, the counsellor can help them find it. If there is no possibility of the relationship continuing, the counsellor can help them make the decision. Some people ask for help because they do not want to hurt their partners by leaving. They think that it might be less painful if they hang on until there is nothing good left between them – whereas they are often just prolonging the misery. In some cases they are influenced by their parents, who feel that divorce is something shameful, and that they should put up with their own pain rather than hurt the partners who have been hurting them.

Counselling helped Mitchell and Joan deal with their divorce better than they had been able to deal with their marriage in later years.

They were both in their early thirties. Joan was dynamic – an emotional, affectionate, sexy woman who was doing very well in her career. Mitchell was very controlled and steady. He liked a quiet life and was unambitious. They had two children, aged eight and six, but this was the only aspect of their life they shared. They had no common interests and their goals in life were different. After twelve years together, ten of them as a married couple, they had grown apart.

Initially they came for counselling to talk about repairing their marriage. But neither of them was prepared to change. Conversations were stilted and awkward, until Joan tentatively mentioned that what she really wanted was a divorce.

Then the communication between them opened up. Once Mitchell agreed that this would suit him too, they were able to talk more freely than they had for years. What they agreed they wanted more than anything was to arrange matters so that the children would not suffer from their decision.

For a few weeks they came for more counselling, during which time they negotiated every aspect of their separation. They agreed about what they would do with the house and what financial arrangements they would make. They discussed Mitchell's access to the children in detail. How often he would see them, how access would be arranged, what they would do about Christmas and birthdays. They also agreed about the boundaries of their future relationship – what amount of contact would be appropriate and what sort of friendship they could expect to have.

When they had worked these matters out to their mutual satisfaction, they went to see a solicitor together to have their divorce papers drawn up. They were shocked when they reported back to the counsellor. The solicitor had told them that it was impossible for him to act for both of them. He suggested that they retained separate solicitors, who would then make sure that their 'interests were protected'. He hinted that one of them was getting a raw deal and might live to regret their informal agreement. They said they received the impression that if they did as he suggested and went to separate solicitors, the solicitors would soon set them at each other's throats. Instead, they drew up the agreement together and took it back to the solicitor to witness.

This kind of co-operation is unusual. It worked for Mitchell and Joan because although there was little relationship left to save, there was a lot of mutual goodwill and no resentment. But even if your relationship is ending with more hard feelings, it is still possible to learn something from the way they acted.

The main point to bear in mind is – what do you want for the future? Do you want to start again happily? Only people who are very bitter do not want this for themselves. The way to ensure a happy outcome is to put to one side your feelings of anger and distress when you are dealing with parting.

These are some of the typical reactions that get in the way of this, and ways of looking at them freshly:

● **Against happiness: you want your partner to suffer.** It is human to want to hurt the person who hurt you, but these natural feelings should be controlled. Feelings or acts of revenge, leading to bitterness and resentment, will link you closer to your partner than the love you once shared. Although some people derive a certain satisfaction from making their exes suffer, this is not happiness. While you are consumed with anger against your partner you are not heart-free to make a better relationship with someone else, or to find satisfaction alone.

● **Towards happiness: you want to stop suffering yourself.**
The way to stop suffering is to concentrate on yourself and your future,
not your partner. Of course, you will have angry feelings as a natural
consequence of what you have been through, but these should not be
acted upon. You should experience them, talk about them – and then let
them go. This is dealt with in Chapter Two, *Coming to Terms with
Loss*. The longer you allow yourself to dwell on your partner's life and
feelings, the longer you will take to recover. Doing things to make you
feel good in yourself, which have nothing to do with your ex, is more
positive.

If you need to think in terms of revenge, remember the phrase 'living well is the best revenge', which means that if you are happily building a successful life you have all the revenge you need. The way to do
this is examined in Part Two, *Working on Yourself*.

Ultimately, you will feel even better if you can get to the point
when you can think of your ex with compassionate understanding.

● **Against happiness: you want to prove your partner was in
the wrong.** This is connected to the first point. You think about your
past relationship only to find more proof that your partner was completely at fault, so that you can fuel your feelings of anger and bitterness. Although there is a time when you need to think deeply about
your relationship, this is a stage that should pass. If you only want to
think about how terrible your partner was, then you will gain nothing
useful from this stage. Chapter Three, *What Went Wrong?* helps clarify
some of these issues.

● **Towards happiness: you are prepared to admit your own
mistakes.** When you can see that there was fault on both sides, you
have made one of the most important moves towards happiness in the
future. As has been emphasised already, it takes two to make a relationship work, and two to make it go wrong. Even if you 'did nothing',
your inaction could have been a contributory factor. When you are able
honestly to shoulder some of the blame (though not all of it!) you will
have learned one of the necessary lessons to help you make a better
relationship in the future.

● **Against happiness: you want the children to be on your side.**
When you are feeling angry at your ex, you can want everyone else to
share your views – including any children you might have together. If
you criticise and blame your partner in their hearing, or try to turn
them against their other parent, you might well succeed in getting them
on your side, but you do this at the expense of their own happiness.

Children taught to hate one of their parents suffer in a number of ways, which are looked at in Chapter Four, *Your Children*.

● **Towards happiness: you want your children to be well-balanced.** If you put your children's well-being higher than the temporary satisfaction of having them on your side, you help them emerge from the ordeal of their parents' separation more healthily. Children need to be allowed to love both their parents to develop into well-balanced adults and to be able to love and be loved themselves when they form partnerships in the future.

● **Against happiness: you want to get the majority of shared assets.** Dividing up the home, possessions and finances is as tricky as the more obviously emotional issues. Sometimes the struggle for assets becomes the arena for all your emotions to be enacted. When you put your energies into getting as much as possible, whether this is fair or not, you create a long-term legacy of bitterness, which, again, can make it harder for you to find happiness.

● **Towards happiness: you want a fair deal.** It is probably never possible to feel that it is completely fair when you are dividing assets. But if your intention is to be as fair as possible you can try to assess whether the bad feelings created by demanding certain things or withholding others are worth what the material things actually represent. If you behave at all times as fairly as you can, you make it possible for you and your partner to show each other generosity in the future – which can never happen if it has become a battle.

When a break-up means severe financial hardship, fairness might be the last thing on your mind. But you can still ascertain whether your motivation is practical, or whether it lies in trying to get back at your partner.

While solicitors can help with the details of a divorce, they are not the best help when it comes to the emotional issues. At the back of the book is a list of organisations that can help. RELATE, of course, can also help you sort out many of these matters, so that you have the best chance for the future. Counselling is particularly useful for determining what went wrong between you, and helping you through the painful process of coming to terms with parting, which is the subject of the next chapter.

# 2

# COMING TO TERMS WITH LOSS

When a relationship ends the emotional impact is very great. You have not just lost your partner, you have sustained a series of related losses. You have lost your role as part of a couple, and all that entailed as you lived together, including the network of friendships and extended family – and even, perhaps, the focus that dealing with a problem relationship gave you. You have lost the daily habits and routines that you built up, which are comforting in themselves. You have lost the sense of security that comes with knowing that you have someone by your side, even if you haven't been happy together. You might have lost your home – either because you left, or because the split meant that it had to be sold. You have often lost the standard of living you were used to, if two households now have to be supported. If you have children you might have lost the daily contact with them if you are the one who left – or lost the support that comes when there are two parents. You might have lost confidence in yourself as a man or a woman now that you are on your own. You have also lost the dream, or vision, that you had of yourselves settling down together for life, leaving a feeling of uncertainty about your future.

It is not surprising, therefore, that counsellors treat the end of a relationship like a death. These losses plunge you into the emotional turmoil of grief. Just like someone facing the actual death of a loved one, you find yourself experiencing the see-saw emotions that accompany bereavement – including shock, disbelief, depression, anger and guilt. Given time, you come to accept what has happened and are able to plan for the future with optimism and hope.

One counsellor talked of two women she was counselling during the same period. Pat was in her late forties, and her husband had recently left her for someone else. Joyce was in her fifties, and her husband had just died. The counsellor says, 'Although on the face of it these were two very different cases, the emotional process was remarkably similar.'

In the aftermath of her husband's death, Joyce didn't feel that life was worth living. She felt totally lost without him. They had always been a couple and done things together. She felt she wasn't valuable now that she was no longer a wife. Although she could drive, her husband had always driven on motorways, and she feared she would never be able to visit her children without him. She veered between feeling guilty that she hadn't been able to keep her husband alive, although she knew there was nothing she could have done, and furious with him for dying, although she knew this was illogical.

Pat's feelings mirrored those of Joyce. She too felt that she couldn't go on, that life held little meaning. She felt that she had failed as a woman, was bitterly angry at her husband for leaving her, and at the other woman involved. Both women alternated between times of weeping despair and depression and angry outbursts.

'Both of them had to learn to build their confidence and find a purpose,' the counsellor says. 'In Joyce's case the turning point was when she decided to tackle the garden, which had become overgrown. She had seen no point in bothering before. With Pat it was getting a part-time job. Although they still had some way to go, they were both looking towards the future, instead of yearning for the past.'

## THE STAGES OF GRIEF

Grieving is a process of emotional adjustment, during which time powerful emotions conflict with each other. There are clearly defined stages to this process, but although each can be explained separately, they don't always come in a tidy order. You don't necessarily finish one stage before going on to the next. They become mixed up, but each has to be fully experienced before you can complete the process.

How long this takes varies from person to person. Some people can adjust quite quickly – to their surprise and, sometimes, guilt. It usually takes at the very least a year, and often much longer than that. But during this time there can be moments of happiness and optimism, as well as turmoil. The progress can involve two steps forward and one step back at every stage. Some days are much better than others.

Your emotions are complicated and ambivalent at this time. The grieving process is not a smooth progression. One day you'll feel happy and believe you are reaching some sort of acceptance and then an anniversary will occur, or you'll hear a sad song, or your ex-partner will do something to distress you and you will be set back. This is normal, and no cause for panic.

It will take the time it takes, and you should not let other people's ideas about how you should be coping affect you. Some people will say, 'You should be over it by now!' but you can ignore them. Being apparently 'stuck' at one stage is also normal. You might have a lot of anger to deal with, or a lot of sadness to experience, and if you find painful emotions hard to handle this will take time. You can only get through them when you are ready. Continuing to feel angry for a very long time, however, can sometimes mean that you are fighting a feeling of sadness. Or being 'stuck' in sadness or depression can mean that you haven't been able to get in touch with your feelings of anger. A counsellor or friend can help you move on by supporting you, but you do the work yourself.

Some people prolong the process because they are frightened by the power of their emotions. They keep themselves very busy, with lots of activity and people around. They feel they must pull themselves together. But you need time to grieve, and you should allow yourself to do so. If you don't, it can hit you out of the blue some months later when you believed you had put it all behind you. As one counsellor says, 'It is fine to "pull yourself together" part of the time, as long as you recognise that it's also all right to let yourself go, even if it means weeping at night when no one can see.'

Understanding the various stages can be a help. Knowing that it is normal to experience these turbulent emotions – and healthy to do so – can give you the courage to endure them and not repress them. It can give you hope to know that everyone experiences what you are going through and that it does end. Life is accompanied by a series of losses, not just the loss of a relationship. You experience the 'loss' of youth, the 'loss' of an ambition that can't be realised, and so on. Everyone who endures the breakdown of a relationship experiences it as a loss, even if it was right that it should end; nevertheless, your own experience is unique. The time can come when you look back and see that you have been strengthened and changed by the difficulties.

Loss always leaves its mark, but it can help you put your life in perspective. You learn more about yourself and others, you reassess your values and what is important. This can lead you to appreciate things you had under-rated, and you can often use what you learn to improve your life in the future.

The stages are now looked at separately. But, as you will see from the following cases, they can overlap.

## Shock

Shock is often the first reaction to the end of a relationship. This is especially so if you have been left, but to a lesser extent it is also the case if you have been the one to leave. Any great change in your life and living pattern is a shock to the system.

Shock manifests in a number of ways. One is a feeling of numbness. You are unable to take in what has happened, and you don't feel anything at all. For instance, Adrian came home one day to find that his wife had walked out – and had taken half the contents of the house with her. He literally couldn't believe his eyes. He stared without comprehension at the empty spaces in the rooms. When he came for counselling a few weeks later he was still in shock, and talked about how he still walked round furniture that wasn't there any more.

When you are in shock, you can't think straight. Nothing seems to make sense, and it is hard to 'hold' a thought. You might repeat yourself or find that you have lost the thread of what you are saying. You become forgetful, perhaps getting off at the wrong bus-stop or not knowing why you have entered a particular shop. There can be accompanying physical effects, such as dizziness, panic attacks, hyperventilation, loss of appetite, and exhaustion.

Shock is a natural defence against the onslaught of emotions that are to come. Your emotions are blocked, and as a consequence your normal reactions and mental processes are affected too. It is also a message from the body to care for yourself during a difficult time, just as the body goes into shock after a physical injury to prevent you from moving in a way that would make it worse. In the same way, while you are in shock you should recognise it as a sign that you should ease up, not do too much, and accept whatever help is offered to you. This stage always passes as the truth sinks in, but it can take from a few days to a number of weeks.

## Disbelief and denial

Even when the first shock has passed it can be difficult to accept that the end really has come. This is true when someone dies, but is even more enduring when that person is still alive. If you have been left by your partner it can be very hard to believe that he or she will not come back. Some people can remain in this stage for many years. One woman, who came for counselling to help herself cope with her own divorce, talked of her parents. Her father had left her mother twenty years before, and had been living for years with someone else. He had no contact with her mother, except through his regular maintenance cheques. But as they had never divorced her mother still harboured the conviction that he would return to her some day.

Although this is an unusual case, some people continue to believe that the parting is not final even when the evidence suggests otherwise.

Although you can come to terms with the truth within a few weeks or months, it can take longer if close contact continues or the ending is drawn out.

For instance, Irene's husband took a year to decide to leave her for another woman. By the time she came for counselling he had been gone six months, but she was still hoping that he would come back. Every week he would turn up to see the children and stay for a while. This hour of his time was so precious to her that even though she suffered for the rest of the week, she couldn't bear to think that it wasn't a sign that he would eventually return. Because she hoped for this so much, she was unable to let herself feel angry towards him.

Other counsellors have spoken of people who continue to have sex with their ex-partners when they do meet. Although some of them say it is 'only sex', underneath they cannot really believe that the relationship is at an end. While they are still having sex they are not free to put the relationship behind them and start again. Counselling helps them understand that the sexual contact must stop before they can move on.

While it is the partner who has been left who is most likely to find it difficult to believe that the relationship is over, the partner who returns for sex or remains too intimately involved, despite saying he or she will never return, also has problems accepting the end.

Counsellors have found that people who get stuck in this stage often do so because they are bewildered about what went wrong in their relationship. Either the ending came as a complete surprise, or they had felt quite able to cope with the dissatisfactions and didn't know their partners felt differently. Usually when they are able to understand what went wrong and how each of them played their part in the relationship's problems they are more able to accept that it is over. Help in doing this for yourself is to be found in the next chapter, *What Went Wrong?*

## Sadness and depression

Sadness and depression are features throughout the grieving process. They affect both partners – the one who has left, even if it was for someone else, will also feel sad and depressed.

These feelings can be even more acute if you were the one who was left. The loneliness that comes with losing a partner is part of this. Even if you are surrounded by understanding friends and family and have a job to do, you might feel unloved, that there is a hole that no one else can fill. People describe a feeling of emptiness, as if part of themselves were missing. It is often this frightening feeling that leads people to jump straight into another relationship, which is an understandable but unhelpful way of dealing with it. Those who find ways of filling that void for themselves develop an inner strength which helps them in the future.

It is healthy and necessary to mourn for what has gone. Some people find it very hard to give in to feelings of sorrow – and they are most likely to try to fend off the feelings by frenetic activity, and avoiding being alone. Although the feelings can be kept at bay like this for a while, they will eventually surface – perhaps months later when you thought you were over it. Some women react like this, but it is more common for men.

This is because it is considered more 'acceptable' for a woman to say that she is miserable and distressed, and to talk to friends about how she feels. After a divorce – particularly if she is the one who was left – a woman is more likely to find that friends and family gather round to give emotional support. Women are also more likely to be lovingly demonstrative with each other. An unhappy woman receives much-needed hugs as well as being given the opportunity to express misery.

Generally, on the other hand, men find it difficult to admit to feeling unhappy and lonely. It is perceived as 'weak' and unmanly. A man who is able to express his feelings is unlikely to be held while he cries.

One counsellor reported a man as saying, 'Other men don't want to know, they're terribly competitive,' and she found that this was a typical experience among her male clients. Or friends feel awkward when another man shows his feelings – as if he has broken an unwritten rule. Other men are likely to turn the conversation to something else when the man talks of his feelings of loss – or they offer a drink or tell a joke. Consequently, men fighting this sadness will often go to the doctor with stress symptoms – complaining about headaches or not sleeping, rather than talking about the misery. One man who felt that he had his feelings under control found that they emerged in a fear of the dark, which he had not felt since he was a child.

It is important to let yourself experience the sadness, and find support where you can from sympathetic people prepared to listen. Both men and women benefit from talking to a counsellor during this time, or from joining a group of other people going through the same experience. Some RELATE centres run such groups, as do other organisations – details of which are given at the end of the book.

Depression can alternate with sadness, but it also sometimes takes over when the truth of the parting sinks in. It marks the understanding that there is no going back – at a time when the future still looks uncertain. It is characterised by feelings of apathy and loss of energy. Again, this is a necessary stage. It occurs when you are coming to terms with loss, before hope can be felt once again, as Nadine found.

She came for counselling after her five-year marriage had ended. For some weeks she was very sad, trying to make sense of what had happened. Then she fell into a severe depression. For two weeks she spent most of her time in bed. As the counsellor says, 'Those two weeks were very important because although they were the lowest point for her, they were also the turning point.' She felt utterly alone, but with that feeling came the realisation that previously she had defined herself through her relationship, that she only felt of value as a wife. During that period she started to think about herself as a person, to wonder who she was and what she wanted. What had started as self-disgust turned into anger, first of all randomly aimed, and then focused into a new energy that propelled her into doing something about her life.

Some people become stuck in the depression for long periods. This was so with Bernard, a forty-five-year-old auditor, who came for counselling when he was in the process of divorcing his wife. They had one child and had been married for twelve years when he found out that she was having an affair. He had moved out of the family home some months before.

Bernard was a quiet, self-effacing man. His manner was anxious and depressed. He was still in the stage of denying what was happening. All he wanted to talk about was getting his wife back. He felt sure that if he approached her in the right way she would see that they could be happy. He was convinced that the affair would end and that his wife would realise that she wanted him. They were still in contact, and Bernard had regular access to his adored child.

Bernard could not feel angry with his wife while he still wanted her back. It seemed like a betrayal, and anger would imply that she had done something wrong, which he didn't want to feel. But after some weeks of counselling Bernard's wife and child moved in with her lover, and he realised that there was no going back.

Now Bernard felt able to be angry. It was the first time in his life that he had ever expressed anger. He had spent his life being reasonable and always doing the right thing. Along with the anger came guilt and self-reproach. He felt that it was his own failure as a husband that had sent his wife into the arms of another man. He felt lonely. He missed his wife, missed his child and missed his home.

After this brief burst of strong feeling, Bernard sank into a depression. His confidence – never high – was at rock bottom. He had lacked confidence as a child and he had been attracted to his wife because she had all the confidence he lacked. He had hoped that some of it would rub off on him, but instead her strength had made him feel more inadequate.

Bernard came for counselling for weeks, his depression remaining unabated. The counsellor urged him to see his doctor, which he eventually did reluctantly. The doctor judged that he need a short course of anti-depressants.

The counsellor says, 'There was an immediate improvement. I was so pleased for him.' Previously Bernard had told no one about his marital problems as he thought they would consider him a failure. Instead he lived for his sessions with the counsellor. But, she says, with the edge taken off his depression he was able to take her advice and tell people what he was going through. He told colleagues at work, and was gratified at how sympathetic they were. He found the strength to leave counselling, at that point, although it saddened him to do so.

Some people remain in this depression for years. Counselling can help you move on. What you need is a renewed faith in yourself and purpose for the future. Part Two, *Working on Yourself,* can also help with this.

## Guilt

Depression is sometimes seen as anger turned inward, so it usually involves guilty feelings. But people often feel guilty about the ending of a relationship even when the depression is not severe. Guilt is likely to be felt by the person who ends the relationship, but it is also felt by the one who was left. In this case it might be experienced as feelings of failure. As you search your mind to discover what went wrong, you will often remember things you wish you had done differently. These memories cause you to suffer, and they are therefore useful as a learning experience. The most positive effect of guilt is the will it gives you to change things in the future.

But there is a less healthy form of guilt, which involves taking all the blame on yourself and punishing yourself endlessly. People do this when they find it difficult to feel anger towards their ex-partners and so assume that everything is their own fault. Castigating yourself in this way serves no useful purpose. What's past is past, and genuine regret must be followed by self-forgiveness.

When you can't stop blaming yourself for what happened you can't complete the grieving process. Much of counselling for Wayne, for example, involved helping him to see the end of his relationship more realistically. Wayne's wife had left him for another man, taking their two children with her. He had adored his wife and couldn't accept that she had gone. Although his wife was being difficult about access he wouldn't hear a word against her. As far as he was concerned, she was wonderful.

The counsellor says, 'I was worried that he was settling into apathy, there was no fight in him.' Instead of feeling angry at his wife, Wayne blamed himself totally for the break-up. He had a good sense of what he had done wrong, and what he could have done better within the relationship, but he did not have an equally sensible perspective on his wife's shortcomings.

It took a lot of work with the counsellor before Wayne ceased blaming himself totally. Although he found it hard to find fault with his wife, he stopped examining his conscience for more ways to heap blame on himself. On top of feeling guilty about the break-up he had also castigated himself for being 'stupid' for feeling so defeated and depressed, and 'worthless' for not being good enough.

Gradually he began to look at ways he could cope, and started to take practical steps towards gaining better access to his children. The counsellor says, 'As he started to look outward it began to be easier for Wayne to stop blaming himself. He learnt to respect his own feelings – to know it was all right to feel depressed and sad.' As the counsellor also remarked, 'It's important for people to accept where they are in the grieving process, and to know that how they are feeling is normal and valid.'

## Anger

It is perfectly natural to feel angry when your life has been turned upside-down by the end of a relationship. Anger is a strong emotion that erupts as a consequence of feeling hurt – even when there is no one to blame for the pain. It is even more natural to direct your anger toward the person who has made you feel humiliated, abandoned, sad, betrayed – or any of the other emotions you experience at the ending of a relationship.

Everyone feels angry in these circumstances, but at what point you start to experience your anger varies. Some people feel angry from the very beginning. Others are much slower to come to anger, as the cases so far have already shown. Anger is energy. It can make you feel restless and on edge, but it can also carry you through the bad times, and motivate you to rebuild your life in the future. As one counsellor says, 'I feel relieved when people can be angry. Sometimes they feel guilty about being angry, but it can be a turning point in the pain.'

This was the case with Nadine who, as already described, spent two weeks of severe depression in bed before she began to feel angry. Before the end of her marriage, she had never been one to express anger. She could remember many times in her life when she had been very sad, but she had never been in touch with angry feelings.

Shortly after her depression ended, Nadine steamed into the counselling room one day in a state of fury. She was angry, it seemed, with everyone – including the counsellor. Counselling hadn't made anything better, so the counsellor must be rubbish! The counsellor was not perturbed by this attack on her. When Nadine had calmed down they talked through all the reasons for Nadine's anger, and Nadine was able to identify positive steps to take. 'She was astounded to realise that she could be openly angry and express it – yet still survive!' the counsellor says. It was even more important for Nadine to recognise that the counsellor could survive her blast of anger – and still feel warm towards her and committed to helping her. Previously Nadine had believed that the power of anger was such that it would chase people away. Free to experience her anger, Nadine was able to move on to recovery much faster.

The difficulty with feeling or showing anger is something that counsellors find is typical. It is hardest for people who have never been able to express anger. Some people suppress their anger when they have been the ones to initiate the break-up. They feel that as the responsibility was theirs they have no right to be angry, despite the fact that they often have just cause. It is also common in people who are devastated by the leaving of loved partners. Feeling angry seems like a betrayal, and therefore they either control their anger or find another target for it. As one counsellor says, 'I see a lot of women who have trouble feeling angry towards their husbands – even if they have left them for other women. They feel angry with the other woman rather than him.'

It is not just women who have this trouble. One man could not feel angry at the wife who left him, despite the fact that she consistently treated him in a high-handed and unpleasant way. It was only when she humiliated him in front of his mother that he first started to feel angry – and when he did so he was able to complete the mourning process.

Some people have the opposite reaction. They are consumed with anger from the very beginning, and can't let it go. Some people are still as angry many years later, which means that they remain emotionally attached to their ex-partners, albeit in a destructive way.

Other people are too free in their expression of anger. As one counsellor says, 'People have fantasies about what they would like to do to their partners – stick knives in them, or ruin their lives. While they stay fantasies these are normal and healthy, the problem comes when they want to act on them.'

Destructive anger that takes the form of acts of revenge or in turning any children against the departed partner seems to prolong the feelings. The energy, which can be used to help you reconstruct your life, is wasted.

The healthiest way to deal with your anger is first to acknowledge your feelings to yourself, and not feel guilty about them. It then helps to express them directly – either to the person concerned or to someone prepared to listen and support you as you do so. A friend, a counsellor, or a group of people in the same situation can be ideal. If you choose to tell your ex-partner, then doing so in a way that does not increase tension by accusations and blame is best. Instead, concentrate on the feelings behind your anger: the sorrow, fear, humiliation and so on. If this is too difficult to do, then it also helps to write the feelings down – either in a letter that you do not send, or in the form of a diary that charts your changing emotions.

You can also channel the energies raised by your anger, as one counsellor explained to a man who was scared of expressing anger directly to his ex-wife, but often felt overwhelmed by it. He found it helpful to work off the energy in a number of ways: swimming and walking were two of the most positive, because they also built up good feelings about himself. But when he was feeling destructive he also found that he could make himself feel better by violent but safe alternatives: taking bottles to the bottle bank, and hurling them inside the bin, or by slamming doors or screaming into a pillow.

If you express your anger, and work with the energy generated, you will eventually find that the anger lessens. It might come back in bursts from time to time, but that is only to be expected, and it won't happen forever.

Gradually, if you have allowed yourself to experience fully all the stages of grief, you will find that the worst of it is over, and you are ready to begin a new chapter in your life.

## Coming through

When you have accepted that the relationship is over with your heart as well as your head, you are on the way to the end of the grieving process.

People who have come through describe a new feeling of 'wholeness'. They no longer feel that part of themselves is missing – but it is even more positive than that. Many couples divide the responsibilities of a relationship. They also take on roles: one person is strong, while the other is weak; one is emotional while the other is restrained, and so on. (This process is looked at more fully in the next chapter, *What Went Wrong?*) When you can stand on your own two feet without a partner you often have to discover new things in yourself – a coping ability, strengths and talents that might have been overshadowed when you were part of a couple. In taking on responsibilities that your partner previously shouldered you find that the pride this gives you increases your freedom to set your life on a course that makes you happy.

Similarly, struggling with emotions that you previously suppressed, or of which your partner seemed to have the 'monopoly' – such as anger or sadness – can make you feel more alive and in touch with your emotions generally. This increases your ability to feel the good things: happiness and excitement. It can also make you more compassionate towards other people in trouble. The difficulties of this emotional time are an indication of the depths of your feelings, and your commitment to the relationship that has gone. You pay tribute to yourself as an emotional person if you respect the painful stages of grief, and do not despise yourself for going through them, or attempt to repress them. Suffering can deepen your capacity to love.

All this takes time and, as has been emphasised, it can take longer for some than others. But you catch glimpses of these possibilities even before the grieving is over. When you are going through a period of feeling good or just 'normal' again, you can build on this by increasing your confidence and self-respect, as described in Part Two, *Working on Yourself*. You can use your new insights to decide what you want out of life, and consider what needs to happen to make you happy. Then, even though some low times might follow, you are moving in the right direction.

# 3

# WHAT WENT WRONG?

There are three main typical reactions to a relationship that has broken down. One is to dwell on the faults of your ex-partner. The second is to try as hard as you can to put the whole thing out of your mind. Although both of these reactions are natural, they don't help you recover healthily from this profoundly unhappy experience. You might eventually regain your spirits, but you still run the risk of having the same things go wrong in future relationships.

The third reaction, which is to try to understand more about the relationship – including what brought you together and kept you together, as well as what went wrong – gives you the best chance of learning what changes need to be made for your life to be happier in the future. It also helps you through the grieving process. Many people are tormented by questions when a relationship first breaks down, particularly people who have been left by their partners. Whose fault was it? What did I do wrong? What could I have done differently? And, in the case of your partner leaving for someone else, what's wrong with me? Wasn't I attractive enough, sexy enough, good enough?

Counsellors who have helped people through this questioning process find that as some of the answers are found, the nature of the questioning changes. They become less concerned with apportioning blame or looking for individual faults, and more concerned with their interaction as a couple. What attracted us to each other? Why did it work when it worked? In what ways did we set up a system that was bound to fail? How did the way we related lead to the crisis that parted us? People who find answers that satisfy them, even if they sadden them, are much better able to lay the past to rest. They can allow themselves to appreciate what was valuable in their partners and their relationships, as well as acknowledging the hurtful and damaging parts. A full understanding allows them to feel better about *themselves* and also helps them see how to do things better in the future – or, at least, how to recognise the pitfalls before they happen.

It is helpful to look in detail at the lessons one person learned, to show how healing this process is. Ted came for counselling on his own some months after his wife, Monica, had told him she wanted a divorce and had asked him to leave. He had started a tentative new relationship with Tricia, but he was still angry, upset and tormented by what had happened. He couldn't accept that the marriage was over. He approached the counselling as he approached problems in the business he ran so successfully: something had gone wrong. He needed to know if it could be fixed, and if not, what had gone wrong and why – so that he could make sure it wouldn't happen again.

Initially Ted wanted to know whether he or Monica was to blame. Could he have done anything better? His opinion was that it was all Monica's fault, but he knew that she felt that he was to blame. He said that if he could understand, he could come to terms with it.

Ted and Monica had been married for seventeen years and had two teenage children. When they met, Ted was already doing well for himself, and Monica was a shy, unconfident girl who looked up to him.

● **Lesson one.** Ted learned that he fell in love with Monica because she needed him and thought he was wonderful – and Monica fell in love with him because he was successful and confident and could look after her.

This set the pattern for most of their marriage. Ted worked hard and provided the family with a luxurious lifestyle. He directed Monica's life like a benign dictator. She didn't think that she was good enough for him. Ted said she ought to make more of herself. He sent her on courses, and encouraged her to take an Open University degree – which she started but then gave up. Too gradually for Ted to notice, Monica began to be depressed more often, and her insecurity increased.

● **Lesson two.** Ted learned that pushing Monica into things that he thought she should do had contributed to making her feel worse, even though his intentions were good. By suggesting that she could become 'better' than she was, he reinforced her feelings that she wasn't good enough in the first place.

Eventually, Monica became so unhappy that she went to a counsellor to sort out her feelings. As she talked about it, she was able to see that although Ted was a good material provider, he was emotionally distant, caught up in his work. Because she felt worthless, she hadn't felt that she deserved more of him. Now she wanted him to come down from his pedestal, become closer to her, and for them to talk about relating differently. With her counsellor's prompting, Monica was able to tell Ted this, and he had become very angry.

● **Lesson three.** Ted learned that his anger stemmed from the fact that his own self-esteem had been dependent on believing that he could take care of all Monica's needs and put everything right for her – and she had to believe it, too. Previously she hadn't dared consider that the very man who looked after her was also making her miserable. It had suited both of them that she thought he was perfect. The fact that *he* was the cause of some of her unhappiness meant that the only way he could put it right was by changing – which he hadn't been prepared to do.

So Ted resented Monica's counselling, and wouldn't talk about it. He hoped everything would settle down. Nevertheless, Monica continued with counselling. She eventually recognised that she could no longer accept the way Ted took charge of her life. She was starting to feel more confident about her own abilities, and stronger in herself. Because Ted rejected her attempts to become close to him, she realised that she no longer wanted to remain married, and she asked him to leave. Ted was as shocked by this as if it were the first time he had heard she was unhappy. His overwhelming feelings were of failure, rejection and fear.

● **Lesson four.** Ted learned that fear of failure was the most important part of his emotional make-up. He immersed himself in work because he was successful there. He had always been less sure of his capacity to be 'successful' in relationships, which was why he had to feel that his partner needed him and that he was the benefactor who could put everything right. Monica needing something he could not give – and then rejecting him – threatened his whole sense of himself.

This also led Ted to understand that he didn't feel that he was loveable for himself – only for his capacity to help someone else. For a long time Monica had not been able to tell him what she wanted and needed – but neither had he been able to tell her his feelings. For, if he had ever admitted to needing anything from her, he would have stopped appearing strong – which, he believed, would have made him lose her. The pity was that his strategy meant he lost her anyway.

With his own counsellor, Ted looked at why he felt so unloveable, and why he was so afraid of failure.

● **Lesson five.** Ted learned that these feelings were rooted in his childhood. His father had died when he was small, after which his mother brought him up on her own. He was the youngest of four, and the others were old enough to be almost independent. His mother, struggling with grief, and left almost alone with Ted, took everything out on him. She was strict and harsh, and kept him tightly controlled. Underneath, she probably feared that he too might die unless she kept him close to her, but he felt unloved and under suspicion. He learned that to escape her wrath he had to be very good and avoid trouble. He worked hard at school and did well. His fear of failure stemmed from his experience that his mother only seemed to love him when he was succeeding. He finally recognised that he also needed 'looking after' and emotional support, but that he had never allowed himself to see this, or ask for it.

By the end of the counselling, Ted was able to look at his marriage in a new way. He now understood why it had gone wrong, and what would have made it better. But he was also able to see that they had both done the best they could for a long time – and for years it had worked happily, each fulfilling what the other had needed. It had stopped being right for Monica, and she had understood why too late. When she did, Ted had been too frightened to meet her halfway. With this realisation, Ted felt profound regret, and wept for what might have been – and what could not be any more. It was too late, and he was sad – but he could now come to terms with the fact that the marriage was over.

As a result, Ted's relationship with his ex-wife improved. He could see the marriage from her point of view, so he was able to forgive her. They could now handle amicably the last hurdle – selling the family home and dividing the possessions and assets. It was a wrench for both of them. They'd invested the time, care and love into the house that they had been unable to invest in each other. In a way, it symbolised their marriage, and when it was gone they would be free to start again.

Ted was also able to use his new understanding to approach his relationship with Tricia. They saw each other occasionally, and both had their own flats. They had no long-term plans, but arranged to see each other only at the end of each meeting. Ted saw that he liked this because of his fear of intimacy, and of what becoming too close would show her about him. Ted recognised that although he enjoyed the time he spent with Tricia, she frightened him because she didn't 'need' him. He realised that if he was not to make the same mistake he had to resist fighting his fears. Instead of making himself out to be strong and in control, he could start by letting Tricia know what he felt.

Now that he recognised that he, too, needed support and care, he knew that the relationship would stand the best chance if they were open with each other. Then he would be able to trust that Tricia liked him for himself – not the self he pretended to be – and he would be able to receive support as well as giving it. Ted wanted this, although he acknowledged that he found the prospect disturbing. Counselling ended with the arrangement that if Ted found making these changes too hard, he would come back to talk to the counsellor again.

You might have noticed that this description of what went wrong with Ted's marriage included few actual incidents. For example, Monica was driven to seek counselling because she was unhappy, but at that moment the unhappiness had reached a peak because of something that had happened. Ted had once again gone on a business trip with almost no prior warning. It was Ted's habit to say, 'Incidentally, I'm off to Brussels in two days, please see that I have enough shirts for three weeks.'

When Monica first saw her own counsellor, she talked about the loneliness and insecurity she felt whenever Ted went away, and the times he had rung up to say he wouldn't be home for supper – just before she was about to serve it. As far as Monica was concerned at that point, Ted's inconsiderate ways were the problem. But they were, in fact, only the symptom. Ted could have been persuaded to behave more considerately – cut down on his business trips, or give Monica more warning about when he would be away or when he would be late – but something else would then have arisen to cause a problem. The *real* problem was the pattern of their marriage: Ted was in charge and was always right, Monica was the insecure, ineffectual partner who fell in with Ted's plans in gratitude for being looked after.

Ted hadn't changed; he had always behaved like this. Monica *had* changed. Earlier Ted's lack of consideration hadn't been so bothersome. It was their pattern of relating that needed to be changed if their marriage was going to be saved.

Apparent problems in a relationship are always a symptom of a larger relationship issue, although it rarely seems like it to the two people involved. As in the example of Ted, it is usually the pattern of the way the couple relate to each other that determines whether problems or difficulties can be handled well – or contribute to the breakdown of the relationship. And, again as in Ted's case, that 'pattern' is usually set at the beginning of the relationship, and has its roots in earlier patterns from the past. Most of this chapter is concerned with detailing typical relationship patterns, and patterns of behaviour set in childhood, into which your own relationships with your partners might have fitted.

Nevertheless, if you are now looking back at your past relationships, it will probably be easier for you to see the symptomatic problems rather than the pattern you followed. If one of you had an affair, or you were driven apart by arguments about the children or money, or because of sexual incompatibility, it might even annoy you to be told that these were merely the focus of your problems, not the underlying cause.

## PROBLEMS AS SYMPTOMS

All relationships have their ups and downs. Even happy couples who maintain their relationships for life have problems – sometimes crises of the gravest proportions. The seriousness of the problem is not the indicator of whether it will disrupt the relationship, it is how it affects the couple involved. For instance, there is the true story of a previously gentle man who killed his wife because she moved the mustard from its usual place on the table, and a counsellor told of a man who left his wife because she had a slow dance with a neighbour at a party. Clearly, these incidents, insignificant in themselves, symbolised something of fundamental importance to the people involved. While it is obvious to us that the 'real' problem in these cases must have lain elsewhere, it can be harder to see that this is also true of more serious problems.

Another extreme example is the true case of a woman who survived a pre-meditated murderous attack by her husband, and pleaded for him to be shown clemency because she wanted him back. The wife of the Yorkshire Ripper also stood by her husband, despite knowing that he was guilty of the most vicious murders. For most people, the horror of these incidents would have been enough to damage their relationships irreparably, but for these women this was not the case. Although the examples are again unusual, they show in an exaggerated form that when the relationship is still satisfying to the partners, no problem is great enough to disrupt it.

In the context of your own relationships, this also holds true. When something caused you to row a lot, it was, of course, upsetting in its own right. But the fact that you fought, rather than resolved the problem, shows that the issue highlighted an unsuccessful way of relating to each other. For instance, one couple who fought most over housework were really locked into a much larger battle over how men and women should live together.

Similarly, sexual problems are often an indication of greater dissatisfactions between a couple, and affairs are often the way people demonstrate disappointment or hostile feelings about their partners – feelings which were already present.

Most relationships go through patches that are dangerously unstable. Perhaps one person becomes ill, money is a problem, there are difficulties with the children, boredom sets in, or frustration. There are also the mid-life issues, such as ageing, children leaving home, or earlier ambitions having to be shelved. All of these things cause very real distress, but when they are the trigger for a couple to fall out and part, there is usually more to it. What all these matters have in common is that they herald great changes – so a relationship based on a particular pattern may no longer work. In relationships that survive these periods – and do so successfully – the couple have usually, knowingly or not, renegotiated the way they live together to accommodate the changes.

It is less clear-cut when the relationship ends because of one part-

ner's violence, addictions, mentally unstable behaviour, or sexual abuse
of the children. For many people there is no question of trying to keep
the relationship going in these circumstances. But, even in these cases,
it is rarely the first discovery of the partner's nature that ends the relationship. Usually there is an accumulation of incidents, leading to the
'last straw', when no more can be taken. It is also true that at some
level the 'innocent' partner had an inkling of the partner's potential to
go off the rails.

This was so in the case of Neil, who had been married to Berenice
for two years. He came for counselling as the divorce was going
through. He had been at his wit's end because of Berenice's increasingly erratic behaviour. She was obviously seriously mentally disturbed and had developed obsessional habits and violent outbursts,
during which she would destroy things in the home. Neil admitted that
he had had a gut feeling before the marriage that something wasn't
quite right but he couldn't put his finger on it. Berenice was certainly
wild and different, but neither obsessional nor violent at that time. Neil
was a scientist, a logical, methodical man who needed help to understand why Berenice had become like this. Although it seemed to the
counsellor that some of Neil's ways of treating Berenice had likely
made her problems worse, he refused to see it. This was the way he
always behaved – nobody else had reacted like Berenice, so it couldn't
be anything to do with him.

What is often found is that this 'gut feeling', as Neil described it,
forms part of the attraction in the first place. Although this can be hard
to accept, it is not a cause for guilt. Again, it is patterns from the past,
imposed by your experiences within your own family, which can cause
you to become fatally attracted to someone who will only cause you
misery. For instance, Neil's mother had also been mentally unstable,
though not to the degree that Berenice was. Neil had vowed to marry a
woman very different, and initially Berenice had seemed so. Whereas
his mother's condition took the form of fears and phobias that increasingly confined her to the home, Berenice had seemed spirited and bold,
if somewhat eccentric. But Neil's 'gut feeling' meant that unconsciously
he had recognised the symptoms of mental instability, and because that
was his experience of how wives were, he found himself falling in love
with her.

Before examining the typical relationship patterns, therefore, it is
helpful to look at what attracted you to your partner.

# WHAT ATTRACTED YOU TO EACH OTHER IN THE FIRST PLACE?

Leaving aside physical attraction for the moment, why did you fall in love with your partner? Or if, in fact, you married without love or moved in together for other reasons, why that person and not another?

It can be hard to separate physical attraction from the other elements that brought you together, and it is, of course, connected. The missing quality that makes you say about one person 'I can see he/she is good-looking, but I don't fancy him/her' is the clue to the mysterious magnetism that leads you to feel the opposite – drawn to someone, whether good-looking or not, who is somehow compellingly attractive to you. Whether you fell in love at first sight, or more slowly grew to feel that you had found 'the one', it is this hard-to-analyse recognition of rightness that contains the essence of the relationship you went on to form.

## Choosing partners

The most important point to remember when you attempt to understand what drew you both together, is that your choice of partner depends on the sort of person you are. And that, in turn, depends on your experiences while you were growing up. Often, what seems so 'right' about your partner are ways of behaving and emotional reactions that are familiar to you, because in some ways they remind you of the interactions in your own family. This can be the case even if those ways of behaving didn't make you happy in the past. You know where you are with them.

The following task is a quick way of seeing the truth of this in a past relationship.

! ———————————— *Task* ————————————

### It reminds me of . . .

Remember aspects of your partner's behaviour that made you particularly angry. Think back in time to see if you can recall any behaviour of a member of your family that made you feel the same way.

!

However, you can also be drawn to someone who behaves in very different ways from what you have experienced in your family, because you hope to be different yourself. Sometimes this very difference, initially attractive, causes you problems in the end. Perhaps your partner had qualities that you admired, and would like to have had yourself. These issues are looked at in more detail later in the chapter, under 'Patterns of Behaviour'.

## *Your feelings about yourself*

Consciously or not (and usually unconsciously) you also choose the person you believe you deserve. Although most of us would say we believe we deserve 'the best', underneath we might feel very different. If you grew up lacking in confidence or not feeling very loveable or pleasant, part of you believes you deserve someone who also feels the same things about you. It isn't too difficult, therefore, for you to accept someone who treats you less than well, or with whom you are unhappy.

Very broadly, the way you feel about yourself depends on how you felt as you were growing up. The quiz over the page is a quick guide to the way your early experiences affected you. Range your feelings on the issues in the quiz between 1, GOOD and 5, BAD; 3 in the middle is OK. Circle the number you choose.

If you score mainly 1, 2, and the occasional 3, it means that you are likely to have felt quite happy growing up, and therefore feel quite secure about yourself and your loveableness as a person. This means that you are more likely to fall in love with people who appreciate you and treat you well. If, by chance, you fall in love with someone who does not, you are less likely to make a permanent relationship with him or her.

If, however, you have many answers that fall into category 4 or 5, you will feel much less secure. The more you have, the more likely you are to question how loveable you are. Indeed, if a lot of your feelings about yourself were bad when you were growing up, your doubts will go very deep – no matter how confident or attractive you appear on the surface. Although you might believe this would lead you to fall for people who make you feel better about yourself, this is rarely the case. Time and again, people who feel unloveable have told counsellors that they are suspicious of partners who seem to think they are wonderful. If they do form relationships with them they are scared of becoming too close to them in case they discover the 'real' unloveable person underneath.

Strange as it might seem, this means you are much more likely to have fallen for partners in the past who made you unhappy in some way, because this fitted in with what you expected unconsciously. At any rate, the less good you have felt about yourself deep down, the more able you are to tolerate behaviour from a partner who makes you miserable.

# ? _____ Quiz _____

## Growing up

|                                                              | GOOD |   | OK |   | BAD |
|--------------------------------------------------------------|------|---|----|---|-----|
| **HOW I FELT ABOUT ...**                                     |      |   |    |   |     |
| ... myself as a small child                                  | 1    | 2 | 3  | 4 | 5   |
| ... how much my mother loved me                              | 1    | 2 | 3  | 4 | 5   |
| ... how much my father loved me                              | 1    | 2 | 3  | 4 | 5   |
| ... how much love I deserved                                 | 1    | 2 | 3  | 4 | 5   |
| ... how happy my home was                                    | 1    | 2 | 3  | 4 | 5   |
| ... my relationship with brothers or sisters                 | 1    | 2 | 3  | 4 | 5   |
| ... my parents' relationship with each other                 | 1    | 2 | 3  | 4 | 5   |
| ... how respected I was                                      | 1    | 2 | 3  | 4 | 5   |
| ... how liked I was                                          | 1    | 2 | 3  | 4 | 5   |
| ... how understood I was                                     | 1    | 2 | 3  | 4 | 5   |
| ... the amount of physical affection I received              | 1    | 2 | 3  | 4 | 5   |
| ... the amount of physical punishment I received             | 1    | 2 | 3  | 4 | 5   |
| ... my friendships with other children                       | 1    | 2 | 3  | 4 | 5   |
| ... my ability to get on with people                         | 1    | 2 | 3  | 4 | 5   |
| ... the loss by death or separation of a person or animal I loved | 1 | 2 | 3 | 4 | 5 |
| ... the way I looked as a small child                        | 1    | 2 | 3  | 4 | 5   |
| ... my body at puberty                                       | 1    | 2 | 3  | 4 | 5   |
| ... my attractiveness as a teenager                          | 1    | 2 | 3  | 4 | 5   |

**?**

## *Your parents' relationship*

To complicate matters further, a factor in your choice is your experience of your parents' relationship. Without even thinking about it, you might assume your own relationship should be similar, so you are drawn to someone like one of your parents. Or you might be determined not to be like your parents, and so choose someone very different. But, as Neil showed with the mentally unstable Berenice, by what seems like an extraordinary quirk of fate you can end up with someone who is very similar underneath. Some of these issues are explored later in the chapter, under *Relationship Patterns*.

These ideas might sound like nonsense, and have nothing to do with how you experienced falling in love. But time and again couples in counselling realise for themselves that some of these elements contributed to them falling in love, even though they had never thought about them consciously before.

It is helpful to see how your early experiences programmed you to feel that your partner was 'the one'. If you can recognise the connection, you can also see where the programming went wrong. Which of the things that attracted you were, in fact, the very things that made you unhappy in the end?

Before looking at the patterns that made you ready to fall in love with your partner – and helped contribute to the ending of the relationship – see if you can recognise if some of the worst characteristics about your partner were what attracted you in the first place, by doing the following task.

**!** —————————— *Task* ——————————

### It stopped being funny

Make a list of character quirks or behaviour patterns that you hated in your partner. Then think back to the beginning of the relationship and see if you can connect them to things you once loved. Some examples of what other people have said are given to start you off.

| Things I hated at the end | Things I used to love |
|---|---|
| He never talked to me | His quiet strength |
| Her vanity | Her beautiful grooming |
| Schoolboy jokes | Always ready to laugh |
| She treated me like a child | Made me feel cherished |

**!**

## PATTERNS OF BEHAVIOUR

As a child, your family train you how to behave. There are the things you learned consciously because you were told them – when to say 'please' and 'thank you', what was right and wrong. But most of what you learned was unspoken. The way your parents behaved to each other and towards you are much more profound lessons. Daily, you saw what happened when people were angry, how love was expressed, how decisions were made and how people got their own way or not. Whether these ways of relating made you happy or unhappy, whether you thought they were good or bad, they are the ways you know best. You fitted in with them because you knew no other ways, and they have become a part of you.

This means that you have taken these basic patterns into the relationships you have made yourself. The ways of behaving that were healthy and helpful will have contributed to your happiness in relationships.

But you will also have brought the ways that were less helpful, causing strife, misunderstanding or unhappiness in your own relationships. Often you are unaware that you are acting out the patterns of the past, and become confused about why the same things are going wrong in your relationship as went wrong in your parents' – and why you seem to make the same mistakes over again in relationships, even when you try not to.

Until you become conscious of the patterns you are repeating the problems will remain. When you are aware of them you are able to change them.

## Dealing with emotions

The way you handle your emotions, and those of other people, can determine the success of your adult relationships. As a child you will have learned how acceptable it was to show emotions, or whether some emotions were more tolerated than others. If you came from a family that believed in control and a 'stiff upper lip', it can be hard for you to express emotions with your partner. Conversely, if your family was emotionally uncontrolled, you might never have learned how to channel your emotions into acceptable behaviour. Some of the main issues are examined now in more detail.

● **Love and affection.** If your family was openly affectionate you will feel quite comfortable showing love – both physically and verbally. If you were given plenty of love as a child then you will have been ready to love your partner and respond to your partner's loving attention.

However, if your family was more reserved, or cold even, you will not have had the experiences that make it easy for you to be loving. Often this means that you have a great hunger for love and demand it openly – or a secret yearning for it that you can't express. Because you weren't given enough love, however, you often find it difficult to know how to show love to someone else.

An example of this is Leigh, who had been married three times, and was about to marry for the fourth time when he came for counselling. It emerged that his family had been constantly on the move when he was a child. He had been sent to boarding school when he was seven, and had missed the loving atmosphere of a family. In the holidays he would become used to being fussed over by his mother – but then he was back to the cold atmosphere of school. He would make friends with neighbouring children when he was home but, more often than not, by the time the next holiday came around the family would have moved and he would have to start all over again. He felt very lonely, isolated and in need of affection. As an adult, he longed for a loving relationship to give him what he had missed. He would enter a relationship with a lot of expectations about how perfect it would be. He knew exactly what he wanted: limitless love and affection, but it never occurred to him to think what he was going to give in return.

His wives had been attracted by his neediness. Initially they had been able to give him all the love he wanted. But, in each case, after they had had children he felt let down because he did not have all their attention. After a period of disillusionment, he would leave his wife for a new woman who seemed to be offering total love. Because his early life had been a series of partings he found it easy to turn his back on a relationship. He went into his marriages almost expecting them to end – as all friendships and relationships had ended in the past.

He came for counselling because he knew something was wrong, but he didn't know what. He couldn't bear the thought that his fourth marriage would end too. Counselling centred around talking about his lack of love as a child, and his unrealistic demands for boundless love from his partners. Although nothing could be done about the past, the counsellor said, 'For the first time Leigh was beginning to think. Before he went blindly in to relationships with his impossible expectations. He could see how he had contributed to the failures of his marriages. We left it that he would return for help if his new relationship seemed to be going wrong.'

You are also affected by the way your parents showed love to each other. If they were affectionate with each other and you sensed that they were happy together you will have been shown a good example of an adult relationship. But if, on the other hand, there seemed to be little love lost between them, a part of you will believe that it is not 'adult' for a couple to continue to be openly loving when they have settled down together. You might then have blocked your own loving feelings – or rejected your partner's loving attentions as immature. This can even happen when what drew you to your partners was the fact that they seemed to be offering the kind of loving you find it hard to give.

! ─────────────── *Task* ───────────────

### Showing love

Think back to how love was expressed in your family – towards you, and how your parents related to each other. See if you can connect this to ways you behaved in your own adult relationships.
                                                                    !

● **Anger.** Anger is a fact of life. It can be triggered by petty irritations or more profound events. Yet its very power can be disturbing. It is impossible for two or more people to live together without incidents arising that cause anger and bad feeling from time to time. You find your own way to handle your angry feelings and those of other people, and each family has its preferred method of dealing with it.

The healthiest way of dealing with anger is to acknowledge the feelings and to understand where they have come from – and then take action based on this insight without blaming or attacking someone else. Most people, however, do not do this. They cope with anger in less healthy ways. The way your own family dealt with anger is likely to fall into some typical patterns.

One way is for your family to repress all outward display of anger. Although the family members continue to feel angry from time to time, it is driven underground. Instead of the anger being expressed, it simmers and is shown in cold hostility, depression and other ways of behaving which mean that the anger is never directly dealt with. If your family pattern was like this, you might well believe that your family members were never angry. Or you might have sensed the anger and have believed that it was not allowed to emerge because its destructive power would have been too terrible. Either way, you will have grown up not knowing how to deal with your own anger except by putting a lid on it. As an adult you might try to be different, but this often means that when your anger boils to the surface you become unrestrained and destructive.

Another pattern is for your family to have been uninhibited in displays of anger. There might have been violent temper tantrums in which cruel and hateful things were routinely said and perhaps objects were smashed. Sometimes family members might have used actual physical violence on each other, though not always. Growing up in a family like this can be frightening for some children, and as an adult you might do your best to avoid angry scenes and your own angry feelings so they become as controlled as if you were brought up in the family that never showed anger. On the other hand, you might reproduce your family's way of behaving, throwing angry scenes yourself as an adult.

A typical pattern is for one parent to be the obviously angry one, while the other never seems to be angry at all. As a child you learn that there are only these two ways to be – and you might become like either one of them.

You will have seen your parents behaving in one of these ways towards each other. You will also have experienced more personally their anger – either directed towards you, or as a response to your own angry feelings. You might have learned to regard anger as being a terrifying force; for instance, when your parents were angry with you, it seemed as if your world was caving in. Or, if you were an angry child, given to tantrums, and your parents were uncomfortable with this, you might have found that you got your own way – gratifying, but also giving you frightening power. Conversely, if you sensed anger that was not openly expressed, but manifested as sulking or withdrawal, you can fear that anger means the end of love.

These are just some examples, and within the main patterns there are an infinite variety of ways that families deal with anger. The complicating factor for your own adult relationships is that your partner might have learned different ways of dealing with anger, which either reinforce or clash with your own. If these are not healthy ways of expressing anger, your adult relationships will have suffered – riven by strife, or stifled by over-control, or unbalanced by one person acting out the angry feelings for both of you.

Dividing up anger between you is one of the more common ways of behaving. Counsellors often find that in couples one is the openly angry one, while the other apparently never gets angry. This can be part of the initial attraction. The angry person is attracted by what seems like the calm serenity of the other. The calm person is attracted by the apparent emotional openness of the partner. What then happens is that couple continue to live out these roles together, usually less than happily. The 'calm' one can be frightened and repelled by the other's anger, and becomes withdrawn and depressed. The 'angry' one can become even more enraged by the partner's lack of reaction. The truth is that *both* of them are angry, but only one of them is able to show it. Unknowingly, the 'calm' one gets rid of his or her own angry feelings by making the other one angry – although this person is so unaware of the anger inside that it is quite unconscious. Therefore the 'angry' person behaves even more angrily than is natural.

An example of how this operates is Isabelle, who came for counselling after her husband left her with no explanation. He had gone to live in a flat and refused to give her his address. One day he was living with her, and the next they were communicating through solicitors.

The counsellor says, 'She was a very sweet girl. Very unworldly and devout. She came to me bewildered, but without an ounce of anger in her.'

Isabelle talked about the appalling treatment she had received from her husband, and the callous way he was handling the separation. She reported that everyone around her was furious about this – her friends, her family and her workmates. Even the counsellor was feeling angry on her behalf. But Isabelle only responded by finding excuses for her husband's inexcusable behaviour. The counsellor says, 'I began to see that she had buried her angry feelings very deep because she needed to feel good and sweet. But she had a knack of igniting it in other people. When they felt angry she was able to feel better, and so defended her husband. As she talked about her marriage it was clear that she did the same thing with him. She was the saint in the relationship and he had been the monster – behaving badly, which he was still doing.'

Another example is Hatty, whose ten years living with Con were characterised by the angry, hysterical scenes she threw. Con only rarely lost his temper. Indeed, when they were arguing about something, and Hatty became hysterical, Con's mood would often change to amused tolerance. After they split up, Hatty was surprised to find that she rarely felt uncontrollably hysterical, despite the fact that she faced a lot of problems as a single woman. In fact, the only times that her control snapped was when she talked to Con on the phone. He was distressed and perturbed by her ability to manage adequately without him – and somehow or other, while they were talking he would wind her up to such a pitch that she ended up screaming at him. As he calmed her down, she would sense that he was in a good mood once again. It took some time before realisation dawned. 'He dealt with his anger by making me become as hysterical as his mother had been in the past. He couldn't express it, so it seems I was forced to,' Hatty says. 'Now that we don't live together I realise that I am not a particularly angry or hysterical person.'

Ways of transforming the patterns of handling anger from your childhood and your past relationships are looked at in Part Two, *Working on Yourself.*

● **Fears and weaknesses.** No one grows up feeling totally strong and confident. Everyone has areas of insecurity, weak points – and downright bad points. It is not human to be perfect. How you handle

! ============ *Task* ============

## Cross purposes

Think about how anger was handled in your family. Was it good or bad – how did it make you feel?

How did you and your partner handle anger in your own relationship? Can you see a connection to your own childhood, and what you knew of your partner's childhood?

Can you see that the way in which you handled anger together contributed to your relationship going wrong? What would you like to have done differently?

!

this side of yourself partly depends on your upbringing. Ideally, you will have learned to accept and tolerate the aspects of yourself that you don't admire – and feel sure that you are loved for the whole human being that you are.

For any number of reasons, however, it is possible that you do not feel like this. You might hate your 'bad' side, hiding the aspects of yourself that you don't like, for fear that they make you unloveable. This might be because, for instance, your parents seemed only to love and approve of you when you were behaving in certain ways and not in others. For instance, a little boy might learn that his father approves of him when he is being sporty and aggressive, but makes fun of him if he cries or wants to read a book. A little girl might discover that she is petted and indulged if she is being good and sweet, but incurs disapproval if she is naughty or angry.

These are common examples, and different families have different requirements. The important point is that if you were made to feel that *you* were unloveable rather than that your *behaviour* was unacceptable, you are likely to have grown up feeling that you have something to hide.

More subtly, it can be because parents were unable to give you enough loving (because of depression, illness, divorce or other reasons unconnected to you) and you presumed it must be your fault, so looked inside yourself for character flaws to blame.

Watching your parents' relationship can have a similar effect. If one of your parents behaved in ways you couldn't like or respect, you might consciously try to get rid of similar impulses in yourself.

You can grow up believing that showing vulnerability or a need for love is a weakness that must be controlled. Sometimes this is because you feel you did not get all the love you needed as a child, and this was so hurtful that you don't want to show you need it as an adult.

It can also be because one of your parents was very put upon by the other, and you fear that the same thing will happen to you if you show any weakness.

It is also natural to find yourself strangely attracted to people who might be openly showing the very characteristics you despise in yourself – sometimes falling in love with them, while at the same time feeling irritated or repelled by them. Or you might choose someone who apparently has none of the faults or weaknesses you despise – and feel very disturbed if they emerge later.

Shirley and Pete show how some of these issues can affect a relationship. They had been married for two years, and had a one-year-old girl. This was a second marriage for Pete, who was thirty-seven. He had three teenage children by his first wife, whom he had married very young. Pete had met Shirley while he was still unhappily married. His wife had developed the habit of looking after him like a child, which he had once needed. Now he felt he had grown up, and with Shirley he felt like an adult.

But throughout their short marriage Pete had left Shirley a number of times to return to his first wife. He said he felt guilty about his children, but Shirley felt there was more to it. She was desperately unhappy about the situation, and was now at her wit's end. She felt that she wouldn't be able to go on if he should leave her again, so they had come for counselling to try to sort it out.

Their relationship sounded very good. They had many interests in common, a lively sexual relationship and enjoyed each other's company. It was a very equal, adult relationship, both acting positively and responsibly. But what was lacking was any recognition that either of them could sometimes feel insecure, 'childish' or have a need to be pampered and looked after by the other. Every now and again Pete would hit a problem with which he would try to wrestle in a grown-up way. But he would then become worried or depressed, and look to Shirley for support.

Shirley would panic. Faced by Pete as a little boy, she would tell him to pull himself together. Far from supporting him, she withdrew emotionally. It was usually after occasions like this that Pete would go back to his first wife. When he had received enough mothering from her he would be ready to return to Shirley.

Shirley, although ten years younger than Pete, never seemed to feel afraid or insecure, although Pete's yo-yo behaviour was making her unhappy. Her own mother had been a timid mouse of a woman, who was ruled by her domineering husband. Shirley had pitied and despised her. From the age of thirteen Shirley had effectively taken over the running of the house, and her father had talked over matters with her, rather than her mother. When she was fifteen her father had lost his job, and had gone from being a strong man to a 'fearful wreck', in Shirley's words. Shirley, therefore, was convinced that weakness of any sort was disastrous. She became as strong as she could be, denying any weakness in herself. When Pete was feeling insecure or troubled, it was a terrifying echo of the past.

After a few sessions, Shirley and Pete were starting to understand the process. Rather than talking through his feelings with Shirley, Pete would wait until they overwhelmed him, at which point he would become childish and demanding. Shirley would find this threatening and go cold on him. Then he would leave. They were talking about how they could handle this differently when the counsellor went on holiday.

When she returned, she received a phone call from Shirley saying that they wouldn't be coming for counselling any more. Pete had started to talk to her about his ambivalent feelings and she had blown up. She thought he was bound to leave her again, so she had told him to go back to his first wife and not to trouble coming back. He hadn't wanted to go. Shirley told the counsellor she could see no further point in counselling.

The counsellor was very sorry it had ended like that. She said, 'The root of it seemed to be that Shirley was denying her own fears and insecurities. She saw them mirrored in Pete, and couldn't take it. If she had recognised that she, too, needed support from time to time, to be vulnerable and cared for, she could have coped with Pete's need too. If she could have taken her turn to be 'childish' she would have known that the world doesn't fall apart when that happens – the need is met and then it goes away. A couple should be able to take turns to parent each other, as well as be adult together. It was a pity because I felt they had an awful lot going for them.'

Just as some people grow up wanting to hide their weaknesses, others grow up fearful of being strong. If you were made to feel less loveable when you asserted yourself or were independent, you can

---

! ——————————————— *Task* ———————————————

## The dark side

Which aspects of your own personality don't you like? How did you cope with that in your relationships – did you hide them, or did they come out anyway?

Imagine how it would be to be loved for all your qualities, good and bad.

!

deny your own ability to look after yourself in adult life, which creates similarly unbalanced relationships.

In the same way, if you grew up being insecure about your abilities and talents, you might fall in love with someone who has the very qualities you wish you had yourself. For instance, someone who seems more intelligent than you, or artistic or good with people. What often happens is that by finding these qualities in someone else you stop yourself developing your own innate possibilities. You daren't 'compete' – as you see it – because you believe you can never do so well. Or if you try, you find that your partner, needing your admiration, feels threatened, and so puts you down for your attempts.

## Asking for what you want

The best relationships involve give and take – and usually some negotiation so that both partners feel satisfied with the amount of give and take involved.

But many people find one aspect easier – either the giving or the taking, and their relationships are less balanced as a result. Again, the pattern for this is set in childhood, and you can often see the connection between your emotional responses now and some of the practical incidents in the past.

The 'plate of biscuits' is an example. Imagine that you and some other children were offered a plate with mixed biscuits on it and are asked to choose which you want. These are some of the typical reactions, and how they might be indicative of your emotional responses in adult life.

● **'I don't mind' or 'you choose first'.** Even though you know exactly which biscuit you would prefer, you don't say. You might look pointedly at your favourite biscuit and hope that someone notices and gives you that one without you having to ask.

What lies behind this response is wanting to be liked, but fearing that you won't be if you assert yourself, or say you want something that might clash with someone else. When someone chooses the biscuit you wanted you feel disappointed, or resentful. Perhaps you have already learned that your parents are more loving towards you when you are undemanding, or you have been slapped down for asserting yourself by brothers or sisters. Or perhaps no one asks for things in your family, but gets their way by manipulating.

As an adult you are likely to respond similarly in more complex circumstances. Telling your partner that you 'don't mind' or asking your partner to choose when you have a clear preference yourself, or not asking for something that would make you happy for fear of confrontation or losing love, means that you set up a situation that can make you unhappy.

Usually you want your partner to guess what you really want without you having to say it. And when he or she fails to do so, you feel that it is because you are not loved enough.

● **'I'd like the plain one'.** You would really prefer the chocolate one, but you choose your least favourite. You eat it without pleasure, or keep asking the others 'is that nice?' while they are eating.

Again you do this because you hope it will make people like you. You want them to notice that you have taken a biscuit that you don't really want, in the hope that they will think you are a nice person. If they don't appear to notice, you might be driven to say, 'I left the chocolate one for *you*, because I knew you liked it.' Perhaps you gained most attention in your family when you were looking soulful or sad, or when you put yourself out for others. Or perhaps the parent with whom you closely identify behaves in similar ways.

As an adult, this can translate into martyrish behaviour with your partner, 'buying' love at the expense of your own happiness. You can't believe that you will be loved unless you put other people's desires first.

● **'Let me go first!'** In this case, you dive in and take the one you want before anyone else can have it, and perhaps eat it quickly so that if there are any second helpings you'll be ready before anyone else.

You do this because you believe that if you don't one of the other children will get in first. The most important thing is to get what you want – it doesn't occur to you to worry whether it will make you unpopular because you believe that all the children are thinking the same way. As long as you're all right, it doesn't matter about anyone else. Perhaps you come from a large family where you have had to struggle for the attention you wanted or the things you desired. Or you might have witnessed one parent consistently getting his or her own way at the expense of the other.

Emotionally and practically as an adult you might be similarly demanding. You think about what you want, and what would make you happy. You might be irritated by demands that conflict with your own desires. It seems to you that considering a partner's needs means that your own won't be attended to. You are likely to be oblivious to 'signals' from a partner who doesn't ask for things directly.

● **'I'd like the chocolate, but if you want it I'll have it next time'.** This is the least likely response. You are prepared to give way in the interests of another child, but can say what you want and create a situation where you will get it at some point.

You can do this because you recognise that the other children have equally strong desires, and you are willing to put yours on hold occasionally for the sake of good relations. You believe in fairness, and are prepared to stand up for yourself as well as give in to others. You have almost certainly experienced healthy give and take in your own family – sometimes getting what you wanted, and understanding why not when you didn't. You have been used to having your own feelings respected, so it is easy for you to respect other people's. You have usually seen your own parents handle conflicting desires in a similar way, and know that most situations can be negotiated so that there is no winner or loser.

You can use these skills as an adult to pursue your own happiness in a relationship, without it being at the expense of your partner's happiness. You get pleasure from doing something that pleases your partner, secure in the knowledge that your turn to be pleased will come.

While it is possible for everyone to learn this way of dealing with their own and their partner's needs, it is usual to be stuck in a version of one of the three less helpful ways. If you have done so in the past, you can probably see for yourself how this contributed to mounting dissastisfaction in your relationships.

! ———————————— *Task* ————————————

### My pattern

Look back at your relationships and at how you were able to ask – or not – for what you wanted. Which was your pattern? How did your partners' patterns fit with yours? Can you see how it could have been different? !

One example of how this very issue can erode a relationship is Judith and Walter. He came for the first counselling interview on his own, shell-shocked and pathetic. He and Judith had been together since they were teenagers, and married for the last seven years; they had two small children. They were both thirty. As far as he was concerned they were fine, until suddenly Judith had announced that she was in love with someone else and was leaving him. He didn't know what had gone wrong.

Judith joined them for the next interview – making it clear that she was only coming to help Walter understand that it was over. She told a different story. She said she had been unhappy for years. She said it was because he'd put so much time into his work, and none into his family – they had hardly seen him. If he hadn't been so wrapped up in his work, she maintained, he would have noticed how frustrated and unhappy she was. He had never done anything to change the situation for the better. Falling in love with the other man had shown her that she must end the marriage.

But although Judith was very clear about what Walter might have done to make her happier, it emerged that she had never actually told him. She said he should have known, should have noticed. Instead, she expressed her grievances by sulking, and occasionally nagging and complaining. Judith was acting out the adult version of the 'I don't mind' or 'you choose first' attitude to the plate of biscuits – expecting Walter to know that things weren't as she wanted them to be, but not clearly telling him.

Judith prided herself on being a good communicator, and she was certainly articulate – but she had never checked that Walter had understood what she was trying to tell him. Walter was aware, of course, that she was sometimes upset and irritated, but he never knew how important the issues were. His own parents had stayed together through many bad patches: Walter just thought it was a fact of married life that the wife must let off steam from time to time.

Counselling came too late to help them. Judith was committed to her new love and completely disillusioned about her marriage to Walter. But many of the things that would have made her happier would have been relatively simple to achieve if she had been able to ask for what she needed at the time.

## RELATIONSHIP PATTERNS

The patterns of behaving that you have learned make it likely that your adult relationships will also fall into a recognisable pattern. The trouble with patterns is that they require a certain way of behaving for all time. So even when they start off well, they do not allow for change, development and growth. Before looking at the typical patterns, their restrictions, and what you can learn from them to make better relationships in the future, it is useful to explore what a healthy relationship is like. This can serve as a model against which to judge your own relationships – and an ideal to aim for in the future.

In a Marriage Guidance Lifeguide published in 1984, the author Geoffrey Fletcher cites the three main aspects of a healthy relationship, as defined by the psychologist, Dr Jack Dominian. These are that the relationship should be 'mutually sustaining', 'healing' and that the individuals should be 'free to grow'. These are worth examining further.

● **A healthy relationship is mutually sustaining.** This means the couple grow to depend on each other for the best reasons: that they know that they both deeply value each other and are concerned for each other's welfare and happiness.

In practical terms, this involves not only working out what makes you happy, but being prepared to make your partner happy. When both partners do this, love increases, and the partnership becomes very satisfying. With concern for each other's feelings comes the will to deal with problems constructively so that they do not come between you. While you will still have conflicts, if you care about each other's happiness you will not want to punish each other, but find workable solutions.

● **A healthy relationship is healing.** The very fact of being human means that we all have bad as well as good characteristics, frailties as well as strengths. With the best will in the world, even 'good enough' parents will not have been able to see that we have no fears or insecurities. As this chapter has shown, the very process of growing up inevitably causes some difficulties or leaves emotional scars.

In a healthy relationship you don't hide aspects of yourself from your partner. You feel able to show your vulnerabilities and your less admirable side because you are confident that you won't be taken advantage of, but will be loved anyway. When this is proved, trust grows between you. You also show your partner that you accept and love him or her just as he or she is. When this is the case, you draw confidence from each other. Love heals the old wounds, helps you enhance your good qualities, and gives you the strength to deal with the aspects of yourself with which you are less happy.

● **In a healthy relationship you are both free to grow.** This means that you always see your partner as an individual, while also feeling close and loving. You know that you do not own your partner, who has feelings, ideas and needs different to yours. You both respect your separateness as much as you value your closeness. Sometimes this means accepting that your partner can find satisfaction in things outside your relationship as well – perhaps hobbies, interests and friends that you do not share, but that you can talk about and participate in at one remove.

Throughout life you change. What makes you happy can change, as can your needs, ambitions and what you see as your purpose in life.

Change is always difficult to handle – your own as well as that in someone close to you. Allowing your partner freedom to grow means supporting and encouraging him or her through the changes, even when you find them disturbing. This involves talking and sharing feelings, so that you both become gradually acclimatised to the changes.

A relationship that has these three elements has the best chance of lasting till death parts you, and of being, on balance, happy and satisfying – though every relationship has its unhappy moments.

However, even relationships as good as these sometimes end. Sometimes the changes that you make mean that you gradually come to realise that you would be happier apart, because your aims and needs have become quite different. This shows that the end of a relationship does not necessarily have to be regarded as a failure. Sometimes your beloved partner dies. Nevertheless, the experience of a healthy relationship like this shows that you have what it takes to make other satisfying relationships – whether romantic or just friendships.

The relationship patterns that now follow lack these elements of loving flexibility. It is the rigidity of the patterns that creates unhappiness and, ultimately, causes the relationships to break down.

## Pattern One: 'You need me, and I will look after you'

In this kind of relationship, one person apparently relies heavily on the other – the 'strong one', who controls the relationship. In fact, they are mutually dependent, both needing to play their separate roles. The strong one draws strength from the weakness of the other, usually because he or she is frightened of feeling weak, and of what he or she might become if control is relaxed, or shared. The weak one is fearful of standing on his or her own feet, while sometimes also feeling resentful of the power of the strong one. Included in this is the situation where the strong one is the 'rescuer', who saves the weak one from circumstances – or from himself or herself.

This kind of relationship can work well, sometimes for years. The one in control draws pleasure from feeling powerful, though underneath is the fear of losing the partner if the control is relinquished. Often, the strong one has problems with self-esteem, masked by an 'I know what I'm doing' manner. The other feels relieved – 'I'm being looked after' – but can't develop or grow. Both secretly fear losing the other, not just because they love each other, but because their entire sense of identity is defined by their roles.

The relationship starts to go wrong when one of them changes. Perhaps the 'weak' one develops some strength and independence, and begins to find the controlling ways of the strong one unbearable. Or the 'strong' one goes through a phase of needing to draw strength from the partner, who might be unwilling to take the responsibility.

Vince and Audrey were an example of this. Vince had 'rescued' Audrey from an unhappy marriage twelve years previously. He had also been married before, and they were both in their late forties. Audrey brought two children from her previous marriage, and later one of Vince's teenage sons moved in with them. They came for counselling because Vince said his feelings towards Audrey had changed. The children had left home and he said he wasn't sure that he and Audrey still needed each other. He had met another woman, a single parent in distressed circumstances. He was on the brink of leaving Audrey and moving in with the other woman.

As they explored their relationship with the counsellor, it became clear that it was important to Vince to feel that he was the provider – that everyone was dependent on him for his largesse. He saw himself as the beloved patriarch. He was well-established in his own business, so materially he could provide everything that was wanted. This was just what Audrey had needed when they first married. Shell-shocked from her first marriage, with two young children to support, Vince was a dream come true.

But four years ago, with the children almost grown-up, things had changed. She had found a job, developed confidence, and felt proud that she could now contribute to the home.

This had rattled Vince, who was disturbed by Audrey's new independence. His response was to become heavy-handed in laying down the law, and Audrey began to resent the way he tried to control her life. Initially their angry feelings centred on money. Audrey began to feel that there were strings attached to Vince's generosity. He needed to be thanked and appreciated endlessly. She felt he was buying her – and that by extension he believed he owned her. Audrey's reaction was to block his attempts to give her things.

Then the children left home, and Vince's view of himself as the patriarch-provider evaporated. It was at this point that he met the other woman, who needed him. If he could rescue her and look after her, then he would once again be the man he needed to feel himself to be.

In this case, there was still a lot of love between Vince and Audrey. They participated in counselling for months and gradually came to understand what had happened. As they began to see the other's side, they were able to make changes in the way they related. Vince saw that Audrey still loved him and wanted to stay with him even though she no longer had the same need for his support, and Audrey stopped feeling threatened by his acts of generosity. In the end, the relationship was so improved that Vince decided to remain with

Audrey. The relationship survived because they managed to leave behind the roles of rescuer and rescued, and develop a more equal and flexible relationship.

● **Influences from the past.** If you have found yourself in this kind of pattern, whether you were the 'strong' or 'weak' one, this is usually because you have developed a fear of weakness in your early years. Perhaps you were over-protected as a child or, conversely, you were expected to grow up and mature before you were ready to. What both the 'strong' and the 'weak' have in common is the belief that without control there is chaos – so either you feel the need to control someone else closely, or you need to feel that someone is taking charge for you.

The most uncontrollable area, of course, is your emotions. Feelings of weakness, panic, fear and vulnerability are particularly threatening. An emotionally intimate relationship exposes these vulnerabilities, so you find closeness difficult. When one of you is dedicated to appearing strong at all times, you never become truly close, because that can only happen when both of you are open enough to reveal all of yourselves. This lack of real intimacy will therefore feel comfortable to you.

You might also repeat this pattern if it was the way your parents related. For instance, Mandy had a domineering father and a mother who did everything in the home and sheltered behind her husband. Mandy was her father's pet. She was pretty, clever and capable and she could do no wrong in her father's eyes. Mandy had despised her mother as a child, and didn't want to be like her. Now, at thirty-five, Mandy was close to her mother and saw things differently. She saw that her mother had been unhappy for many years, but had been too weak to assert herself.

What this meant was that Mandy had no idea how a healthy, close and balanced relationship operated. She didn't want to be like her mother, so the alternative, as she saw it, was to be like her father – in charge and dominant. Nevertheless, she was also affected by her child's-eye vision of how women (her mother) behaved – which was to do everything for their men. The result was that Mandy became a rescuer – always falling for weak and troubled men, and then putting herself out to look after them, build them up, and set them on their feet.

Mandy came for counselling on her own, soon after her third marriage failed. She had now met someone new. She had been knocked back by the end of her marriage to Liam, and was terrified that it meant that she would never make a relationship that lasted. She wanted to know where she had gone wrong before, and how to avoid the pitfalls in this new relationship with Chris.

Mandy was quick to see how her parents' marriage had formed the pattern that she was following. She needed to be the rescuer, but she also wanted them to become strong partners, like her father. Her first husband had been a drop-out, and she never succeeded in making him settle down, so she eventually divorced him. Her next husband had a depressive illness, for which he was eventually hospitalised. She had supported both of them.

With Liam, she had felt, she had had more success. He had been unemployed, in deep debt, and drinking heavily when they met. She dried him out, paid his debts, got him to retrain, and he had found a job. Unfortunately, this job was in another city.

Liam took up the post while Mandy stayed behind to work out her notice. When she joined him, having found only poorly paid, part-time work in the new city, she discovered that he had started drinking again and his job was now on the line. It was at this point she knew that he could never be 'saved', and they were in the process of divorcing.

Then she met Chris. He, too, was newly divorced, and still grieving for his lost marriage. They started an affair, in which she played her 'rescuing' role in helping him feel better. He wanted her to move in with him, but by now she was very scared – which was when she made her appointment to see a counsellor.

Once she recognised the pattern, she could see that in some ways Chris was different. He was dependable and solvent, although very emotionally needy. But she soon recognised that there was one element in the pattern that was the same. Her need to be the 'strong' one meant that while she was prepared to give Chris emotional support, she would not share her own problems with him. What she had denied through all her relationships was her own need to be looked after. She thought that if she acknowledged any weakness then she would become like her mother.

The first step for Mandy was being able to confide in women friends about her difficulties, unhappiness and fears, which she had never done before. But she told the counsellor that Chris had enough troubles of his own, and she didn't want to burden him. It emerged, however, that Chris had been urging her to share her feelings. He wanted to get closer, but she was holding him off.

The breakthrough came when Mandy understood that her insistence on being strong had contributed to the failure of her relationships. She felt strongest when the men were weak. As she had seemed invincible, they had never understood how unhappy they made her. Now that she had found a man who had some strength, the final step was to show him that she needed his support. By the time Mandy left counselling she had started to confide in Chris. Although it made her feel vulnerable, she was valuing this new closeness. She wasn't ready to move in with him, but was waiting to see how the relationship developed before committing herself.

● **Lessons for the future.** Breaking this pattern is possible when you recognise what lies behind it – your fear of weakness. But when the relationship breaks down you can see that the pattern never truly protected you. The following task is useful to help clarify some of the issues.

═══════════════════ *Task* ═══════════════════

### The chink in the armour

If you were the 'weak' one in previous relationships, ask yourself whether you ever allowed or encouraged your partners to be less than strong? If they showed a chink in their armour, did you panic until the illusion was back in place? Did you show your resentment of their strengths by attacking them verbally or physically, while believing they could never be hurt? Or did you leave if they seemed to be needing some strength from you?

If you were the 'strong' one in previous relationships, ask yourself what you thought would happen if you stopped acting strong? Did you trust your partner enough to accept you when you had doubts or fears? Did you ever feel lonely or despairing because there was no one there to help you?

Truly strong people recognise and accept their own weaknesses (which everyone has) and do not fear them. A weakness is not a failing, it is simply a human response to certain circumstances which seem out of your control. Weakness can be many things: it can be fears you harbour, it can be admitting that you don't always know the answer, it can be acknowledging that you sometimes need support or help. It can also be showing you are upset, hurt, worried or panic-stricken when the occasion arises.

On the other hand, 'weak' people have to develop their own strengths (which everyone has) so that they can form more equal relationships. Strength is not the same as aggression or power-wielding. Strength is trusting yourself, it is the capacity for endurance, and the ability to extend a hand to help someone else. These issues are looked at in Part Two, *Working on Yourself*.

While you don't have to deny a future attraction to an apparently weak or strong person, what you must not do is let the pattern where one is in control become established. This means both partners letting each other see their weaknesses, and helping each other develop their strengths. It means sharing, negotiating and talking, rather than letting one person take charge of the entire relationship.

What this kind of relationship also teaches you is that both partners need to learn how to care for themselves. The weak one looks to the strong one to do the caring, and the strong one doesn't admit that he or she needs looking after.

Sometimes the pressure on the one in charge to be strong eventually tells, and then he or she recognises a need to be cared for. For instance, David, a forty-two-year-old man, came for counselling because he was confused, scared and depressed.

David had been divorced for five years, and was now married to Lindsay, another divorcee with two children. He was unhappy in the relationship and wanted to leave, but he couldn't sort out what had gone wrong.

According to David, he came from a very loving and affectionate family and when he had met his first wife he had wanted to share this with her. She had been sexually abused in her poor and deprived family, and she blossomed during their marriage. But as she did so his sexual feelings for her went. Eventually she left him for another man.

When he met Lindsay she was equally needy. She was an emotional mess after her divorce, and her children had taken it badly. Again, David took over the caring role. But as Lindsay started to recover, David found he stopped wanting sex with her and wasn't sure he loved her.

When the counsellor asked about his apparently ideal 'loving and affectionate' family, he found that David received love at a price. His parents had been sickly, and David had to be ultra-good so as not to upset them. Later, he looked after them. He had learned that his needs were not important, and that if he was going to be loved then he had to earn it.

What this meant for David was that he knew where he was with someone who needed support – he felt loving and strong. But when his partner did not need him he felt insecure, unhappy in the relationship, and his desire for the woman went. He was a 'giver' because he needed approval. But what he hadn't recognised was that to be able to give generously, you also need to be able to receive – and ask for – what you need. To love others effectively you have to feel your needs are important too, or, as the counsellor said, 'to love yourself'.

David finally learned that he needed to care for himself. He recognised that he had exhausted himself caring for the people in his life, but he had never given the women the chance to care for him in return; and he had cut them off by rejecting them sexually. Although his relationship with Lindsay could not be saved, David had learned a lot. He was working on his self-esteem, and had recognised why he had been driven to form his relationships – and then disrupt them.

## Pattern Two: 'What I say goes – you just have to live with it'

Superficially similar to 'you need me, I will look after you', this pattern also has a strong and a weak partner. The main difference is that there is less pleasure in this relationship for either partner. The boss – male or female – is not concerned with looking after the partner, or rescuing the partner, but with having his or her own way. Usually the boss despises the partner, whose role is to do as ordered and to have no needs of his or her own. In this situation the 'strong' partner is usually, but not always, a man, who also wields power by being the bread-winner.

The weak partner goes along with this, but without the same satisfying feeling of being cared for. This partner's self-esteem is very low so he or she feels that this treatment is deserved. Although resentment might be felt, and occasionally expressed, it is not done with any belief that it will make a difference. The weak partner feels lucky to have a partner at all and believes there is no other option.

Fear operates here, as well. The 'strong' one has the bully's fear of being stood up to – when this happens, the strength crumbles. The 'weak' one has a fear of being left alone; anything is better than that.

Sometimes this relationship continues, unhappily, until one partner dies. Occasionally the strong one becomes weak – through illness, say, and the roles flip. Now the 'weak' one takes up the role of command and does so in the same bullying, uncaring way as the other did. Otherwise, it will change when one of the partners becomes fed up. The strong partner might discard the weak one when it suits him or her – or one humiliation too many might finally drive the weak partner away. This is what happened in the case of Flora and Derek, who came for counselling because Flora's doctor suggested it. Derek was reluctant, but thought it would be 'interesting'.

Flora was being treated for depression because Derek was having an open affair. On the weekends he would leave Flora and go to stay with his mystery mistress, who lived in another town. Derek, a good-looking man, smiled as he told the counsellor, 'No man is monogamous. It doesn't affect my marriage; it is just extra.'

The counsellor wanted to know what Flora thought about it. She was hesitant and apologetic when she said, 'I would feel better if Derek finished the affair.'

'No question of that,' Derek said. 'You just have to learn to live with it.'

To the counsellor's surprise, Flora accepted this without a murmur. 'If that's what you say, then I will try, but I'd like to be able to feel better about it.'

It is not the counsellor's job to advise or suggest solutions. She or he must work with the 'agenda' the couple set. This couple's agenda, therefore, was that they wanted to stay together and for Flora to come to terms with the arrangement Derek had made. In view of the situation, the counsellor was surprised that they continued the counselling for many more months. Derek enjoyed talking about himself, and Flora worked hard to understand their marriage and to accept the situation. She remained unhappy, but her hope was that as Derek chose to stay with her, he might eventually tire of his mistress and be hers alone.

There is no telling how long this might have continued, but one day Flora received a phone call from Derek's mistress. She wanted Derek full-time, and wanted Flora to let him go. The shocking truth was that the mistress was Flora's own sister. This double betrayal was the final straw. In her rage and misery, Flora threw Derek out of the house and told him never to come back. She started immediate divorce proceedings.

Still they came for counselling, but this time separately. Flora was initially traumatised, and frightened about what the future held. How would she manage to look after herself, let alone her children? Gradually, however, she learned to cope, and a year after counselling ended she wrote and told the counsellor she was engaged.

The greatest change was in Derek. His mistress deserted him as well, and now he wanted his marriage back. The counsellor said, 'He seemed to shrink physically. Everything had fallen apart for him, and he was less able to cope than Flora was. She had learned something from the experience, but he had learned nothing. "Things" had gone wrong – there was no recognition that he had done anything wrong.'

● **Influences from the past.** Both partners in this pattern have usually endured distressing and damaging experiences in their past. The strong one has usually had very little nurturing loving as a child, or was ruled by a dominating parent in a household where one parent was in charge. What he or she has learned is that the only thing that works in relationships is to rule by fear, without understanding the place for trust and love. Under this is usually a person who yearns for love but hasn't learned the healthy ways to give or accept it. Their philosophy can be summed up as 'It's a dog-eat-dog world'; that is, if they don't dominate they will be dominated.

It is similar for weak partners in this set-up, who usually felt unloveable as children for one reason or another. Additionally, they probably learned that if they were demanding or assertive, matters were worse for them. Such people are likely to have painful memories of 'putting themselves forward' and being rejected or bullied.

Sometimes their own parents' relationship followed this pattern, so their picture of what an intimate relationship is like involves one person being subjugated by another. If they reject the weak role in their own relationships, the only option they can see is to become the bully.

There were some of all these elements in the backgrounds of Ronald and Jackie. Ronald's mother died giving birth to him. He was looked after by some uncaring relatives, who had children of their own and found him a nuisance. When he was five, his father remarried, and Ronald was sent back to live with him. The new wife resented the difficult little boy that Ronald had become, and his father was a stranger who did not know how to handle him. Three years later his father died, and his step-mother bundled him straight back to the relatives. By this time Ronald was a very disturbed boy, and they couldn't cope with him. He was sent away again, this time to boarding school. He had never had any experience of being loved, only of rejection.

Jackie had a superficially more stable childhood. She came from a large family, where she was the eldest of nine children. Her mother was weakened by her many pregnancies, and constantly ill. Jackie spent most of her time looking after the younger children. Her parents' relationship was along this pattern – her father was domineering, and her mother was terrified of him. The only 'love' her father showed Jackie was when her mother died, and he started to abuse her sexually.

When Ronald and Jackie met, she was a suspicious, overweight girl who worked as a secretary. She had never had a boyfriend. Ronald was a good-looking labourer. Jackie couldn't believe her luck when he asked her to marry him. Jackie gave up work, and was soon pregnant – she was happy to be able to give Ronald what he had never had: a family. Ronald was bullying and demanding but to Jackie this was normal and she felt she deserved no better. She put up with him stoically. Eight years later, however, she made an appointment with a counsellor.

Becoming a mother had changed Jackie. She had her children's happiness to fight for and she couldn't stand to see them being made miserable. More significantly, her secretarial experience had been seen as valuable for the Parent-Teacher Association at the school and she had become involved. She was respected there, which built her confidence. A year previously she had found herself a good job. She was now stronger, and not ready to put up with Ronald any more. She wanted to leave him, but he wouldn't hear of joining her for counselling.

Jackie told the counsellor that if Ronald would change, everything would be all right. The counsellor gently pointed out that that the only thing she could control was herself. It would be nice if Ronald could change – she could wish for it and ask for it, but she couldn't force him to change.

During the sessions, the counsellor asked Jackie to show her marriage symbolically using a bag of stones that the counsellor kept for the purpose. Jackie picked out stones to represent herself, her children and Ronald – and placed them as they were in relation to each other. She also used stones to represent other important people in her life. When she was finished, the stone that represented herself was surrounded by children, friends, colleagues, brothers and sisters, while Ronald's stone stood alone. It was painful for her to see so graphically how isolated Ronald was. The counsellor asked her to move the stones to represent things as she would like them to be. 'Like a game?' Jackie asked. Then she had a realisation, 'I can see that our relationship has been like a game in which Ronald made up the rules. I was quite happy to follow them. Now I have changed the rules, but he is still playing by the old ones!'

It was shortly after this that Jackie found the courage to leave, though she mourned for Ronald. In her last session she told the counsellor, 'Ronald's going along the lines he's been programmed for. He'll never change to become happier because he doesn't know what happiness is.'

● **Lessons for the future.** If relationships of this kind lie behind you, it is unlikely that you remember much tenderness or pleasure in them. It is, perhaps, more difficult for you if you were the strong one to see how destructive it was, because you always got your own way. However, sex was likely to have been infrequent and unsatisfying, and your partner is likely to have been depressed and hostile. If your partner ended the relationship, it is important for you to recognise how your behaviour contributed to the parting, and not see it as an inexplicable, unpleasant attempt to hurt you. In future, you will develop a more rewarding relationship by learning to see your own weak side, and accepting and sharing it. This, in turn, will mean you are offered more of the warmth and love that can heal the wounds of your past.

If you were the weak one, it is perhaps easier for you to see that it would be unhealthy for you to let this happen again in the future. You need to recognise that you allowed yourself to be dominated by not standing up for yourself at an early point in the relationship. Both of you will have had difficulty understanding that there are other ways to live together than by one person controlling the other.

!
======================== *Task* ========================

**Win – win**

Think of one or two incidents from past relationships in which one of you got your way at the expense of the other's happiness. See if you can devise a solution that would have involved a compromise that might have suited both of you.

!

The other problem that both of you shared is that of low self-esteem and of not feeling loveable. If you are going to make better relationships in the future, one of your first tasks will be to work on your feelings about yourself, which Part Two can help you do.

## Pattern Three: 'We are everything to each other'

On the surface, this looks like many people's idea of a perfect relationship. The couple seem to think the same on every issue, like to be together as much as possible, sometimes even dress or look alike. They don't argue, can finish each other's sentences, and might even stay literally 'in touch', holding hands or sitting very close together.

This makes an attractive, romantic picture, because it is what most people experience when they first fall in love. During this early stage of a relationship a couple can't bear to be parted, derive most of their happiness from being together, and feel almost like 'one'. Many people would like their relationships to stay at this stage for ever, and are disappointed when, instead, this intensely involving mutual admiration passes. In most relationships, this is followed by a time of adjustment, when the couple realise that there are differences between them, and that they are not perfectly complementary. As we saw earlier, in a healthy relationship the couple develop a new closeness. This involves recognising and understanding each other's separateness – loving each other 'warts and all' – and allowing each other what is sometimes called 'personal space', while remaining intimately committed.

The couple who remain apparently as entwined as young lovers, however, find the idea of any differences intensely threatening. To be apart, or to disagree, makes them feel that not only their love, but their very lives are at stake. The result of this is that they repress any feelings, ideas, or needs that are not identical to their partner's. So, although they seem extraordinarily close, the relationship lacks intimacy. They do not really know each other because they daren't be themselves – or show any aspect of themselves that threatens the idea that they are twin souls.

Although this looks loving from the outside, and the couple believe it is what loving is about, the couple are, in fact, fearful and unrelaxed. They cannot develop as people because any small move towards independence is seen as disloyal.

Some couples stay locked in this togetherness until death parts them. Usually they do so less than happily, because circumstances will inevitably prove that their idea of perfect unity is an illusion. For instance, if they have children it might become obvious that they have responsibilities and emotional attachments separate from the relationship. This is experienced as a disappointment and a threat, but rather than deal with the feelings, they are driven underground. The couple continue to act towards each other as if they are 'one mind in two bodies', but the fear increases.

In other cases they break up after a long time because one of them develops in such a way as to find the relationship suffocating, and the other can't change. Others go through a series of relationships that break down as soon as they realise that they can't derive all their security and needs from each other. It can't be love, they believe, unless they have found their entire world in each other.

This was the case with Karen, who had been married three times, and had a child by each marriage. She came for counselling because she was in her fourth relationship, which looked as if it was about to end.

Each marriage had started off with this kind of exceptional closeness. When Karen met her first husband they both felt that they had found their 'other half'. After two years together, they had a baby – and within a year her husband had left her. He had felt unable to share Karen with the child, and became sullen and resentful, accusing Karen of not loving him any more. Karen was devastated by his defection, but was thrilled when, four years after this, she met her second husband. Again, it was intensely romantic. Karen felt she had 'known him all her life'. Her child was, by this time, at school, and Karen was so wrapped up in her new husband that he came first in her life. A year later they too had a baby. History repeated itself chillingly. Her second husband couldn't take Karen's involvement with the baby. He started an affair with someone else, and by the time the child was three he had moved in with the new woman.

The same thing happened with her third husband. At the start of the relationship, which was marked by exceptional closeness, her previous children were no problem. But soon after having a child of their own everything fell apart and it was just a question of time before he moved out.

Karen was now in her early forties, and the three children were grown up. She had lived with this new man for a while, and had no plans to have children of their own. Nevertheless, now they had passed through the romantic, courting stage, he was becoming increasingly jealous of her relationships with her children. He maintained that they were more important to her than he was.

During the counselling Karen was able to see that the men she fell in love with all wanted a totally exclusive relationship in which nothing else mattered. As far as the men were concerned, love shared was love lost. But why had she chosen them?

It became clear to Karen that this was her view as well. In the early, romantic phase, she was able to believe that the relationship between them was the single most important thing in her life. But with the arrival of each new baby she was caught up in a rush of maternal love, which made the men feel excluded from her heart, so that they were unprepared to love the children that had caused this. Although the men left Karen – and each time she was very upset about it – the truth was that she too felt that the relationship had crumbled because she ceased to feel that the man was number one in her life.

While Karen was still having counselling, her live-in lover left. Shortly afterwards, Karen left counselling too. The counsellor had hoped that if Karen could understand that a relationship could be satisfying even when it wasn't emotionally exclusive, she would have a better chance of making a lasting relationship in the future. But Karen had not wanted to see this. She preferred to hope that she would eventually meet the 'right man', with whom she could say, 'We are everything to each other.'

● **Influences from the past.** Needing this kind of relationship is a result of great insecurity. You have usually grown up questioning whether you are loveable. Because you doubt this, you need to feel that you are all-important to your partner. If your partner needs any independence, or disagrees with you, or has other important relationships (even family or friends) you feel unbearably threatened. You only feel valuable or 'whole' when you have someone 'completing' you, who not only needs you but approves of everything about you. When your partner is not a clone of yourself, it appears to you there is something bad in the relationship – and bad about you.

In your own family there is likely to have been difficulty with anger. Either it wasn't expressed in your family, but you felt the dangerous simmerings of resentment, or there was a lot of open, frightening (to you) anger. In either case, you have probably grown up yearning for a peaceful, harmonious relationship, which you will go to great lengths to form. Rather than disagreements seeming natural, they can appear to be the thin end of a wedge that will prise your relationship apart.

Sometimes your parents had this kind of over-close relationship, in which they presented a united front, so you have always expected the same for yourself. Or perhaps you were the child of divorce, and determined not to have the same thing happen to you. If you have a great fear of parting, then the only alternative can seem to be a closeness in which only total agreement and unity is allowed.

The upbringing of Bridget and Nigel shows the way their own relationship was shaped by their experiences. Their parents' marriages had both been very similar. They were frightened of their fathers, who were both strict, cool and unaffectionate. Both their mothers were distant, too. What their fathers said went in the household – and their mothers seemed to agree with the laws the fathers laid down, but both Bridget and Nigel felt their mothers were also scared of their fathers. They had grown up feeling unloved, and they had never seen their parents behave lovingly towards each other.

They had both been married before. It had been the first time that either of them had experienced feeling loved. When those marriages had broken down they had been deeply hurt, more convinced than ever that they were unloveable.

Nigel and Bridget had met fifteen years previously, shortly after their divorces had come through. They comforted each other, fell in love, and eventually married. Neither of them wanted to repeat the mistakes of the past and they soon developed an exceptionally close relationship. They never argued and were very careful of each other's feelings. They spent every available minute together, and after some years they had a son.

They were devoted to their child, and their relationship continued as before. They strove to do things differently from their parents, showering the boy with love and maintaining a constant, polite atmosphere in the home, where there was never a cross word. Then, a year previously, a new colleague had joined Nigel's electronics firm, a woman who shared his interest in technical matters, about which Bridget was ignorant. The relationship was perfectly innocent – she was some years older than Nigel and happily married, but Nigel was delighted with his new friend.

Bridget was as devastated by Nigel's friend as if he were having an affair. She had met the woman, and had seen for herself that it was a simple friendship, but this did not stop her feeling total panic and fear. The fact that Nigel should enjoy the company of anyone else, particularly another woman, had hit at her self-esteem. She felt shut out from part of Nigel's life. She had been unable to have sex with him any more, so they had consulted a sex therapist.

They told the therapist that their sex life had been regular previously, but Bridget had only ever tolerated it. She saw it as a way to reward Nigel when she was pleased with him. She also believed that whenever Nigel touched her he wanted sex – even if he just took her hand or put his arm round her shoulders. She would never touch him, even casually, in case it 'gave him the wrong idea'.

Because they were concerned about the sexual problem, the therapist worked by giving them tasks to help improve their sex life. But while this was happening the nature of their relationship pattern was exposed.

Bridget was encouraged to tell Nigel about the kinds of touching she found difficult and why. For instance, she would freeze if he came up behind her while she was washing up or ironing and put his arms round her or touched her breasts. Any unexpected caresses, particularly to sexual areas such as breasts, thighs or bottom, had the same effect. Bridget had to tell Nigel what touching she was comfortable with. She said she had to know he was about to touch her, and felt she would be all right if he put his arm round her when they watched television.

Nigel was encouraged to put his side. He explained that he needed cuddling and didn't always want sex. The therapist intitially 'prescribed' some evenings cuddling in front of the television, which they did, and which they both enjoyed. The therapist described this as a major breakthrough.

The reason this was so profound for them was that it was the first time that they had acknowledged any differences in the way they felt – and their relationship had survived. Previously it would have been unthinkable for Bridget to say that anything Nigel did was unpleasant to her. She was only able to do so in the context of counselling, and because his independent act of making friends with someone else had so shaken her.

From then on, the therapist said, they both began to tell each other what they did and didn't like about sex – and were able to accommodate each other's differences. But it also gave them the courage to open up generally.

As they became more affectionate and genuinely considerate towards each other, they started talking about other things – childhood problems, hurtful experiences in the past, fears they harboured now. They grew to know each other more completely than they had in all their years of marriage, and inevitably other differences between them emerged. They were stunned to find that, instead of forcing them apart, they actually felt closer. Bridget was able to come to terms with Nigel's friendship, and not feel threatened by it any more.

● **Lessons for the future.** The fact that Bridget and Nigel were able to save their marriage – and transform it for the better – contains clues to how you can break this pattern in future relationships. The most important is recognising that differences between you are natural, and that allowing them free expression brings you closer than denying them.

Part of this is understanding that the complete togetherness of the courting stage can't last – and shouldn't last. It no longer feels loving, and it becomes stifling if you can have no independent thoughts, desires or interests.

As with all these unbalanced relationships, self-esteem and confidence are at the root. The better you feel about yourself, the more able you will be to believe that someone loves you, even if you disagree, or have some parts of your lives that remain separate.

In the future, while you can still aim for harmony and peace in your relationships, you must discover that you can achieve this without denying your own individuality. Taking each other's feelings into account can only truly be done when you *know* what those feelings really are, not when they are suppressed. Loving negotiation is what satisfying harmony is based on. When your differences are tolerated you can feel more securely loved than when you act in unison out of fear.

!————————————— *Task* —————————————

**Best and worst**

Think back to your relationship. What was the best part of your togetherness? When did you feel this? What was the worst part? When did you feel this?

Identifying the unpleasant feelings is an important step, as it can spur you into not repeating this pattern again. !

*Pattern Four: 'You are so wonderful, you can do nothing wrong'*

In this kind of relationship, one partner is put on a pedestal by the other. So long as the illusion that the superior partner is perfect can be maintained, this is deeply satisfying to both. In most ways it is similar to pattern one, in which there is a strong and weak partner – except that in this case it is sometimes the apparently weak partner who is on the pedestal. The partner who is adored and admired might even, objectively, have many faults, which the admirer refuses to see, or mentally transforms into virtues.

For instance, it would be hard for an outsider to understand why Bruce idolised Helen. Throughout their twenty-year marriage Helen had suffered from depression. They had two teenage children, and ten years previously Helen had tried to kill herself. Some months ago her depression had again became so severe that Bruce had sent her on a cruise. When she returned, she announced that she had met someone else and she left him.

At this point, Bruce came for counselling. He talked endlessly about his marriage and Helen. He saw her depression as a sign of her deep sensitivity and fragility, a response to his clumsiness. Such a delicate person shouldn't have been asked to be a wife and mother. It emerged that she had had affairs before, but he saw this as his fault, too, and had forgiven her.

Helen was always tantalisingly remote. She had been in analysis for most of their relationship, but never shared her insights with him. She rarely confided in him about anything. Helen had consistently rejected Bruce's attempts to help or comfort her. She was contemptuous of him, and he accepted her valuation of him as correct.

As counselling continued, Bruce slowly began to see Helen in a more realistic light, but it was almost as painful for him to do this as it was to lose her. He started to see himself more positively, and understood that when Helen devalued him it reminded him of his childhood, when his parents only rewarded him with attention when he did chores for them.

Gradually, while saying that he still loved Helen, Bruce was able to be more detached about her. He saw that he hadn't dared see her as less than perfect for fear that this might cause friction between them and she might reject him – which she had done anyway. After maintaining that all he wanted was for her to return, he started to see that his future would be better without her.

Soon after Bruce had realised this, Helen contacted him. She had broken up with the other man and wanted to go back to him. Bruce, stronger and wiser, said he would only take her back if she would join him for counselling, which she was not prepared to do. Therefore Bruce decided, with much sadness, that he would not have her back.

This kind of relationship works as long as the illusion can be maintained. And, as Bruce's example shows, the admirer can willfully ignore very obvious faults, or rationalise them, to keep the illusion in place. However, if the worshipper becomes aware of the idol's feet of clay, this can change. Either he or she wants to leave the relationship, or the opportunity opens for a more realistic relationship to be formed. But the 'idol' needs to participate in this. As was the case with Helen, there can be great resistance to looking at the relationship in a new way, as counselling would have forced Helen to do.

Sometimes the idol tires of being worshipped, and leaves the relationship because it is never going to be more equal.

● **Influences from the past.** Look again at the influences that shaped the partners in pattern one (page 71). Many of the same influences from the past operate here. Although both partners suffer from lack of self-esteem and fears of not being good enough, it works in different ways. The 'idol' needs to be with someone who thinks he or she is perfect, despite knowing that it is not true. Helen's depression, for instance, was a clear sign that she did not share Bruce's ideas that she was perfect. They are terrified of partners who see them for what they really are, for they fear that then they wouldn't be loved at all. They maintain their positions on the pedestals by keeping a distance between themselves and their partners so that they will not be found out.

The worshipper copes with bad feelings about himself or herself by investing the partner with all manner of virtues. The only way worshippers can feel good about themselves is by basking in the reflected glory of partners they see as ideal.

These couples have often seen a similar pattern operating in their parents' marriages. This was the case with Angie and Leo.

Angie had been brought up to believe 'your father is always right'. Her mother treated him with a reverence that Angie resented. 'Right' always seemed to involve Angie in doing things that made her unhappy. Women were second-class citizens in the home. Angie longed for her father to approve of her, but he just wasn't as interested in her as he was in her brothers, and he belittled her achievements.

Leo was the youngest of three children. The elder two went to university, but he was not academic and left school at sixteen. He did well at work, but his father was disappointed in him and he felt a failure. Leo's father was a remote figure who had a number of affairs. Although Leo didn't know this officially, he sensed it. In his family everyone pretended things were fine and good when they weren't. The illusion was what mattered. Leo was determined to be different from his father – he wanted to be straight, honourable and admirable.

They met when Leo, aged twenty-four, hired Angie, aged twenty, as his secretary. Angie immediately developed a crush on him. She was dazzled when her 'hero' asked her out, and two years later they were married.

Angie became pregnant immediately and gave up work. Soon afterwards they moved to a new area. She was unable to believe her luck that Leo had married her, but she was lonely. She began to 'eat for two' and put on a lot of weight. After the baby was born the weight stayed on, and while she was thinking about dieting she became pregnant again. After the second baby was born she was two stone overweight.

Angie was disgusted with herself, and couldn't imagine why Leo wanted to stay with her. As far as she was concerned he was the perfect man – she didn't recognise the fact that he paid little attention to her except to comment disparagingly on her weight. Instead of spending his spare time with his family, Leo threw himself into 'good works', for which he could be respected and admired.

One of Leo's projects, to raise money for a hospital, involved time spent in another city. While there he started an affair with a professional fundraiser working on the same project.

Acting like this did not fit with Leo's image of himself. In a surge of guilty conscience he told Angie about it. But the affair didn't stop. Leo continued to work on the project and visit his mistress, who was so much more compelling than his self-effacing, overweight wife. Angie knew the affair was continuing. She knew Leo stayed with his mistress when he was away. She thought it was no more than she deserved. Someone as dynamic and attractive as Leo couldn't be expected to remain faithful to her.

Nevertheless, Angie was unhappy, and Leo continued to be tortured by guilt, so they arranged to see a counsellor. At their first appointment, the counsellor was struck by the difference between them. Leo looked fit and confident. Angie was drab, still wore pregnancy smocks, and looked unhappy and downtrodden. The session was hard going. They talked in monosyllables, unable to speak freely in front of each other. The counsellor suggested that it might be better if she saw them separately.

Angie came first. She talked of Leo's perfection and her own inadequacies. She said that she told Leo that she was on a diet, but she was a secret binger – hiding the evidence from him by taking the rubbish to a tip before he could see it. She begged the counsellor not to tell him.

When Leo came he too had secrets from Angie. This had not been his first affair. Whenever he became involved in a good cause he 'found himself' sleeping with a woman on the project. He was disgusted at himself. He was doing what his father did and couldn't seem to stop himself. Yet what he longed for more than anything was to be a respect-worthy, moral and charitable man. He asked the counsellor not to tell Angie, as he feared she would become suicidally depressed. Meanwhile, he wasn't sure he wanted to stay with her or whether to leave and live with his mistress.

With these restrictions it was hard for counselling to progress. It was even more difficult when Leo took three months' unpaid leave to work for the hospital full-time – and moved in with his mistress for the duration.

Angie's reaction was that she would use the time to make herself a better person so that Leo would want her on his return. She started a diet and the results were immediate. 'An attractive woman emerged week by week,' the counsellor said. 'Angie bought new clothes, changed her hair and make-up and started to feel good about herself.' She also joined a fitness class, where she made new friends and became so good that she eventually taught some of the classes herself.

The curious thing was that as Angie's self-esteem rose, her image of Leo as perfect started to tarnish. It was as if she had previously decided that as Leo was all good she must be all bad. As soon as she started to see the good in herself, she allowed herself to recognise Leo's faults. She became outraged at the way he had treated her, which had made her feel that her life was over at the age of twenty-six.

When Leo returned, amazed and gratified at the change in Angie, she no longer wanted him back. She believed that his need to be adored and admired by her would gradually erode her new-found self-esteem. Instead, she wanted to build on it – without him. The counsellor said, 'They might have been able to save their marriage if both wanted to. But with Angie aware of his imperfections, Leo would have had to confront full-on the side of himself that he already despised.'

● **Lessons for the future**. This relationship pattern is only possible when both of you have made an unspoken 'pact' that one is good and the other bad. As the bad one, or worshipper, you have to recognise that you have strengths, talents and honourable qualities as well. Instead of looking for them in someone else, you have to develop those you are ignoring in yourself. As the good one, or 'idol' you have to realise that everyone has faults and can be loved as much for these as for their virtues. Your own failings are doubtless distressing to you, but they won't go away simply because you pretend they are not there, or if partners in the past have not seen them.

Both of you have suffered from lack of confidence, and it is building this that will help you break the pattern in the future. Two rounded human beings who accept their own good points and bad will neither need to appear perfect nor look for people who seem to be faultless.

**!** ─────────────── *Task* ───────────────

**It could be me**

Think back to your relationship that followed this pattern. If you were the worshipper, which attributes did you most admire in your partner? How can you develop these for yourself? If you were the adored, which failings did you see in your partner? Do you have any similar failings yourself? **!**

## Pattern Five: 'Look how I suffer to make you happy'

In this kind of relationship one of the partners maintains that there is nothing that he or she will not do for the other. These people put their own needs aside and will often make great sacrifices to ensure their partner's happiness. Their partners, in turn, treat them like door-mats, make demands on them and are ungrateful for the sacrifices made.

The truth is that martyrs do not make their partners happy, no matter what they do. Their own suffering is so blatant that their part-ners feel guilty. But there is resentment, too. It is impossible to feel happy around someone who is unhappy. The resentment can cause their partners to behave even more badly and uncaringly. Although the martyrs are prepared to *do* anything for their partners, their partners do not feel it is a sign of love. Indeed, it becomes clear that martyrs are most comfortable when they are unhappy, and much of the martyrdom is self-imposed.

These relationships can break down when the martyr recognises that he or she doesn't need to be so unhappy and yearns to have a healthier relationship, but the partner can't cope with the assertiveness of the erstwhile martyr. Or the partner of the martyr finds the burden of guilt and resentment intolerable and wants to end the relationship. Because of the pattern of the past, these people will often do so with even more cruelty than average.

This was the situation with Barry and Rhona. Barry sought coun-selling on his own, distraught because Rhona was divorcing him. They were both twenty-eight years old and had been married for seven years. They had two daughters.

Barry had no wish for a divorce, but he was particularly bewil-dered because he had no idea why Rhona was unhappy. Even more inexplicable was that she cited cruelty as grounds for divorce – she said he had knocked her down the stairs. Barry said that she had fallen down the stairs while he was at work one day, but he maintained that he had never once lifted a finger to her.

As he talked about the marriage, the counsellor could well believe him. Barry had dedicated himself to Rhona and the children. He was the first up in the morning. He made breakfast for everyone, and brought Rhona hers in bed. He washed and dressed the children and took them to school. He did all the shopping by himself after work, and would cook the evening meal when he arrived home. After this he would put the children to bed. He did all the housework and washing. Despite the fact that Rhona only worked part-time and Barry had a full-time job, the only responsibility she took was to pick the children up from school.

Barry catalogued these details in a long-suffering monotone. He said he was happy doing these things, but the expression in his voice told a different story. He wanted the counsellor to explain how a woman looked after like this could be unhappy. Was it a sign that she was going mad that she had accused him of pushing her down the stairs? The counsellor suspected that Rhona might be having an affair, but Barry denied the possibility.

Barry came for counselling for a number of weeks. He had moved out, but was still going back every day and doing everything as before. Halfway through counselling he discovered the counsellor was right – Rhona had been having an affair. She had hoped that by divorcing him for cruelty she would be able to banish him from her life and keep the house. She thought that she could easily push him around over this, as she had pushed him around during their life together.

In fact, fear of losing his children – and of her incapacity as a mother if she got custody – galvanised Barry. He found clear evidence of her infidelity and sued for divorce in return.

Rhona left to live with her lover, and Barry returned to the house and continued to come for counselling. The counsellor said, 'I was able to understand why Rhona found living with Barry unrewarding. He gave her his power, but she wanted an equal partner. However, Barry changed. He had to take responsibility, not just carry out orders. He began to take pride in himself and look smarter.'

Friends rallied round to help Barry with the children, and accepting help was something new for him. 'He learned that people could still like you when they do things for you – it didn't have to be all one way.'

● **Influences from the past.** If you have become involved in relationships like this, there is often a similar pattern in your parents' relationship. Although this is unlikely to have created a happy atmosphere in your home, it seems natural to you. You will then either be prepared to martyr yourself to someone else, or make unreasonable demands on a martyring partner. In Barry's case, his mother had gone into hospital when he was two, and she had never fully recovered from her serious illness. His father did everything for her out of duty, but resented it.

You are also more likely to take on the martyr role if you were brought up to believe that your value lay in being good and helping other people.

Coral grew up thinking that women should be good and look after their men. She came from a close family in which the women supported each other, but their roles were to wait on their men hand and foot. Her adored mother and grandmother had not been happy in their marriages but they had put up with their lot. Coral's mother and grandmother had also demanded good behaviour at all times from Coral, whereas the boys in the family were tolerated if they were a bit wild.

Coral married Andy when she was twenty-two and he was twenty-three. After a honeymoon first year of marriage, Coral had become disillusioned. She looked after Andy almost as if he were a child – she cut his hair for him, chose his clothes and didn't let him lift a finger in the house. She complained about this constantly, but did nothing to change matters. She didn't think she loved Andy, but there had never been a divorce in her family. What would her mother or grandmother think? The only way in which Coral asserted herself was in refusing to have a baby, which Andy wanted.

Then, five years into their marriage, Coral's grandmother died. This was a blow to Coral, who had loved her very much. But it also made her think of her grandmother's wasted life looking after a man she had not loved. It made her wonder whether she wanted the same for herself – and to what purpose she was being 'good' and following the family tradition. She told Andy that she wasn't sure they had a future, and suggested counselling.

Andy accompanied Coral to the counselling, but very reluctantly. The counsellor said that he was like a spoilt child. He sat hunched, with his arms crossed and refused to listen or participate in any of the sessions. His only comment was that he didn't think anything was wrong with the marriage. But, he said, 'If she's decided it's over, then it is.'

After three unfruitful sessions, Coral took matters into her own hands. She took a job working away for a year, and told Andy that they could use the time to think about whether they wanted to stay together.

Oddly enough, once Coral had left, Andy said he wanted to continue counselling. Over the course of a few sessions he began to realise that he depended on Coral rather than loved her. He came to the conclusion that he had looked on her like another mother – and the way she looked after him had contributed to keeping him like an overgrown child. He said he now wanted to grow up, and he didn't think he would want to stay with Coral when she returned.

● **Lessons for the future.** If you have found yourself in the position of martyring yourself for a loved one, you have to recognise that as a way of showing love it backfires. It is uncomfortable living with a martyr, and it creates a bad atmosphere in the home. Becoming happier by looking after yourself, too, is much more positive for your relationship. What you will probably have found is that you have lost touch with what you want and need to make you happy, because you have not been in the habit of thinking about it.

One counsellor talked of Rhiannon, who was almost prostrate with exhaustion looking after her husband and large family. It was hard for her to remember anything that had ever given her joy. But, after some deep thinking she made a list of things to do in the future: have a bath with the door locked so she wouldn't be interrupted; go shopping alone without children in tow; take up embroidery again; visit an exhibition on her own; arrange to see old friends – which she hadn't done since her second marriage; manicure her nails; read a good book. She wasn't going to do all of these in one week, but regularly make time for one or two. She recognised that to do any of them she would have to stop taking the burden of everything on herself and encourage her family to share responsibility with her.

She expected her husband to resent this, but the opposite happened. As she perked up and calmed down by making time for herself their relationship improved.

Working on your self-esteem in other ways helps, too. As you grow in confidence it is easier for you to recognise that you can be loved without taking over the care of another. In fact, you will be shown more care and respect if you can demonstrate that you respect yourself.

The partner of the martyr often seems tyrannical and ungrateful, but this hides similar insecurities – mainly that a fear of taking other people's feelings into account can only happen when you completely deny your own. You can avoid the trap of making people martyr themselves for you in the future by recognising that it is not the only way to stop becoming a martyr yourself. The alternative is sharing responsibility and caretaking, and you will find this much more rewarding. Just as martyrs have to learn consult their own feelings and say no at times, you have to learn to be sensitive to your future partner's feelings and say yes to requests of you. Building your self-confidence will help you see that freely doing something for someone else does not put you in a 'one-down' position, but makes you both equal.

!————————————— *Task* —————————————

## Switch roles

In your imagination switch roles with a partner you had in the past. What must it have felt like to be the martyr (or the bully)? In your new role, what would you have done differently to make the relationship happier?

!

## *Pattern Six: 'If it's going to work, it will – if not, too bad'*

What all of the patterns so far have had in common is that there is little true intimacy and closeness, even if, superficially, there seems to be. In this pattern it is much more obvious.

In relationships like this the couple have something they share. In short-term relationships it might be a very good sex life, or a romantic vision. In relationships that last longer, it might be the children and the home. But there is not the deeper-based emotions or the growing together that comes when couples are close in other ways. Each partner feels emotionally separate because they look outside the relationship to meet their needs – perhaps through work, family or friends. When what they share is strongly uniting they stay together, but when it is not they are able to walk away from the relationship, sometimes with less pain than other couples.

It is the fear of the pain that comes with parting that stops partners in this sort of relationship becoming close to each other. They are scared of investing too much love in their partners because it threatens their security to need someone too much. While their relationships remain happy, they feel fine. But when problems or unhappiness arise the pain is intolerable and they are likely to cut their losses. When duty binds them together, through shared concern for the children, say, they make no attempt to resolve unhappiness, but invest more energy in the things outside the relationship that make them happy. For instance, becoming more involved in work, voluntary activities, affairs, or in gaining support from friends or family.

Perry and Erica had this kind of relationship. They had been married for six years. It was Erica's second marriage. Her first husband had been violent, and after that relationship broke up she was reluctant to trust a man again.

Perry was very different. They had lived together like love-birds, leaving each other romantic little notes, speaking on the phone several times a day. Erica used to rush home from work to devise special meals, and she dressed herself up glamorously each evening, with sexy underwear – they would often play games in which she would seduce him.

Suddenly Perry announced he was having an affair with a woman from work, and he moved in with her. Erica, desperately upset and shocked, came for counselling.

For the first session all Erica could do was cry. How could such a loving relationship simply exaporate? An affair had been her worst fear, which was why she had gone to such lengths to keep Perry interested in her. Over the next few sessions Erica talked generally about her life and attitudes. She thought men were pretty awful and treated women badly. She had retained her own career so that she wouldn't be 'the little woman at home'.

She turned up for one counselling session white-faced and trembling. Perry had sent her two copies of a formal letter listing their shared assets and how they should be divided. He asked her to sign one copy and return it. This was the man who, just weeks before, had called her up from work to say that she was the sexiest woman alive and he couldn't live without her.

Over a few more sessions of counselling, Erica was able to understand better what had happened. She realised that they had been united by the idea of themselves as two people madly in love for life. Underneath, however, Erica was suspicious of Perry and concerned to keep him from straying – which she was sure he would otherwise do. She had not let him get too close, therefore; she had to maintain the illusion of the sexy, always happy woman. She had been acting a part, and so had Perry.

Two people pretending to be something they are not can never become close, and a passionate sexual relationship does not necessarily mean intimacy. Fundamentally, Erica knew Perry as little as he knew her. Perry had decided to play the game with someone else, and his feelings for Erica switched off like a tap. It was not Erica he had been in love with, but the role she played. Erica could see that she had not been acting out of love for Perry, but fear; she had been attempting to manipulate him so that he would behave in a way that suited her.

● **Influences from the past.** It is the issue of pain that determines the theme of this relationship. Usually the partners have been deeply hurt in the past in a close emotional relationship – often a childhood attachment to a parent that was disrupted by illness, death or some sort of rejection from a loved mother or father. When this happens they also become convinced that they are unloveable. Because of this they are more comfortable in distant relationships where they do not feel too deeply. Loving someone and, especially, needing someone feels very dangerous because in the past it made them suffer very much.

If this is your pattern, it might also have been reinforced by your feelings about your parents' relationship. Usually you have seen one or both of your parents made very unhappy, either because they divorced, or one of them died, or because their relationship followed this or another of the patterns described. Either consciously or not, it is likely to have made you decide that close relationships are a source of pain. This means that intimately opening yourself up to someone is very hard for you. If they saw what you were really like, would they be able to love you? And if you came to need them and rely on their love, wouldn't it be too traumatic?

These were some of the reasons that Amelia had a series of relationships that were characterised by a lack of closeness. Her mother had suffered a long post-natal depression after her birth, and could not look after her. Later, when her mother recovered, they still did not become close. It was generally recognised that Amelia was 'daddy's girl', and her mother left the nurturing to him. But Amelia's father demanded standards of behaviour from her that made her fear him. She preferred her mother, and wanted to be close to her, but her mother was more involved with Amelia's brother. When Amelia was eight her parents divorced. It was frightening and painful for Amelia. They moved from their house to live with Amelia's maternal grandparents in a small village, where Amelia had no friends. Shortly afterwards her brother, with whom she was close, was sent to boarding school. Then her cat was run over. Amelia's father gradually lost touch with the family. In a short space of time, it seemed to Amelia that she had lost father, home, brother, cat and friends – everything she had ever loved. Her mother remarried, but that relationship became unhappy, and Amelia felt unwanted by her step-father.

As an adult, therefore, when Amelia fell in love, she also felt frightened. She experienced this fear as a consuming sexual jealousy. Her lovers could never convince her that they loved her. She felt sure that they would leave her. She was constantly suspicious that they were having affairs, about to have affairs, or wanting to have affairs. She threw jealous scenes, which created a bad atmosphere; but gradually the relationships would become calmer. This was because, oddly enough, as Amelia's jealousy soured the relationship she felt better. When the men seemed to love her less the thought of losing them was less terrible. At the same time, she tried to stop herself caring about the men. Rather than become closer to them, Amelia would create even more distance – throwing herself into her work and her other friendships. After time, when the love was less intense, Amelia was more tolerant and less jealous. Gradually the relationships would fade away into friendship, and they would split up. Each time this happened Amelia's life was almost unchanged; she had kept her men on the fringes of her life, uninvolved with family and friends, so when they were no longer around it hardly seemed to make any difference.

Amelia had had four such relationships, each lasting around five years. She eventually came for counselling when the last relationship split up. She was forty-one and had never been married or had children. She badly wanted a baby before it was too late, but knew that she would have to change her pattern if she was going to form a lasting relationship, for the child's sake. Counselling involved understanding why she had behaved as she did, and building up her good feelings about herself so that she would be more able to trust a man to want to stay with her – and so be prepared to forge an intimate relationship in the future.

---

## *Task*

### Turning points

Think back on relationships that have been distant like this. Can you remember a turning point, at which you could have become closer? Remember how you acted then, and think of what you might have done or said that would have produced a different outcome.

---

● **Lessons for the future.** In order to risk being close, like Amelia you have to learn to like yourself. You might be confident in other areas, and confident about your ability to survive alone, but in your heart you can't believe someone will love you. As you become more sure that you are loveable for yourself, your fear of being hurt by love will lessen. If, in your next relationship, you allow yourself to draw close to your partner, the initially fearful feelings will fade. Showing your need for love, and exposing your vulnerability will allow a loving partner to give you the love you have craved and feared. In turn, becoming close to partners means that you can't see them (or treat them) as potential pain-inflictors, but as people who also need your love, warmth and respect. While no one can promise that any relationship will last for ever, by allowing yourself to love and be loved, you give it the best chance.

After reading these relationship patterns you are likely to see that your past relationships fit one pattern more than another, although you might see elements of more than one in your own life. Some hints have been given for future relationships so that you do not feel you are bound to make the same mistakes over again. This is also looked at in Chapter Eight, *Starting Well*. But, as your feelings about yourself are the most important element in determining the relationships you make, it is transforming those that will help you most. This is dealt with fully in Part Two, *Working on Yourself*.

# 4

# YOUR CHILDREN

The break-up of their parents' relationship is always difficult and distressing for children. Even when your relationship with your partner has been bad for many years, and even when home-life has been unhappy and strife-torn, the majority of children would still overwhelmingly prefer to be living with both their parents in the situation that is familiar to them. Only a tiny fraction of children welcome separation or divorce, and these tend to be older children who have suffered at the hands of a violent parent of whom they live in fear. The wish that their parents were back together can remain unchanged for many years – even when the children have recovered from the immediate consequences of the parting and are generally happier and doing well. Fantasies about parents getting back together can persist even when both parents have found other partners.

This does not mean that you should not end a relationship that has broken down. If your best efforts to improve matters have failed then you and your partner might be happier apart. In these circumstances you might feel that your children, too, will be happier, and assume that they can handle the new situation without too much difficulty or unhappiness. But, while this can be true eventually, particularly if you deal sensitively with the changes and become happier and more positive yourself, the fact is that the parting and the aftermath is still devastating for children of any age.

Sometimes you can resist recognising that a step you have taken to improve your life is upsetting for your children. The chapter *Coming to Terms with Loss* detailed adult reactions to the end of a relationship. Children also feel this range of turbulent and conflicting painful emotions, with the great fear that goes with being young and not in control of their destinies. As with adults, these feelings can last for many months or years, although the way that they are expressed might be different. Over time, you and your ex-partner can help your children come to terms with the changes, and if you keep their best interests at heart they will develop the wisdom, compassion and flexibility that can follow from suffering. As you become happier yourself, and life settles into a more stable pattern, your children will respond by becoming more happy and secure themselves.

While parents who actively welcome a separation can find it hard to recognise that their children are suffering, parents who are less happy about it can have a different problem. If you had no choice in the matter, because your partner left to be alone or because he or she has found someone else, your own anger and distress can become mixed up with your children's. In this situation you might be very alert to your children's unhappiness and use it to punish your partner by denying access, or by turning your children against your ex. But children need contact with both parents, and need to feel free to love them both. Otherwise they continue to feel unhappy long after they could have adjusted, which threatens their emotional, social and educational development – as well as making the formation of adult relationships more difficult for them in the future. Many counsellors see mature adults having problems in relationships who are still heart-broken because of events surrounding their own parents' break-up many years before. Although children can't be protected from their own reactions to the immediate crisis of separation, there is a lot that can be done to ensure that they do not continue to be haunted by the misery in later years.

At a time when you are suffering yourself it can be especially difficult to be available for helping your children. What follows are some guidelines to help all of you through the break-up and beyond.

## TELLING THE CHILDREN

Surprisingly often children know nothing about the break-up until the day one parent leaves. Many parents try to shield their children by keeping them in the dark until the last possible moment. However, the sudden departure of one parent, and the abrupt changes this means in their lives, is intensely shocking to children who are unprepared. Even after the separation, many parents tell their children very little about what is happening and why – and what the consequences are for the future. They sometimes do this because they are not ready to deal with their children's sorrow and anger as well as their own. Some parents believe it is better to tell 'white lies' – that the absent parent has gone on holiday, is ill, in prison or away working. They believe that this is a gentle way of preparing the children for the truth eventually. But it can be even more frightening for the children, who are already witnessing the distress and upheaval of the new situation, without being able to make sense of it.

## What children need to know

According to their age and ability to understand, children need to know as much as possible about what is happening. Although they might be very sad and angry, it is easier for them to deal with the facts than with what they imagine if they are not told. Even young children sense the changes in the home, the increase in stress and unhappiness, and their fears will grow when they are not told what it is all about.

● **The decision to part.** If you and your partner have been talking about parting, then you should involve your children when you have reached the decision. There is often a time lag between deciding to separate and the move that follows. If you can, explain together to your children what has been decided. If this is too distressing, at least allow the children the chance to talk to you both separately while you are still in the same home. The children need to know the main facts of the situation, not all the wrongs and rights on both sides. They also need to know that you will answer any questions they have as truthfully as you can. Although this might be difficult for you, because the children beg you to reconsider, or cry, or become very angry with one or both of you, it is still in the children's best interests to be told at this stage.

If the parting is sudden, and one partner leaves without warning, you will not be able to prepare your children before the event. Nevertheless, you still need to explain the situation as fully as you can, and as soon as possible. Children of different ages will need different explanations. But there are certain typical questions that all children will have.

● **'Why is it happening?'** Although your relationship might have had its problems for a long time, most children will not have realised quite how bad the situation is. They need to be given an appropriate explanation according to their age. The temptation to give a blow-by-blow account of the wrongdoings of either partner should be avoided, but the children should be given clear reasons why you can't live together. For instance, younger children might be told, 'You have probably noticed that we have been arguing a lot and have been making each other unhappy. We have decided that it would be better if we lived in different houses.' Older children might be ready to cope with more detailed explanations, but it is still important to stick to the facts and not to blame one another.

Younger children, especially, can feel that it is their fault that this is happening. Perhaps they believe they were behaving badly – or that the parent who leaves is cross with them or doesn't love them any more. Even older children can worry that they didn't do enough to keep peace in the home, or added to the strain by their own behaviour.

Children of all ages need to be reassured that this is something between the parents, and that they are not at fault. Neither should they be told that you are doing this 'for them', because most would prefer that you should stay together. Additionally, they need to know that they are still loved by both parents, even if one has chosen to live else-where. For instance, younger children might be told, 'Your dad and I don't love each other any more, and he has met a woman he wants to marry instead. But he still loves you very much, and will always be your dad.'

Some parents try to soften the blow by making the parting sound more amicable than it is. For instance, one counsellor talked of a child who was assured that his parents were still very good friends, when in reality there was a lot of bitterness between them. Far from reassuring him, he was puzzled and disturbed, and he found it more difficult to accept that they would not get back together in the future. It was to his teacher that he said, 'What I can't understand is why they can't go on living together if they are such good friends. Good friends can live together.' When the mother was told this she explained to him that adults need more than friendship to live together, and she also modified the explanation by saying, 'When we live together we get angry at each other a lot. We are only able to be good friends when we live sepa-rately.'

● **'What's going to happen to us all?'** The announcement that their parents are separating is like an earthquake in children's lives. Reality as they know it has changed in a substantial way, and they can be frightened of what other changes might be in store. Children need to know the practical consequences of your decision. They need to know where they are going to live and whether anything else is going to change in their lives (such as school). If they are going to be staying on at home, this might seem self-evident to you, but it is not necessarily so to them – after all, one member of the household is leaving and they can't be sure that they won't, too. They also need to know where the absent parent is going to live; children can worry about the safety and lifestyle of a parent who leaves.

Younger children worry that if one parent can leave then the other might as well. They need to be reassured that they will be looked after and that the other parent will be staying with them. This needs saying even if they don't ask. Sometimes children harbour the fear that they will be abandoned, but are too frightened to put it into words.

● **Answering questions.** Most children will have a lot of questions they want to ask you about the separation, which will vary according to the age of the child. Some of these questions will be distressing to you, but it is important to answer them to the best of your ability, and not make the child feel bad for asking them.

Children must have confidence that you will never tell them an outright lie. A lie always damages their faith in you, even if your intentions are good. As one counsellor says, 'When your parents have parted, and your life is shifting, you desperately need some solid ground. The truth is solid. When you can trust your parents to tell you the truth you know you have at least one foot on safe ground. Then you can cope with more uncertainty. When you suspect an untruth, your imagination goes wild.' Remember, what you tell them now offers a framework for their understanding in the future. If you don't tell the truth at this stage, you might have to modify what you have said when they are older. It can be shocking for them to find out later that the version that they were originally told was untrue.

There are ways of telling the truth that are acceptable. The best way is to concentrate on facts and your own feelings – not to run down your partner or burden your children with details that are too intimate. Even difficult issues, such as your partner's violence or sexual abuse can be dealt with factually: 'Dad used to hit mum, and that was wrong, so it is better for us not to live together.' Or, 'Dad used to touch Nicky in ways that were bad. I couldn't allow that, so I had to take you away'.

Occasionally, under duress, you might say cruel and damaging things about your partner: 'He's a stupid, selfish man, who doesn't care about any of us' or 'She's a liar and a whore'. Hearing these things is harmful to your children and will make matters worse for them. It is helpful, once you have cooled down, to tell them that you were angry and upset, which made you say things you regret. Children can understand this, but it shouldn't happen too often.

## YOUR CHILDREN'S GRIEF

All children grieve when their parents break up. Except in very unusual circumstances, your children are far more tolerant of a difficult atmosphere in the home than you are. On the one hand it is something they have become used to: they won't have enjoyed the rows you had, but they might well have accepted them. It is also usually the case that even when parents are unhappy together, they still retain reasonably good relationships with their children.

One parent leaving is therefore a great blow. Even when a distant, stern or less-loved parent goes, the children feel keenly the absence of this very important person. The immediate upheaval of the separation can make home seem even less happy – and certainly less secure – than it was when you were together, however many rows there were. Children of all ages feel rejected by the parent who has left. Children feel that *they* have been left – that the parent who goes did not love or want them enough to stay around. These feelings of rejection can fade eventually, if you explain the situation sufficiently, and if regular contact is maintained. But meanwhile children feel as lonely and sad as adults, as if a part of themselves were missing.

The sadness is accompanied by the fear and powerlessness that children feel. They can do nothing to stop what is happening, however hard they try. Some children become very depressed because of this. Most children also feel bitterly angry – sometimes at life, fate and everyone. But the anger can be directed mainly at one parent – not necessarily the parent at 'fault', but sometimes the one with whom they feel most secure.

Often parents simply fail to see how angry and unhappy their children are. This can be because you are so wrapped in your own feelings at this time that you don't notice. It is also sometimes because the children feel unable to show you what they are feeling – either because they don't want to upset you, or because they think you will be angry with them or will stop loving them. One counsellor says, 'Parents will report that their children are behaving badly or aggressively, and I say, "Do you think it's because they are angry at what happened?" and the parents look completely amazed.'

Marissa came into counselling to try to cope with her recent separation. She had been left with two children aged eleven and nine. She was very tearful and frightened. She had been so used to keeping her feelings under control that the strength of her emotions unnerved her. As a child she had been put down by her parents, who were always telling her to 'smile' or to 'take that expression off your face'. She had become used to hiding her feelings and thinking that she was no good.

Marissa found great relief in the counselling. She discovered that she could express her bad feelings and that it was all right to do so. She experienced anger as well as grief in her reactions to her husband and her parents. She was overwhelmed by sadness about what the situation was doing to her children.

The counsellor encouraged her to allow the children to share the grief. She had been blocking all their attempts to talk about it before. She had cried in private, but told them that she was 'fine'. She would often say to them, 'You're not really sad!' When she was able to realise that she had been making her children suppress their emotions, just as her parents had made her suppress hers, she was able to change.

The counsellor says, 'As she was able to open up to me, so she was able to help her children open up – and they all benefited. Marissa also became able to share her feelings with friends, which she had never done before. All this made her stronger and more able to help her children cope.'

When the children's feelings are not dealt with or are ignored, they can continue for a long time, making adjustment hard for all concerned. For instance, Bill came for counselling with his second wife, Cecilia. Most of their problems were being caused by Bill's teenage daughter, Lorraine, who lived with them.

Lorraine was very angry, and this was expressed as hatred towards her step-mother. Bill, who felt very guilty about the end of his first marriage, was unable to stand up to Lorraine, and although his sympathies were with Cecilia, he was never able to intervene to make the situation better.

When Bill and Cecilia had married they had just hoped that everything would be all right. Lorraine's feelings of pain, anger and jealousy were ignored. Lorraine's mother had walked out on her family, and as far as Lorraine was concerned her father's second marriage could mean she had lost him, too. Cecilia had tried to make friends with Lorraine at first, but the girl snubbed her, and before long they were at war. In the end, Bill was torn in two. He finally opted to leave Cecilia because he felt his first duty was to his daughter.

The counsellor believes that the outcome might have been different if Lorraine's feelings had been handled better. 'Her anger should have been acknowledged as rightful – but it should also have been made clear to her what the boundaries were. They could have sat down and talked about everyone's needs in the situation, and made it clear to Lorraine that she was not going to be given the power to destroy the relationship.'

## Age and response

Once you accept that your children will be suffering as much as you are, you can become alert to their feelings. Children of different ages show their feelings in different ways. All children of school-age are likely to show some falling off in school work, although for many this is short-lived. Some children experience more difficulty with other children – either shunning friends, becoming shy, or indulging in some bullying behaviour. With the co-operation of the school these matters can be monitored, and with sensitive handling it will usually pass.

The following is a rough guide to the other ways that children might respond to the break-up, and how their behaviour might change, according to the age they are when you separate. There is likely to be overlap between the age groups, so make sure you read the one below and above your children's current ages.

● **Up to five.** Some relationships break up when the children are very small, before they can talk or even realise what is happening. Babies might not show signs of distress, so long as they continue to be looked after well by the parent at home. Nevertheless, you have to bear in mind that as the children grow older they need to know about your relationship and what happened. Sometimes they might not ask directly, but they will certainly be thinking about it. One mother reports, 'My daughter had no conscious memory of us living together. But when she was nine I discovered that she fantasised about us getting back together.'

From about the age of two-and-a-half, children respond more directly to the separation. This is the age group that finds it difficult to understand that the separation has occurred because of problems between the parents. They are likely to believe that their own behaviour caused the parent to go away. They need frequent explanations and reassurance. They are likely to show symptoms of fear, becoming more clingy and whiny with the parent who stays with them. Bedtimes might become especially difficult, as the children are reluctant to let you out of their sight. They are likely to want to avoid activities that they previously enjoyed unless you are with them or in sight at all times. The best way to cope with this behaviour is to tolerate it and be available as much as possible until it passes. Even if you can't do this, you should not become angry with the children, or their anxiety will increase. They need a lot of reassurance and comforting routine.

Little children might also regress: falling back in toilet training, needing security objects and old favourite toys. The children are simply showing that they need more care and attention during this time, and if they are given it they will eventually get back on course.

Many children become more aggressive for a time – either towards the parents, brothers and sisters or other children. While this behaviour should be guided, and the children should not be allowed to hurt anyone, they should not be punished. Some children, on the other hand, become excessively fearful that aggression will be turned against them, and become unhealthily restrained and 'good' for fear of attack, or of being left. Either way, the children benefit from being encouraged to express their anger verbally, with someone who will listen without blaming them.

Some children show through their play or fantasies that they have high hopes of the parent returning, or a strong desire for it. They should not be told off or discouraged from this. You can say, 'You *wish* dad would come back', and then go on to explain gently again that this is not going to happen.

● **Six to eight.** This age group is likely to show more obvious sadness than the younger ones. Boys and girls will cry a lot. They understand more about the separation than the little ones, and mourn it openly. All children of this age will feel great sorrow, though some will try to hide it from you. The children will be missing intensely the parent who has gone, and might idealise the departed parent, even if their relationship had not been particularly good. They should be encouraged to show their feelings, and be assured that it is all right to cry and be sad.

This can be hard for you to handle if you are feeling angry or sad and depressed yourself. But try to remember that if the children are punished for missing their parent, or made to feel guilty about it, the sorrow will be driven underground and last for much longer – perhaps turning into depression. These sad feelings often mean that the anger these children feel is not expressed towards the parent who has gone – but to you and other people, however unfair. The anger does not mean that they love you less, but it quite natural and has to come out in some way. This will eventually pass if the children are allowed to express their anger fully, but in acceptable ways that do not cause injury to other people.

Because these children are old enough to understand more, there can be a temptation to tell them the sort of details that will get them on your side – particularly if they appear to blame you with their angry behaviour. This is bad for all children, but is especially hard on this age group, who find divided loyalties even more difficult to handle than older children. While it might make you feel better, the children will feel split in two, which will add even more to their pain and sadness. Children of this age will try to remain loyal to both parents, even if they are not being asked to take sides, and need as much help as possible to do so.

The children in this age group, too, will be feeling frightened, and the initial shock might make them behave strangely, becoming forgetful or panicky. Some children turn to food for comfort, or worry that they won't have enough to eat.

● **Nine to twelve.** These children, feeling themselves to be more grown-up, struggle to cope with and contain their powerfully mixed feelings. They often feel very ashamed of what has happened in their family, even when they know that other children experience the same things. Because they no longer feel 'little', they might try very hard to assert themselves and bring you back together again – either by nagging and making you feel guilty, or by more subtle means.

Sometimes children of this age start behaving in dishonest ways; for instance, lying or stealing. To their minds, parents have done something 'wrong', and they feel less constrained about doing bad things themselves. In a way, this behaviour is letting you know that they are confused about morals and limits that previously seemed clearly defined. Of course this is worrying, but this realisation can show you what is needed: firm assurance about what is acceptable and what is not, without over-reacting. Once they know that you are still concerned about their behaviour and that you are in control, the stage will pass.

Above all, children of this age feel terribly angry about what has happened – more obviously and intensely than children of any other age. Unlike the slightly younger children, they are less likely to be divided in their loyalties, but will usually direct most of their anger at the parent they believe is 'to blame', and sometimes at both parents. They will often be very open in their angry behaviour – shouting, acting up, and directly trying to annoy or control. If the parent who has left was the authority figure in the home, this can be especially marked. Their high level of general anger can result in physical symptoms, such as headaches or stomach pains. While these should always be checked by the doctor, they will usually become less frequent as the anger subsides.

Because children of this age tend to take sides, trying to enlist their support will often succeed. They can turn against a parent with whom they previously enjoyed a good relationship. Although it can be tempting to use a child in this way, it is very damaging to the child at the time and for the future. By using them to reflect your own anger, you increase their own – and can make it last much longer than is healthy for the development of the children.

● **Thirteen to eighteen.** Adolescents are usually experiencing emotional turbulence of their own, unconnected to their parents' separation. They are aware that the end of their childhood is in sight, and they are unconsciously preparing for the time when they'll leave home. They are often in conflict with you over a number of issues, and tend to regard you as powerful authority figures, or role models, or as annoying presences that they simply take for granted.

Because this is such an emotional time anyway for these young people, they have an extra need for security in the home. Even when they are openly fighting you, your rigid attitudes (and comforting reassurance) offer a safety all their own. Therefore, when you separate they are profoundly shaken. Neither of you seem reliable any longer, and home no longer seems safe and familiar. When they are going through ups and downs of their own, your emotional distress can be particularly disturbing for them.

Their grief-related reactions can be very similar to your own. The mourning, sadness and depression; the shocked inability to get on with things as normal. They, too, will be angry and will show it openly – sometimes aimed at your 'selfishness' in putting your own needs before theirs. Often their anger will be intensified if you try to make them choose sides; and because they seem sophisticated and old enough to take it, you might burden them with far more details about the relationship and your own anger and unhappiness than is suitable. Sometimes they will react by distancing themselves from both of you, and throwing themselves into their school and social life outside the home.

Children of this age might react in two main ways: either acting older than their years, or retreating back into more childish behaviour. All these young people worry more – about you, about their future, and about their own relationships. Some will become more thoughtful and helpful, sharing responsibility in the home. Others, so disenchanted with what is going on, keep away as much as possible and behave coolly to you both. Usually this is to allow them to come to terms with what has happened, and later they are likely to become warmer towards you again.

Children who become more childish will be more clingy, and prefer the company of younger children. Their schoolwork might fall off for a while. Given plenty of reassurance, they will usually catch up later, though some might need professional help. If the parent who lives with the children leans too heavily on the adolescents it will be harder for them to grow up and grow away as they are supposed to do at this age.

Some children respond by jumping into a sexual relationship, or a series of sexual relationships – either for comfort or to 'show' parents who they believe are behaving badly. Rejecting you can also take the form of rejecting your values – getting involved with a bad crowd, taking drugs or drinking.

Children of this age need as much stability as you can give them. They need support for their own feelings, and clear rules of behaviour. It will be harder for them to adjust if you draw them into your battle, and might harm their educational progress at an important time. They benefit from being encouraged to help in the home and to share responsibility, but they should not be manoeuvred into taking over or made to feel that they should look after you.

● **Adult children.** Grown-up children who no longer live at home are likely to be equally distressed by your separation. If they are married themselves, it will cause them to worry about the future of their own relationship. Some will try to interfere to get you back together. On the other hand, others might be able to understand better than younger children your need to be apart. One woman, with three grown-up daughters, two with children of their own, found that they actively encouraged her to leave. She had stayed with her difficult and abusive husband for years, and her daughters were angry at her inability to make the break. When she finally left, they offered her consistent and warm support.

## SUPPORT FOR THE CHILDREN

Children of any age need all the support that they can get during this time. Whether they are showing signs of distress or not, they will be feeling insecure, disturbed and unhappy. Security of life as they have known it is temporarily disrupted, and their parents are suffering deeply, so life seems frightening and unsafe. Just as you should be casting round for help for yourself, children's needs should also be considered a priority.

### Help from you

This is unquestionably one of the toughest times to be a parent. No one walks away from a separation feeling strong, positive and happy. However difficult your relationship was in the past, the ending is rarely accompanied by pure relief. With everything changing around you, all your energy might be directed to keeping going.

Nevertheless, some thought must be given to your children. You don't have to hide your grief and bewilderment in order to give your children the help they need. Above all, they need plenty of reassurance that they are still loved. Children of all ages need more cuddling and comfort – and words of love. You should make allowances for regressive or difficult behaviour by letting them know that you understand the strain they are under.

They also need to know that they are allowed to express their own feelings of sadness and anger, and that they are not expected to bottle them up. Spending time each day talking to the children together and separately is important, so that they feel able to share fears and worries as they arise. While you can't make everything 'all right' – and don't need to pretend that you can – listening sympathetically goes a long way to soothing the worst of their troubled feelings. Children should also be encouraged to ask questions on matters that are troubling them, and you should let them know that you will answer what you can.

This is a tall order, and some days you will be better able to handle them than others. When you can't cope, it is helpful to tell them directly by saying things such as, 'I'm feeling too upset right now', 'I need some time to myself', 'I'm feeling irritable and on edge today so I'm rather snappy'. This is better than controlling your feelings until they burst out in a way that frightens the children, or makes them feel guilty.

If this does happen, however, you can apologise to the children when you are feeling better. Children tend to be forgiving, and appreciate parents who can admit when they have done something wrong. They are likely to follow your example and say that they are sorry when they act in ways of which they are later ashamed.

## Help from others

It is too much to expect you to carry the whole burden of supporting your children at this time, and you should not feel reluctant to mobilise as much support as you can from other people.

● **Family.** A breakdown in your relationship can have repercussions in the wider family. Your own family might be split about it, and you might fall out with your partner's family. You have to remember that for the children's sake it is best to try and foster good relationships where you can. The children are still related to your partner's family, and losing contact can be painful for them, and for the relatives who love the children and are parted from them by the situation. If your children have developed good relations with grandparents or other relatives, they can offer invaluable support. Spending time in other households where the children feel relaxed, and where life is going on pretty much as before, can restore a feeling of stability in their lives. It can be comforting for them to be fussed over by loving and sympathetic relatives, and gives them a break from the unhappiness that home represents for a while. Some children might be happy to stay with relatives for short periods, but they should not be forced to do so if it distresses them to leave you.

● **Friends.** Older children who have developed good relationships with the families of friends might also benefit from time spent with them. Some find it a relief to be able to talk about what is happening with people who are not emotionally involved. If your children want to visit or stay with friends more frequently, you should let them – even if you feel you want them around you all the time. Anything that helps them cope better will eventually benefit you.

● **School.** You should let the school know what is happening, and if your children spend time at a nursery, childminder or playgroup, you should also tell the carers there. Your children's behaviour is likely to change, and the teachers and carers are helped by knowing why this is. Some children become more obviously sad and clingy, others become more aggressive. All children will find their concentration disturbed, and their work performance will suffer as a result. When the teachers and carers know that there are problems at home, they can take appropriate action. They can keep an eye on the children, and be more tolerant and sympathetic about your children's behaviour. Kindly teachers can offer extra support, by giving your children an opportunity to talk privately about what is happening. They can also keep an eye on your children's progress and behaviour and keep you informed about what is happening.

● **Professional help.** Sometimes the greatest help can be given by a professional trained to work with children. There is no shame attached to your children seeing a professional; it does not mean that they are 'mad' or 'sick', simply that extra help can enable them to move on faster towards recovery. While children can find expressing their emotions difficult to the people they know and love, it can be easier for them to do so with a trained outsider.

Some parents seek help for their children at an early stage, to help them over the first shock and upset. Others only do so after a long time, when the children still seem depressed or are behaving very badly. Either way, seeking help can be useful for you, too, as you are likely to be given some advice on handling the children at home.

You should be able to get details of local professionals from your children's school, or your doctor.

## PARENTS APART

It is very different being a parent when you are separated. Previously you might not have thought much about your relationship with the children, or your partner's relationship with them. Decisions to do with the children are taken informally, with or without much discussion.

When you live separately, however, these matters change. Your children are relating to you as individuals, and decision-making becomes a more thoughtful process. It is hard to disentangle your feelings towards your ex-partner from your children's needs. It can take great courage and forbearance to put aside your own hurt and anger in the best interests of your children. Sometimes it takes effort to remind yourself that if you want them to be happy in the future you must work as co-operatively as you can with your ex-partner.

## Access

Children need both their parents. They need to be allowed to see both of them, and they need to be allowed to love them. Regularly seeing the parent who leaves is vitally important for their emotional health – and also for their feelings about themselves. Children who, for one reason or another, lose contact with the absent parent not only suffer continuing unhappiness because of this, but they also feel rejected. They grow up feeling not good enough and unloveable. This makes them insecure, and it also affects their ability to make happy and lasting relationships when they are adults.

Seeing the absent parent is not necessarily a happy business at the beginning. Children have varied reactions. Sometimes it seems to open the wounds that are healing: they cry a lot before or afterwards, and seem to have trouble settling down. Other children behave badly and aggressively to one parent or another, during the visiting times or afterwards. All of this is quite natural, and with steadfast reassurance it passes.

But some parents believe that this means the access should stop. They think that it is less upsetting for the child not to see the absent parent. Either the parents at home forbid access, or the separated parents find the behaviour, and their own feelings, too hard to handle, so stop trying to see the children.

Although the children might seem superficially more settled in these circumstances, it is no solution. The children's feelings are driven underground, sometimes to become an enduring depression. Or they feel guilty about the consequences of their behaviour, which leads them to feel bad about themselves. However difficult the children are around the time of access visits, the visits should still be allowed to continue. Tackling the children's feelings that lead to the bad behaviour can help. Acknowledge that you understand that they are feeling angry or sad, and ask them if they want to talk about it. It is not useful, however, to add your own feelings and observations at this time, if it means you criticising or accusing the other parent.

If the absent parent is violent or sexually abusive, the situation is more complicated. Surprisingly, even in these cases studies have shown that it is better if the children are able to maintain contact with the parent, although it is essential that the visits are supervised, and the parent is not left alone with the children. However inadequate or disappointing the absent parents are, children make better adjustments to the immediate situation – and are more emotionally and psychologically healthy in the long term – if they can continue to see them. There is more about handling access visits later in this chapter.

Children who have the most frequent access to the absent parent often adjust much more easily. There is no such thing as too much access as far as the child is concerned, although this can be difficult for the parents.

Ultimately, you have to decide what pattern of access suits you best. Ideally, there should be a mixture of the absent parent seeing the children in their own home, taking them out, and staying at the absent parent's home. When you are living very far apart, the children might stay with the absent parent for longer periods, perhaps during the holidays. As children become older, there needs to be some flexibility in the arrangements. The children need to be involved in planning visits, and have the option to change some of them to accommodate plans of their own. Frequent telephone calls or letters when it is difficult to meet also help.

## *The parent who disappears*

In some cases one of the parents disappears – either immediately following the separation or some time afterwards. This is distressing to children of all ages, and also to the parent who is left dealing with the children's misery and anger. Even in these cases it is best to refrain from attacking and running down the absent parent, however angry you might be yourself. Your children need the reassurance that it is not lack of love for them that has driven the parent away, but the parent's own problems and inability to handle the situation.

Nevertheless, the hurt and rejected feelings run deep. As one teenage girl said to her mother, who was trying to offer reasons for her father's silence, 'I don't want to be understanding! I'm too young to have to worry about him! I want to be angry!' The children should feel free to express whatever feelings are raised by the absent parent's departure, without you reinforcing them with angry or disgusted reactions of your own. Your role is to reassure them that they are still loved and wanted by you, and to support them through their own unhappiness. This is a situation where professional guidance is often useful to help your children sort out their feelings and express them.

Your children also need help in understanding the situation even if they have no memory of the absent parent. Some parents say that their children never ask questions about parents they have never known. However, they will undoubtedly have thoughts about the other parent, even if you are unaware of this. Sometimes they have picked up the idea from you that asking questions on the subject is unwelcome. Be alert to this, and be prepared to open the topic if you sense there is something they need to have answered. Sometimes their interest is disguised by general questions about mothers and fathers, or about other couples they know.

## Decisions to do with the children

When absent parents continue to see the children, they also need to be involved with the decisions that affect the children's upbringing. Absent parents who feel fully involved in their children's upbringing, and know that their opinions count, are most likely to continue to see their children regularly.

In a divorce, 'joint custody' means both parents have equal responsibility for the major decisions that affect their children, and this is usually the best option for everyone.

Even if you do not have joint custody, or were never married, it is still best if you can agree to talk over matters that affect your children and make decisions together. Obvious issues include which schools your children go to and major items of expenditure. It might also be useful to agree on standards of behaviour and issues to do with independence. You won't be able to agree about everything, but if you keep in mind your children's best interests, you can usually compromise.

While you continue to feel angry at your ex-partner, or intensely sad about the break-up, discussing matters to do with the children can be hard. It is worth thinking of these discussion as comparable to the talks you have with your children's teacher about their future. In these cases, you and the teacher might not like each other, or understand each other's lifestyles, but these feelings are irrelevant: you put them on one side while you discuss your common interest – the children and their education. While this is easier said than done with your ex-partner, you should agree not to bring up other issues when you are involved with making decisions to do with the children.

## THE PARENT AT HOME

In many ways the parent at home has the greater burden as far as the children are concerned. You are the one who has to manage the daily routine, and deal with their feelings as well as your own. This takes a lot of strength at a time when your reserves are low. The most stressful time will eventually pass, but meanwhile there are some things you can do to make it easier for your children.

Stress for the children is minimised if you can keep routines as close to normal as possible. Bedtimes and mealtimes should follow the usual pattern, except, perhaps, when you are making special concessions. For instance, an unhappy child might be allowed to stay up later for extra comfort, or given extra time and attention at bedtime. On the whole, though, they need to feel that there is continuity and that life goes on as before. If you are forced to move, or to find work when you previously stayed at home, it is obviously more difficult to continue the routines you used to follow. You must try in these cases to structure a new, reliable routine when you can, which will help you as much as the children.

## Time with the children

In the first few months after a break-up the children often need more of your time than usual. If circumstances have forced you to find work, or change your working hours, this can be difficult. However, as your distress will sometimes mean that you are emotionally unavailable to them, you should make the most of time that you do spend together.

Although there is a temptation to keep your own feelings at bay by seeing sympathetic friends, or boosting your confidence by going out on dates, you should be sensitive in the way you do this. Your children will be even more anxious if you go out a lot while they are still unhappy. Younger children might fear that you are not coming back. Try to make sure that you are around at bedtime as much as possible, which is when children's fears and unhappiness are most likely to surface. Children often have more nightmares around the time of separation and feel better if you are around when they wake. It is perhaps best to invite supportive friends round to your house so that the children know that you are still there. When you go out you should arrange babysitters with whom your children feel secure and relaxed.

However much you might want to date or find a lover during this time, it is best to wait. From your children's point of view it is disturbing to be aware of a new partner or succession of partners. Just as important is the fact that you are at a particularly vulnerable stage in your life, and becoming involved with someone else now can backfire.

## Handling your own feelings

Your children know that you are suffering, even if you attempt to hide your feelings from them. It is often better for them to see a more open display of emotion. There is no harm in letting them see you cry, or in telling them that you are sad or angry, or that sometimes you find it hard to cope. However, it is frightening to children to be exposed to the full range and power of your emotions.

While it is fine to show that you have feelings, children of any age are not equipped to cope with some of the things you feel. Children are particularly burdened and scared if you admit to suicidal thoughts, or even wild statements, such as, 'I wish I were dead!' Their fear for you makes it harder to deal with their own problems and feelings.

Just as difficult for them to deal with are your angry, bitter and vengeful attitudes towards your ex-partner. Children are aware that they are 'half mum and half dad', and they have looked up to you both in different ways. If they are now asked to believe horrible and demeaning things about one of their parents, they suffer intensely.

On one level they know that you will feel betrayed if they continue to love their other parent, which will make them feel emotionally torn in the most painful way. On a more profound, less conscious level they are likely to grow up feeling that there is something bad in themselves – the part of themselves that comes from the other parent. This can go so deep that, as adults, they can't even remember why they feel like this. Whatever the temptation, therefore, you should resist the impulse to enlist your children in an emotional tug of war – they will suffer more than your ex-partner does. This does not mean that you have to pretend that you don't have negative feelings towards your ex-partner, but your children are not the people to tell the details to, or to hear your views on the character, personality and shortcomings of him or her. They are entitled to have their own views and feelings, based on their own perceptions.

However, these feelings are natural, and you need the chance to express them. Other adults, or perhaps counsellors, are better able to help you when you are really angry or despairing than your children are. Make sure that you have people you can talk to about all of this, away from your children.

● **Your attitude to the other parent.** As far as possible you should try to separate the fact that your ex-partner is someone who has hurt you from the fact that he or she is a parent to your children. This is most difficult to do when that person is still in your life as a continuing presence for your children.

Access visits are most likely to stir up feelings that you need to control. Having your ex-partner in the house, or seeing your children go off for a visit, can make you feel sad, angry, and raise memories of all the hurts and slights that have led to your separation.

You can help yourself in a number of ways if it is disturbing for you when your partner visits the house. One is to invite a friend or family member to be with you at the time, and to make yourself scarce. Another is to arrange for someone else to be with the children at access times, and to go somewhere else until your ex-partner has gone. It is best to avoid bringing up grudges when your ex-partner is there to see the children. Problems to do with maintenance or other issues should be saved for a time when the children are not around to see you argue and become distressed and angry. Bear in mind that it is best for the children to have a pleasant and relaxed time with their other parent, as it will help them come to terms with the situation.

Children who seem reluctant to see the other parent are often picking up on your anxiety about the situation. Encouraging them to go and enjoy themselves will make them feel better about it. Reluctance that persists, however, should be explored in detail, to discover what is so disturbing about seeing the other parent. Ways to make the children feel better about it should be tried: perhaps taking a friend along, or arranging the visits in places where they feel secure, such as a grand-parent's house, or under supervision. Forbidding access is very much a last resort, when there is a very bad relationship between children and parent. In every other circumstance, the children have a lot to lose.

When your children go off with your ex-partner for an outing or to stay the night, try not to create problems when they leave. Again, they will benefit from feeling free to be excited and happy on this occasion. Resist the temptation to cross-examine them on their return about what went on, who was there and what was said. Allow them to tell you in their own way, if they want to. It is difficult for them if they believe that you require them to spy, or if you show distress at what they have been doing. It can, of course, be very galling for you if your children return full of excitement about what they've been up to, and with tales of the generosity of the other parent, who has given them treats. It is tempting to point out what you do for them, which, although less glamorous, is more onerous. But, again, it is better to hold your tongue – or complain to someone other than your children.

Remember, children are not stupid, and they usually come to understand how much you do for them in relation to what the other parent does. Consider how much better it is for them to feel that there is a ray of sunshine in the gloom of the separation – the fact that they are having special treatment that they might not have had when you were together. How much better that there is some of aspect of the situation that marks an improvement, so that they do not constantly mourn the separation!

Similar forbearance should be shown when your ex-partner is involved with someone else. Again, it is human to want to know all about the new partner, and to hope that your children have unpleasant things to say about him or her. It is better all round, however, if you maintain your reserve. Your children might well not like the new person who is taking their parent's time and attention, but it is not for you to make the situation worse with your comments. Try to see it from their point of view if they do, by chance, like the new partner. It is better for them not to be made unhappy by the involvement. Most children are suspicious of their parents' new attachments, and often feel very threatened and sad because of them. They will be happier altogether if they can accept new people in your lives and feel that they can like them.

Ultimately, your parenting relationship with your ex-partner needs to be worked on, even when your relationship is long over. Over time it can change and develop as you and your partner (and your circumstances) change. With care, respect, and an eye to the children's welfare, you can work together successfully as separated parents, which will help your children more than anything to come to terms with the situation.

● **Your attitude to your children.** It is natural to look to the children for love and support when you have been left on your own with them. You often need reassurance as much as they do. It can, in fact, be quite good for them to know that you need their help in practical matters around the home, and some children grow in maturity when they have to take on responsibility.

However, it is burdensome for them if you rely on them too heavily, or want them to take over because you can't cope. While older children can be assigned to help with the little ones, they should not be expected to look after them totally. Neither should you curtail all their social or other activities because of what you require them to do. It is much better to draw on support from other adults if you possibly can.

Similarly, while you will obviously look to them for love, you should not make them feel totally responsible for your happiness and well-being. While you will all draw comfort from increasing the amount of cuddles and affection you give each other, you might also find this extends to sleeping together from time to time. This is fine as a temporary arrangement, but should not become a habit. Children who feel duty-bound to replace their absent parent by becoming, in effect, your partner, are being put in a position that is too responsible for them. Their own development can be affected if they believe that their main purpose in life is to make you happy, or give you a reason for living. Children who have felt this can feel humiliated and betrayed as you become better able to cope and re-start your social life, or find a new partner.

This was one of the problems for Bill who, as mentioned before, broke up with his second wife because of his daughter's behaviour.

When Bill's wife had walked out on him, Lorraine was twelve. She was desperately hurt by her mother's departure, and Bill looked to her for all his emotional needs. Lorraine's mother had been a powerful woman, as Bill's mother had been. Lorraine, while feeling duty-bound to comfort her father, also assumed her mother's role as the dominant influence in the home. She dealt with her father the way she had seen her mother do.

In fact, Bill had so taken for granted that women were the 'strong' ones, that he had failed to see how manipulated he had been in the past, and how Lorraine was being forced to duplicate this pattern. Despite her strength, Bill saw Lorraine as a 'poor baby' who should be shielded from distress.

For four years, all Lorraine's emotional energy went into caring for her father – no wonder she felt so angry and rejected when he found someone to marry. Although she succeeded in coming between her father and his second wife, it was not a happy victory for her. She was still focused on replacing her mother, when she should have been building up to an independent life of her own. She had proved that her father's attachment to her was strongest, but in a way that was not good for her development. No child should feel that she has the power to determine her parent's life and actions. And by 'seeing off' the other woman Lorraine needed to continue to fill that space in his life. Although counselling could not save Bill's second marriage, it did help him learn how he should handle Lorraine in the future, to break the unnatural tie so that they could both live lives of their own.

## Problems with children

There are always problems with children – it comes with the job of parenthood. Some are special to the separation, however, and have already been looked at. There are some others that need closer examination.

● **Scapegoats.** When one child is more difficult than another, or that child reminds you of your departed partner, you can find yourself picking on him or her. At this emotional time you are not always acting rationally, and some of your feelings can be displaced inappropriately on to a child.

Catch yourself if this happens – and tell yourself that difficult behaviour is a sign of stress and unhappiness, so the child needs more – not less – love. Similarly, remember that your child's resemblance to your ex-partner is no reason to make the child even more miserable.

If you find it hard to break out of this behaviour, then you might need outside help if it is not to cause harm to the child. Counselling can help with issues such as these, and organisations that focus on parent/child interactions are listed at the back of the book.

Sharon came to RELATE when she was breaking up with her

husband. Although the counselling focused on helping her come to terms with the separation, much of it also concerned her two children, particularly the boy – Ross. While she gave her little girl lots of loving attention, Ross got the brunt of her bad feelings. She said he was very naughty and uncontrollable, but as she talked, the counsellor was able to help her identify what was behind it.

Sharon's own mother had treated boys and girls very differently. Sharon had been brought up to believe that all girls were good and boys were a problem. When the little girl was difficult Sharon was indulgent, but when Ross acted up, she became intensely irritated. It didn't help that he was the spitting image of his father.

It became clear to the counsellor that Sharon wasn't giving Ross any clear idea about what was and wasn't allowable behaviour. When he began to irritate her, she would first of all plead with him to stop in a gentle and ineffective way. Then suddenly her temper would snap, and she would scream and hit out at him. Sharon was able to recognise that her first requests were confusing to a small boy, who had no idea that she was angry until she started shouting. Sharon realised that she had to be very clear and firm when she meant 'no', so that Ross was in no doubt that she meant it.

It also emerged that Ross received more attention when he was being naughty. Sharon was very free with her cuddles for her daughter, but was not inclined to fuss over Ross. Once Sharon saw in what way she was contributing to Ross's difficult behaviour, she was able to change it. She was firmer with Ross, but at the same time gave him more affection – and during the course of counselling, her relationship with him improved measurably.

● **Your children's attitude to the absent parent.** Some children remain intensely loyal to the parent who has left. As has been said, it is desirable that children are able to be loyal to both parents, but this can occasionally cause an additional problem. Even parents who are managing quite well to cope with their divided feelings can be unreasonably upset when one of their children seems to take sides with the absent partner. This can happen at any age, but is perhaps most likely during adolescence, when children tend to show rebellious behaviour towards the parents with whom they live.

It can be difficult to remember that a child who becomes aligned with an absent parent is suffering, when you are most aware of aggressive behaviour towards yourself. It needs patience to deal with this situation and a realisation that you shouldn't take it too personally. An older child or adolescent sometimes needs you to make the first move towards forgiveness when this happens. At a rebellious age, children can find it difficult to apologise or give up a stance they have adopted.

It can sometimes happen that the child is only trying to have a good relationship with both parents, but you perceive it as a rejection of you. This was the case with Annabelle, whose sixteen-year-old son, Craig, maintained a strong relationship with his father, despite that fact that he had behaved very badly towards the whole family.

Annabelle was extremely angry and bitter, and had good reason to be. Her husband was a very good-looking man, but mentally unstable. He had lost all their money, and had ruined her relationships with friends and family. He had had a number of affairs, which he had flaunted openly in front of Annabelle, before finally leaving her for another woman.

Although that relationship broke up, he did not return to Annabelle. Instead of dealing with her anger in a rational way, Annabelle was taking it all out on Craig. The boy was the only member of the family who continued to visit the father and defend him. The two younger children didn't want to know their father. Whenever Annabelle spoke to her ex-husband she became enraged, and she turned on Craig. On one occasion when she was particularly incensed, Annabelle threw all Craig's precious computer game disks in the bin. Craig, an intelligent, reasonable boy, was so desperately upset that he put his fist through a plate-glass window in the living room.

In the event, this dramatic action shocked Annabelle into realising that something had gone very wrong. She was already having regular counselling with RELATE, and she talked these matters through with the counsellor.

In an unusual move, the counsellor received permission to talk to Craig on his own. It turned out that the boy was heartbroken by the separation – far more disturbed than his younger brother or sister. Over the years he had become used to his parents rowing, and was able to switch off from it. He had also known about his father's affairs, and knew that his parents had managed to rebuild their relationship in the past. He had hoped against hope that they would be able to do so again. Craig felt that it was his responsibility to keep his father involved with the family, all the rest of whom had turned their back on him.

Craig had come to terms with the fact that his parents weren't going to get back together, although he still wished it were possible. Craig did not idealise his father, in fact he was angry that the loss of the family money meant that he had to change to a school that was not as good as his previous one. He passionately wanted to maintain his relationship with his father, however, whatever his faults might be.

Craig was upset and angry that his mother was taking everything out on him. When the counsellor asked how he reacted when this happened, he said, 'I withdraw.' He made the connection himself that this was what his father used to do, and therefore it was guaranteed to make Annabelle even more angry.

Craig found great relief in being able to talk to the counsellor. This one session helped him feel much better about the situation. They discussed alternative ways he might react to his mother, and what he could do to improve matters between them.

In her sessions with Annabelle, the counsellor also worked on ways Annabelle could cope with her angry feelings without taking them out on Craig. Many months after the counselling ended, Annabelle got back in touch with the counsellor to report how much happier she was generally, and how unrecognisably better her relationship was with Craig.

## Discipline

Discipline can sometimes go out of the window in the early days after a separation. You might fear alienating your children if they are angry towards you and seem to blame you for what has happened. If they are very sad, you might not want to add to their burdens by telling them off. Some parents, already feeling vulnerable because of the loss of a partner, now fear losing their children's affections if they lay down the law.

It can be especially difficult when the partner who has left was the disciplinarian. If you delegated the responsibility for keeping the children in line to the other parent, the children can respond by acting up when that parent is no longer around.

Sometimes you just feel too weary to put your foot down, and so let the children behave as they please.

You need to set down limits as soon as possible after the first shock is over. Your children might complain, but you won't lose their love or loyalty. All children feel more comfortable when they know how far they can go and what is acceptable behaviour. It can, in fact, feel quite frightening to children when they are not controlled – with everything changing around them, and adults behaving so unpredictably, they can feel threatened by chaos. Children who worry that what their parents are doing is wrong can doubt their own capacity to know what is right.

Some older children, disturbed by the loss of clear rules, mimic the departed parent by attempting to boss the parent who remains, and the rest of the household, too. Ultimately they are relieved when the parent once again takes over.

It can sometimes be helpful to enlist the children in drawing up the new house rules. Explain that you all have to live together as amicably as possible and share the responsibility for things working well. When children are asked to suggest rules they can be surprisingly strict. They are more likely to respect rules that they have assisted in devising.

If you continue to have difficulty keeping control, it could be that you are still bewildered and disorganised by what has happened. Seek help from other adults, the school, a counsellor, or one of the organisations listed at the back of the book.

# THE ABSENT PARENT

When you are the one to leave, the changes in your life are substantial. You lose your home as well as your partner, and your relationship with your children changes abruptly. Instead of taking each other for granted and being casual in your contact, seeing each other now becomes charged with extra significance. You now have to concentrate on each other rather than just simply being together. You miss your children's daily routine, and the sorts of things you automatically knew about them – small pleasures, fleeting worries, as well as the more important events in their lives.

This can be very distressing for all of you. When you do see each other in the early days after the separation everyone is emotional and tense. It is impossible to recreate the ease you used to feel with your children when you only see them occasionally. You want your times together to be happy, but they might be fraught with anger and sadness. It is not surprising that some parents in your position find this too difficult to cope with. They can't bear the changed relationship, so they stop seeing the children, or see them only rarely.

If you were the one who initiated the separation you might also be feeling very guilty about the impact it has had on the family. In this situation, too, absent parents stay away from the family home (and therefore their children) because the guilt is more intense when they are there. Or you might stay away because you want to avoid your ex-partner's anger and grief, or daren't risk opening up your own hurt feelings.

While all of this is quite understandable, the fact remains that your children need you. They feel desolate and rejected enough as it is, and knowing that you make the effort to see them, even when things are difficult, is very important in helping them come to terms with what has happened.

## Continuing involvement

Remaining involved with the children benefits you, as well as them. Some parents find that they are able to make better relationships with their children now that they have to give them concentrated attention at the times that they do see them. If you were a more remote parent in the past, who left your partner to do most of the caring for the children, you have the chance to get to know them better than before. Indeed, some parents only realise how much their children mean to them when they are no longer living together.

Even if your experience of seeing your children is less happy than this, you should persevere. It is the single greatest contribution you can make to their well-being now and for the future Their confidence will be profoundly shaken if you stop seeing them. It is never too late to pick up the threads of your relationship. Although it is best to maintain steady contact from the beginning, you can still get back in touch and increase visiting times if you have let it slip for a while.

To help keep pace with the changes that your children are going through, you should also attempt to make it easy for your partner to consult you on their welfare, and the decisions that have to be taken about the children's future. Most schools are also happy to send both parents copies of school reports and letters to do with the children's progress. Attending parents' days and special occasions, such as sports and drama days also helps.

Some parents make heroic efforts to keep in touch with the children, even when it is very hard for them. Denis's wife left him suddenly and without explanation, taking their three children with her. She moved to a city a long distance away, and for the first few months after the separation Denis commuted every weekend to stay at a bed-and-breakfast near the children. He would arrive at midnight on Friday, and return home on Sunday afternoon. The strain eventually became too much, and he was not able to maintain this level of contact.

In circumstances such as these, the children need you to explain to them why you are visiting less, and need to be reassured that you still love them and think about them when you don't see them. Where possible they should come to stay with you from time to time, and you should try to keep in touch by writing letters and telephoning them. If you find it hard to be regular about visiting or keeping in touch, explain the reasons. Although they will still be sad, it helps them to have an explanation that they can understand. For instance, you can say, 'Sometimes when I am very busy I become forgetful. But I still love you very much, and feel bad when I know that I have made you sad.'

You should, however, make every effort to be regular and consistent with your children. You should be prompt at turning up when you say you will, and give plenty of warning if there is some reason that you can't. One little girl, who spent many Sundays waiting in vain for her father to turn up to take her out, carried a heavy burden of rejection into adulthood. She would dress up and wait eagerly for the promised treat, not wanting to move away from the window in case she should miss him. She became increasingly nervous on the occasions that she did see her father, fearful that any difficult behaviour on her part would send him away for good. She never dared tell him how unhappy his erratic behaviour made her.

## Handling your children's feelings

Children respond in different ways to the separation and in their reaction to the absent parent. Your children might be unhappy when they see you – nervous, clingy or even angry. Some might be sullen and awkward. At the very least this can be disturbing for you – and can also be frightening. You can fear that it means that you are losing your children or that they will stop loving you.

What you must remember is that this is a very stressful time for them, and their behaviour does not have any real relevance to their underlying feelings about you. It is a reaction to the situation, and to the unhappiness, distress and upheaval all around them. It is often precisely because they love and need you so much that they are angry and difficult.

The temptation can be to 'buy' their happiness with special treats and activities. While this does no harm in small doses, and can be very gratifying to the children, it is not the most helpful way of dealing with the situation. Above all, the children need to feel that you love them and care about them however they behave. Showing your affection openly and being tolerant of difficult behaviour is even more healing than a present or an exciting outing. Where possible, it is good to spend some ordinary time together, when you can sit around and get on with other things, as well as activities you do together.

Time to talk also helps. Let your children feel free to express their anxieties, distress or anger while you offer warm support. However, you shouldn't push a child to talk who doesn't want to, neither should you demand explanations for feelings or difficult behaviour. Some children are not sure why they feel or behave as they do. Instead, make it clear that you know they are feeling mixed-up, and that you respect their right to feel as they do.

Your children are also likely to have a lot of questions, particularly in the early days. Some children will beg you to return and might want to know why you won't. These questions are distressing, of course, but if you answer them as honestly and fully as you can, your children will eventually be satisfied that they know all they need to know. Remember not to blame or criticise the parent with whom they live in your explanations, but answer their questions factually, or in relation to your own feelings.

Children are also likely to want to know how you are feeling and coping in the new circumstances. Again, be truthful, but don't over-burden them with very strong emotions. You can tell them that you are sad and angry sometimes, but they also need reassurance that you are managing. You don't have to pretend to be happier than you are – but neither should you believe that it is better for them to think you are sad all the time. Worrying about your welfare can make it harder for them to come to terms with what has happened.

## Your attitude to the live-in parent

Whatever your feelings for the other parent, remember that it is hurtful to the children to hear critical comments about the parent with whom they live. Your time with them will be more stressful and miserable if you insist on talking badly about the other parent. Remember, this time is for you and your children, and should not be seen as an opportunity to get your own back at your ex-partner. Try not to be drawn into a battle, even if they report things that have been said about you.

Neither should you question them too closely about what goes on in the home. A genuine interest in them is one thing – a desire to find out things you can use against the other parent is another. If they do tell you anything that disturbs you, however, it is not helpful to complain to them about what you hear. You should reserve your concerns for when you talk to your ex-partner, preferably at a time when the children are not around to become involved.

If you make them anxious, or critical of their other parent, then home-life is likely to be even more difficult and distressing for them. Encouraging them to defy the other parent also makes adjustment difficult. Any serious worries about how they are brought up should be tackled in a way that promotes the best outcome for the children. This means not antagonising your ex-partner, and making sure that any suggestions you make are seen purely as being in the children's best interests, not as an attack.

## New partners and your children

It is hard for children to adjust to new partners in their parents' lives. If you are already seeing someone else it is best not to include them in the visiting in the early days. The children are hungry for your attention, even if they behave badly, or even if they seem to be ignoring you. They will be made even more unhappy if they have to divide your time with someone else. Of course, your children need to get to know your new partner when he or she becomes important in your life. But even so, if you only see your children occasionally and for short periods, you should make sure that for most of that time you see them alone. More details on how to handle this situation can be found in Chapter Nine, *The Family Network*.

## THE YEARS TO COME

Eventually your children will settle down. Although some of the stronger emotions persist for a long time, they will become less obviously distressing. If you have managed to avoid burdening your children with your angry and blaming feelings towards your ex-partner, they will be better able to accept the finality of the split – and they can go on to make good relationships with you both. As you become happier yourself, you will be better able to handle the situation, and cope with your children. If all goes well, your relationship with your ex-partner will develop in such a way that you can co-operate satisfactorily over issues to do with the children. However, there are a few things that you should bear in mind, which are dealt with briefly here.

### The children's need to understand

As your children grow older, they will continue to think about the relationship between you, the parents – probably long after you yourself have put it behind you. You are still their parents, after all, and you once all lived together. As the children change and mature they will still be trying to make sense of it all: what went wrong? Was it ever right? Who was to blame?

Questions you answered to their satisfaction when they were younger are likely to come up again, as they enter a new phase of development. If you have always told the truth, you can enlarge on it according to their increased ability to understand. With a new perspective yourself, you might also be able to fill in details about the 'good times', which will have been harder for you to think about during the period of adjustment surrounding the separation. It is helpful for your children to know the good as well as the bad. They understand more and learn something useful about relationships for themselves.

Sometimes your children will see things differently as they grow older – have more compassion for the parent they believed was to blame, for instance, or become more critical of the parent they thought was innocent.

The re-assessment over the years can be irritating and occasionally upsetting for you. But you have to remember that the subject is never a closed book for your children. The fact remains that your union – and your separation – have been of crucial importance to your children's development, and will continue to be so for the rest of their lives.

## Changing relationships

Your relationship with your children will have its ups and downs as it does for parents who remain together. When things are bad you might continue to believe the separation is to blame. But children have great powers of recovery, especially if they can rely on your steadfast love and support. As you become stronger and happier, your children will benefit from the improved atmosphere.

Older children might spend more time with the absent parent, and sometimes you might all decide that it is better for the children to live with the other parent for a while. Access arrangements, anyway, should be reviewed regularly as children develop, and their own wishes and plans should be taken into account.

Access continues to be important, even when the children have busy social lives and other interests. An adolescent feels vulnerable, even when he or she appears to be arrogant or aggressive. If the absent parent disappears at this time, it delivers a great blow to the child's self-esteem and confidence.

## Long-term problems

Some children are worse affected by your separation, and for a much longer time. This is especially likely if *you* continue to harbour angry or depressed feelings for years, or if the other parent disappears. Because you see your children every day, you might be the last to notice that long-standing emotional problems, such as depression or anxiety, have settled in. Looking at the children's rate of development or educational progress might provide clues that you otherwise miss. This is why keeping in touch with the school, and consulting the staff about your children, continues to be useful.

Help for yourself to overcome your own feelings will benefit your children. RELATE sees individuals as well as couples, and can help – as can other forms of counselling or therapy. Professional help for children who continue to be depressed or difficult, or who are lagging behind, can be very useful.

# Part Two

# WORKING ON YOURSELF

# 5

# HAPPINESS, CONFIDENCE AND INDEPENDENCE

The end of a relationship can be a new beginning. Without the constraints of a partnership you can concentrate on your own needs and take steps to construct a more satisfying way of living and relating to other people, which includes any children you might have. It is a chance for you to take a fresh look at yourself and at your life.

There is a Buddhist saying, 'Out of the greatest suffering comes the greatest good.' No one wants to suffer, and these words might raise a hollow laugh. But it is true, if you let it be. The suffering caused by breaking up with your partner is a combination of loss and stressful change. Your life can't be the same afterwards. The choice is yours whether you find value in it.

This is a new idea to some people. If you believe that people or circumstances 'make' you unhappy, and the reverse – that you only become happy when other people do something to make you so, or when nice things happen – then you live your life at the mercy of events. In fact, the most reliable happiness comes from within, and is under your own control. Similarly, unhappiness can be used as a spur to make their lives better by people who are strong inside.

This is easy to say, but what does it mean? How can you 'control' your own happiness or become strong inside? Ways to do this are examined at length later in this chapter, but the issues behind them can be summed up here.

Very briefly, your happiness comes under your own control when you take responsibility for it. On one level this means recognising what steps you can take to make yourself happy – not in the sense of acquiring possessions or attracting people to you but in the more fundamental sense of adjusting your daily life in small ways to make it more satisfying and pleasurable. Of course, things that upset you continue to happen – a separation is one of them – but in the midst of misfortune you can choose how you react to events.

We have all been inspired and amazed by tales of people in terrible circumstances who have regained their good humour, optimism and determination. People with grave physical disabilities who have accomplished extraordinary feats, for instance. Or people who have responded to a personal tragedy by starting support groups for others in similar circumstances. While these people are exceptional, we can all learn from their underlying motivation: a drive to make sense of their lives, and to find value in experiences that are difficult, unfair or tragic.

These people have not denied or suppressed their suffering. Instead they have come to terms with it, and used it to give them a purpose. Finding your own purpose, and living your life in accordance with it, is one of the main factors in bringing your happiness under your own control.

The inner strength that helps people deal with their suffering in creative ways can be summed up in one word: confidence. When you trust yourself, respect your emotional reactions and retain a conviction that you have the ability to endure and cope with life's difficulties, then you can handle almost anything that happens. It is a fortunate fact that even if your self-esteem and confidence have never been high, or have been dented by your separation, it is possible to build both up. This self-created strength gives you more than the ability to deal with unhappiness, however. It gives you an inner security that frees you to take more chances and dare to make changes that will bring your life closer to the way you want it to be. The exciting bonus is that the more you do this, the more confident you become, and the more possibilities open up for you, as shown later in this chapter.

## TOWARDS HAPPINESS

Happiness can be defined in a number of ways. This is because it means different things to different people. It is also because there are degrees of happiness. At one end of the scale there is ecstasy – that bubbling excitement that comes when delightful things are happening and everything seems wonderful. Marvellous though it is, this is a passing feeling. You become used to anything in the end, and ecstatic feelings eventually fade. There is the more ordinary kind of happiness at the other end of the scale: a quiet contentment and feeling of well-being when life suits you just as it is. Even this feeling can't last forever. Human nature is such that after a while contentment slides into boredom. Even when nothing has gone wrong, you feel a restlessness – less contented because you want something new to happen.

It is the same for the degrees of happiness in between: the happiness of a good night out with lots of laughter, or the happiness when you receive good news. You experience the feeling, and then it passes.

Annoyances or greater upsets change your mood for a time. Difficult periods, however, help you appreciate the times of happiness.

The most indestructible form of happiness is the 'quietest' of positive emotions. It is an inner certainty that you are doing your best, living in accordance with your principles, and making the most of whatever circumstances you find yourself in. Although there may not be accompanying feelings of elation, excitement or even the passive pleasure of contentment, this is the most solid, reliable feeling of all. Even so, there are still times when you doubt yourself, or when things get too much for you – so this inner certainty is not always consistent either.

The passing nature of happiness – and, indeed, of all emotional states of mind – means that you can never reach a point where you are completely happy for ever. What you can do, instead, is make more space in your life for happiness, by understanding what makes you happy, and by taking steps to make it happen. When you are in emotional turmoil after a break-up, however, happiness can seem very far away. Some people wonder whether they will ever be able to feel happy again.

Happiness returns slowly. There can be happy moments even in the midst of grief, however fleeting. Some will be genuine bonuses out of the blue – something happens or someone does something to give you a little joy. But if you are going to reach a stage where you are more happy than not, and where you have some control over your level of contentment, then you will have to start to think of ways of achieving it.

## Immediately after the break-up

Some people attempt to grab at happiness after a separation. Because they have lost a partner they believe that finding a lover will fill the chasm of emptiness they carry round inside. Relationships started too soon after a separation can run into difficulties, however; and the disappointment this creates can send you even deeper into despair. Again, it is an example of looking for happiness outside yourself, rather than learning to create your own.

There is no such thing as instant happiness that will hasten the end of the grieving process. What you can do, however, is start to lay down the foundations for future happiness by starting to take care of yourself.

● **Don't deny your feelings.** Finding happiness in the future involves understanding your feelings and respecting them, whatever they might be. When you can experience your sadness, and know why you are sad, or express your anger, and understand the reasons for it, you are closer to knowing what makes you feel bad. This results in a better sense of what makes you feel good. If you have become used to keeping a lid on your feelings, you can reach the stage of not really knowing what makes you happy – or finding yourself in a situation that you believed would make you happy, but not feel anything at all.

After a separation you will be feeling more of the turbulent, negative emotions, usually very strongly. While this is unpleasant, experiencing these feelings releases them. If you have struggled to contain them in the past, it will release even more. As you recover, you can find all of your emotions fresher and more accessible to you – meaning you can fully enjoy happiness when it comes.

---

! ================ *Task* ================

### Today

Check on your mood from time to time. What are you feeling? Tell yourself, silently or aloud, what it is: 'I am very angry', 'I am depressed', 'I am panicky', 'I feel anxious', and so on. Even if this seems silly, acknowledging your feelings to yourself is an important step towards dealing with them.

It can also help to keep a journal of your feelings. At the end of each day, write down what you have felt and what seemed to cause it. !

---

● **Look after yourself.** Acknowledging your feelings also involves monitoring your physical feelings. Some people pride themselves on keeping going when they are exhausted or under par. 'Listening' to your body is far more sensible – pushing yourself beyond endurance results in listlessness and an increase in depression, as well as a slower recovery rate.

The very process of grieving is tiring and you should take this into account. If you can take time off to recuperate, then you should. If you can't, you should make as much time to rest as you can. Go to bed early, take naps and rearrange your schedule to do as little as necessary. Ask people to help you with anything that is difficult or stressful.

Paradoxically, it can also help to build in some exercise, even if it is just a long walk three or four times a week. Strengthening your body helps you cope generally. When you are very angry or restless it can help if you release the feelings in a physical way, by some kind of sport, gardening, or even pummelling some bread dough.

You should also try to eat healthily and regularly. Your emotional state is linked to your physical well-being, and if you stop eating enough, or binge on comfort foods that are not good for you, you lose the stamina necessary to help you deal with your strong feelings. Smoking more, or drinking more heavily, can also make you feel physically under par when you need every available ounce of energy.

! ——————————————— *Task* ———————————————

### Relaxation

Make a daily habit of a few minutes deep relaxation. This can be useful first thing in the morning before you start, or later in the day when you find some quiet time. Twenty minutes is ideal, although ten will do.

Either sit in a comfortable chair, or lie down. Close your eyes and breathe deeply and slowly. Mentally check your body: are any of your muscles tense? Consciously release them until you feel your body becoming heavy and relaxed. Try not to think about your problems or what you have to do. Instead, imagine a peaceful scene: a meadow, a beach or a wood. If thoughts intrude, brush them away – tell yourself you will deal with them later. When your time is up, open your eyes and continue to breathe deeply. Don't jump up immediately, but look around until you 'come to'.

Taking ten minutes to do this when you find yourself feeling angry, panicky or anxious during the day also helps, or when problems threaten to overwhelm you.

You can sometimes find that solutions to problems pop into your mind after a relaxation session.
!

● **Treat yourself.** Develop the habit of asking yourself every day or several times a day – 'What would make me feel better now?' Choose something that is possible and pleasurable, however small. What makes you feel better can change according to your mood or circumstances. It might be as simple as a cup of tea, or a long bath, or a chat with a sympathetic friend over the phone. It might be going to a film, or taking a walk – or getting a disagreeable chore out of the way so that you can stop worrying about it.

The idea is to pick a small treat that carries no negative

consequences. Eating a box of chocolates, for instance, is no good if you feel disgusted with yourself afterwards. Getting drunk doesn't help if you feel hungover and depressed by your lack of control later. Buying something you can't afford is also a mistake if it leaves you feeling guilty or broke. There is always something that you can do to shift your mood slightly towards feeling better, without leaving you feeling worse later – whether it is spending a quiet half-hour reading, watching a gripping 'soap', having an evening out, or writing a letter for a job application.

Don't avoid this issue by thinking that the 'only' thing that would make you happy is impossible – your partner coming back, or an expensive item you covet, or leaving a job that you hate. The aim is to feel better than you do at this moment, not to reach for unattainable happiness.

This simple and harmless habit can have much greater repercussions than are immediately obvious. Many people have long stopped thinking, 'What do *I* want?' or 'What would make *me* feel good now?' Indeed, if you have problems thinking up small treats for yourself, you are probably one of them. Although this might not seem very important, it has a larger impact on your life than you realise. If you never think about these matters you are likely to slide into the habit of going along with other people's demands and requests, whatever they might be. People who do this, and feel taken advantage of or angry, usually never consider whether they want to say 'yes' or 'no' before they do. It is only afterwards that resentment sets in, and they realise that they have agreed to something that doesn't suit them. Starting to question what you want as a treat, can lead to a quicker recognition of what you do and don't want in other circumstances.

Treating yourself has another important long-term beneficial effect. When you regularly improve your mood by taking your desires into account, you raise your general level of contentment. If you know that you can make yourself happy in small ways you are less easily cast down. More than that, it creates a pattern of thinking that increases your chance of happiness. You can eventually take larger steps: instead of 'What would make me feel better now?' you can ask yourself what is possible and achievable over a longer period: 'What can I set in motion that would make me feel happy later?', 'What changes do I need to make that will help me feel good?'

When you have been used to living with someone and taking their needs into account – or putting their needs before your own – it can take a real effort to develop the habit of thinking of things for yourself. Valerie came for counselling for nearly a year after her seventeen-year marriage broke up. Alongside dealing with her grief, the counsellor

!——————————————— *Task* ———————————————

**My treats**

If you find it hard to think of treats for yourself on the spur of the moment, it can help to take time to make a list of the kinds of things that you enjoy. Write down everything – from small to large – and keep it handy so that you can consult it at moments when you are lost for ideas.

!

encouraged Valerie to find out what she wanted from life, and for herself.

The counsellor says, 'It sounds a small thing, but the turning-point for Valerie was realising that she could choose what she had for breakfast. For years she had joined her husband in his choice of cereal, tea, toast and marmalade. When they parted she continued to have the same things. One day she realised that she didn't actually enjoy this: she wanted croissants and coffee. It was an exciting moment for her when she made the change. After that breakthrough everything changed for her.'

● **Giving space to happiness.** What is it that enables someone to say, 'I like my life'? Whatever else it may be, you can be sure that it also includes a daily pattern that is broadly satisfying, which means priority is given to things that make the person happy.

People who usually find contentment in their lives don't just give themselves treats to help overcome gloom and sadness. It is natural to them to pursue actively what gives them pleasure. They are good to be around because they enjoy life.

This is what you should aim for in the long term. As treating yourself becomes a habit, you experience directly the value of making sure that your life is pleasurable. By the time you have worked through the stages of mourning your relationship you will be ready to welcome happiness, and take steps to make yourself happy.

When Jack broke up with his wife, Lydia, after fifteen years of marriage he felt that the meaning had gone out of his life. At that point, the only thing that he could imagine that would make him happy was to have her back. Trailing a poor second was a desire to find someone else to take her place quickly, particularly as he felt lonely and sexually deprived.

Jack had kept his feelings on hold for most of his life. When the counsellor asked him what he was feeling, he often had to confess that he didn't know. However, his bursts of strong anger, and his times of desperate sadness made him confront feelings that he never knew existed. As that happened Jack was startled to realise that he couldn't remember ever truly feeling happy – or even simply enjoying himself.

In his talks with the counsellor, Jack began to experience a feeling of profound emptiness. Everything he had done had been for Lydia, or with her in mind. He believed that thinking about himself was a sign of selfishness, and selfishness had been frowned on in his family.

Jack found it surprising that as he experienced his painful emotions he felt a certain liberation. He began to feel at home with himself, to 'know who I am'. It was at this point that the counsellor was able to encourage him to look at interests and activities that he would like purely for himself.

Jack remembered that in the past he and Lydia had gone swimming together. He had learned to dive because Lydia fancied accomplished divers, and found it a turn-on. Jack had never thought about whether he enjoyed it or not. He experimented by going swimming alone, and found that he enjoyed himself enormously. It became part of his regular routine. He also decided to take up the guitar. Lydia had been the musical one in the family and had laughed at his attempts to pick out tunes on the piano. He now found that he had a talent for guitar. This gave him pleasure, and he also found practising chords soothing when he was feeling low. Both of these activities became part of his weekly agenda. For the first time in his life, Jack was finding that he could make his life enjoyable, even when there was no one to share it with.

At the end of counselling, Jack said that he was still keen to find another woman, and still felt that he missed a regular sex life, but he had made a decision not to rush into a new relationship. He said he wanted time for himself, to use the freedom to experiment with his own life. He wanted to ground his sense of security in himself and know what made him happy before looking for someone else.

Another example is Yvonne who, like Jack, was learning through counselling to find pleasure in her daily life after a long period of despair when she broke up with her lover. One day, towards the end of counselling, she bounced into the counselling room to report that she had taken herself off to the seaside the Saturday before. 'I called a friend and asked her to join me. She came up with excuses about ironing that had to be done and a parcel she was expecting.' Yvonne went on her own, taking a cheap coach ride and a packed lunch. 'It was chilly, but exhilarating. I wandered along this almost deserted stretch of beach, and revelled in feeling free. I sat on a rock and ate my lunch, and then warmed up later with a steaming cup of tea in a café.'

When Yvonne returned, her friend rang up to moan about her boring day, and to say that she wished she had come along. She said she would join Yvonne on the next expedition. 'I thought, "that used to be me"!' Yvonne reported to the counsellor. 'Always postponing pleasures until "next time" – and then postponing them again. Not now! I've learned to live in the moment!'

A simple way to check on whether you are organising your life in order to give yourself the maximum chance for happiness is to identify how much time you give to the various elements in your life each week. Then you can see whether it needs reorganising in any way to make it more satisfying for you. The following task can help you do so.

! —————————— *Task* ——————————

## My life

Draw a large circle. Divide it up into segments of various sizes according to how much time you spend on activities during the week. This should include all the things you have to do; for instance, work, household tasks, time with the children (if you have any), voluntary commitments. Also create segments representing the amount of time you spend on things you enjoy; for instance, reading, gardening, sport, hobbies – even resting or bathing. Also, if relevant, a segment to show how much television you watch.

Then draw a second circle. In this one allocate the segments and their size to show how you wish you were spending your time.

Then compare the two circles. Are they very different? If so, then your life is not organised in the way to give you maximum satisfaction. Think if there is any way you can change what you are doing now to reduce the time you spend on disliked activities, and to increase the time you spend on the things you enjoy.

!

● **Will I become selfish?** This question inhibits many people, as it did Jack. If you are used to putting other people first it is hard to believe that you can make yourself happy without someone else suffering as a consequence. But you don't lose consideration for others just because you start considering yourself.

If you have many responsibilities and calls on your time it can take a certain amount of juggling to free yourself to do the things that give you pleasure, but it is possible. Where other people are involved, such as children, it can also involve negotiation. You want to soak in the bath, but they want your attention? Explain that you are going to feel much better and happier when you have spent an hour by yourself, and you will be ready to read to them or talk to them after that.

It is inevitable that your desires will sometimes clash with other people's. That's life, and is no reason to stop thinking about your own needs. As long as you are prepared to put others first sometimes, and maintain your right to put yourself first at other times, you set up a healthy pattern of give and take. Remember, when you consistently deny your own needs you are not a comfortable person to be around. It benefits others as well as yourself if you can become happier and more contented.

## Discovering what you want in life

While you still might not be completely over the break-up, at some point you will find that it is not occupying all your energy and thoughts. This is the time to stop focusing on the past and to turn your attention to the future. What do you want to happen in the rest of your life? How would you like to be?

The happiest people are those who have a purpose: a goal, or a set of beliefs that gives meaning to their lives. Drifting along without this means that your happiness is always vulnerable to outside influences.

Living as well as you can day to day is important. But longer-term happiness involves a broader vision that you can work towards. Many people forget this – and, worse than that, actually limit their own potential by putting themselves down. These are people who brush aside daydreams of things they would like to do, or ways they would like to be, with the thought, 'I am not good enough/clever enough/ attractive enough/nice enough/strong enough, (or whatever) to do that.' Or, when offered an opportunity of some sort, turn it down, saying, 'I could never do that/I haven't got the time,' and so on.

If you find yourself doing this, you might congratulate yourself on your modesty or your realistic evaluation of yourself; but it is self-limiting. You are not the best judge of your own capabilities and potentials. Think of it this way: by limiting yourself, you are saving yourself from the effort of having to try, or the pain of not succeeding. The very act of working towards something, whether you achieve it or not, gives you a motivating purpose. It is people who do try, and who are prepared to cope with some failure, who are able to surprise themselves and other people.

!

================= *Task* =================

## I can, and I will

How often do you find yourself thinking or saying 'I can't do that!', 'I'm not good enough!', and other self-defeating phrases? Catch yourself when you do and stop. Instead, say 'I'll try!' or 'I'll give myself the chance to be good enough!' Remember, anything challenging takes practice – perfection isn't instant, and neither is it a realistic goal

!

Having a goal, whatever it might be, can create excitement as well as purpose in your life. When your day is dreary, aggravating or even unpleasant, a goal gives you reason to look beyond the here and now. There is something on the horizon worth aiming for. It is a reason to endure what you have to put up with, because you know there is hope for the future.

● **Dreams and ambitions.** People who accomplish most in their lives, personally and professionally, allow themselves to dream. In the privacy of their own minds they fantasise about the way they would like things to be, without censoring their own thoughts because they are 'silly' or 'unrealistic'. Without a dream, a vision, something to aim for, you are most likely to settle for second best. For instance, in career terms there are always examples of bright and able people who inexplicably reach a plateau. Everyone around them can see they have the potential to go far, but somehow or other they stick at a level below their potential. Usually these people have gone as far as they 'dared' to dream, and can't imagine aiming higher.

A dream beyond your grasp, therefore, has a purpose. It acts as a motivating force, gives you the courage to try, and the ability to spot openings that you otherwise might ignore.

This is true in your personal life, too. If your dream is to be married, then finding someone willing to marry you might seem enough. But if your dream is to marry someone with whom you can build a healthy and satisfying relationship, you are likely to choose more carefully, and also to question what you can bring to the marriage to make it good.

So don't dismiss dreams as childish. It is essential to allow your imagination free rein if you are going to be happy in the future.

The broader your vision, the better. The most helpful goals define the essence of what you want rather than the specific details that might lead to it. Only one person at a time can be prime minister, for instance, but a goal to be an influential person in society who can change things for the better, opens up many possibilities. It's too easy to discourage yourself by thinking, 'I could never be prime minister because of the following reasons . . .' But a goal to do something to leave the world a better place challenges you to find ways of fulfilling it. The person who sticks at a post below his or her capabilities might well go further if the goal is 'to develop my potential at work until I reach a position where I am satisfied.'

A narrow goal, where your ambitions rest on a specific job, qualification, achievement, salary level, house, and so on, invites failure. If you don't reach it then you feel bad and are likely to stop trying. A broad goal, on the other hand, can be reached by many means. When one route is closed to you, then you look for another.

Dreams, goals and visions can be very personal – to do with the kind of person you want yourself to be, and the meaning you want your life to have. Religion can be comforting and inspiring when it offers a model of excellence in human qualities, as well as answers to the more profound questions of life and death. Even without a specific religious faith, however, many people aspire to become the best person they can be, and to seek value in the difficulties as well as the joys of life. These goals are just as motivating, ultimately, as the more practical issues of family and work.

! ———————————— *Task* ————————————

### My dreams

Take time to think what would make you satisfied with your life. Daydream about how you would like life to be. Then write down your dreams – as many as you wish. You can be as specific as you like, and you don't have to think about how you can achieve them.

Then look at your dreams individually, and try to define the essence of what it is about them that is satisfying and will make you happy. If you dream of acting, for instance, is it because you think fame will bring you the respect of others? Is it that you think you will become very rich? Or is it that you enjoy the experience of acting?                                                                    !

Having a dream doesn't guarantee that you will attain it. What it does do, however, is give you a standard, something against which you can measure your life as it is now, and a direction – so that when presented with choices and opportunities you can take the path that leads where you want to be going.

This principle applies to all dreams. The desire can spur you to take action. The pleasures and rewards of doing so can make each day better, so that the quality of your life improves from now. When that happens, you can cope with the disappointment that comes when certain dreams can not be realised. Perhaps you discover you can't have children, when you have longed to be a parent, or you don't achieve the fame you have sought, or you don't find another partner. While you need to mourn the passing of a dream, when the quality of your life has improved, you do so from a position of strength.

Remember also that dreams can change. What seems attractive at one stage in your life can seem less so later. Thinking about the way you want your life to go is a continuing process. Sometimes you will reach a goal and want to expand your vision to encompass more, at other times you will change your focus totally, choosing a new goal.

Flexibility and adaptability are qualities that allow you to maintain your level of happiness, whatever the circumstances. If you are too concerned with keeping things as they are, or are too narrowly focused on a particular goal, then it can make you nervous and unhappy when things change. When you are prepared to adapt your ways of behaving, and your goals, according to circumstances, then you are able to 'roll with the punches', it also makes you alert to possibilities and opportunities that can improve your life.

## Making dreams reality

When you know broadly want you want to happen in your life, it gives you a clearer idea why you might not be happy with the way things are now. If the way you live your life bears very little relation to the way you want to live it, and doing what you do is never going to lead you closer towards your vision, then you will feel discontented and hopeless.

Once you have isolated what you do want, then you know what needs to change. For instance, if you want to be rich but have a dead-end or low-paid job, your goal remains forever out of reach. You will be frustrated and unhappy in work that occupies a large slice of your life. Training for a career that offers more money and the potential to go further is one solution. The very fact of taking action that makes your goal a possibility will make you feel happier and more positive, even when it is still a long way off. In the same way, if your dream is to be a writer, but you 'never have time' to do any writing, then your dream becomes a source of disappointment and frustration. Even finding three half-hours during the week to write uninterrupted will make the realisation of your dream a possibility.

Perhaps your dream is more down-to-earth: You know you would feel happier if you had more time to yourself. Acknowledging this to yourself forces you to look at the reasons for your life being so hectic. Do you feel obliged to do whatever is asked of you? Do you have difficulty saying no, or in making requests that would free you of certain responsibilities? Your dream will be within your reach when you tackle these issues. The way to do so is examined later in the chapter.

The secret of reaching your goal, or of drawing nearer to it, is to look at what *you* can do to make it happen. Dreams that remain dreams involve you saying, 'If only so-and-so would . . .' or 'If only such-and-such would happen . . .'.

For instance, if your dream is to find a new partner and settle down happily, or to find someone with whom you can start a family, half of the equation is the 'luck' of meeting the right person at the right time. But what else can you do? Going out and meeting people is part of it, but the rest involves work on yourself. This includes getting over the relationship that has finished – but it is still more than that. It is also finding motivation in your daily life, taking pleasure in what you do, so that you are not 'on hold' until the right person comes along. When your life is full and satisfying people enjoy your company, whether it be friends, family, or a potential new partner. When, on the other hand, all your energies are focused towards finding someone new, your very determination can be off-putting. And until you succeed you are likely to find life unrewarding and depressing.

The goal of making a good relationship, therefore, must include personal goals to become happier in yourself and a determination to make your life fulfilling meanwhile.

Working towards a dream involves a succession of much smaller steps. Some people draw up a 'plan' – a series of moves over one year, or five years, to bring them closer to their goal. While this can sometimes work, life is changeable. Outside forces can disrupt a plan, and if you depend on it you will feel defeated. Or when an opportunity comes along that is not part of the plan you ignore it. A rigid plan also allows no room for your dreams and focus to change. A better way is to think of changes you can make right now, and review your options when you have done so and seen how they are working.

A move in the right direction, however small, is a move towards happiness, and a move away from feeling that you are a victim of cir-

---

**!** ================= *Task* =================

**A step at a time**

Think of one small change you can make in your life now that
will put you on the road to realising your dream.

**!**

---

cumstances and fate. Whether you will take the first step, or continue
to take further steps – and whether you will continue to try when some
of them fail – depends, above all, on developing confidence.

When you have confidence your life opens up. The fact is that
even failure is experienced differently by people who feel good and
strong inside. When something they have worked towards doesn't
come off, confident people are able to say, 'That didn't work!' rather
than, 'I'm a failure!' A confident person who doesn't achieve an objec-
tive still feels unhappy and cast down. The death of the dream still has
to be mourned. But when your self-esteem remains intact you find the
energy to try again when the mourning period is over. Until you find
that confidence, it is all too easy to decide never to risk failure by never
trying again.

## DEVELOPING CONFIDENCE

When an important relationship ends, your self-esteem takes a bad
knock, however confident you were before. If you have never felt very
good about yourself or secure in your abilities it is even worse.

The death of love inevitably leads you to question your value,
your attractiveness and your loveableness. The longer you were
together, the more devastating this can be. As one counsellor says,
'When a relationship goes wrong people can have an overwhelming
feeling that they are not good enough for the outside world. They have
been rejected by the person to whom they were closest. I've seen a number of women, especially, for whom it was as if half of them disappeared and they thought that the half that was left wasn't good
enough.'

Sometimes it is lack of confidence that keeps you with a partner
even when you have been unhappy for a long time. It is often lack of
confidence that stops you from tackling the issue of your unhappiness
with your partner because you dare not rock the boat. Lack of
confidence in your own abilities can make you fear being on your own

because you can't believe you will be able to cope. If you looked on your partner as being stronger and more able than you, then the idea of taking charge of your life and happiness can seem terrifying or impossible.

This was the case with Fiona, who had been married to Martin for eighteen years. They had four children, and Fiona stayed at home to look after them. Martin was a doctor, a well-respected man, known for his devotion to duty and his compassion with patients and staff. At home, however, things were very different. Martin was irritable and contemptuous with his family. He wasn't interested in Fiona and spent little time with his children.

Fiona felt intensely lonely and inadequate. She also felt resentful, but never dared show it. Instead her feelings turned inward. She was depressed and hesitant. She feared Martin and she was also angry with him.

Gradually they grew further apart. Martin started an affair with a colleague and soon afterwards he told Fiona about it. She was distressed and frightened, and begged Martin to join her for counselling at RELATE.

At the first session, Martin was calm and reasonable when he talked to the counsellor about his affair. He said that Fiona had virtually forced him into it by her withdrawn behaviour, and that he had realised that she would never be able to be everything he needed in a partner. He could not envisage ending the affair. Fiona, looking at him with terror, said, 'If that's the case, then you must have the affair. I don't mind if she is giving you something I can't.'

Martin, in his turn, looked at Fiona with contempt. 'Look at yourself,' he said. 'You have no self-respect. How can you expect me to respect you?'

It became clear to the counsellor that their relationship had deteriorated so far that Martin's vision of himself as a caring, compassionate man did not extend to being concerned about hurting Fiona; however, he seemed to want to goad Fiona into taking action. It didn't suit him to be the one to initiate either a reconciliation or a parting.

The counsellor said to Fiona, 'You are prepared to accept that Martin's affair will continue?' 'Yes,' Fiona agreed. The counsellor went on, 'You mean you are prepared to have two out of ten, say, instead of eight out of ten?'. 'Yes,' Fiona agreed again, with increasing reluctance.

They came as a couple for two more sessions. At the second session, Fiona's anger suddenly flared up. 'You have no right to be in the postion of caring for people,' she raged. 'Underneath you are cold – cold even with your own children.'

It seemed to be what Martin was waiting for. Without a word, he got up and walked out of the counselling room. He went home, packed a bag and left Fiona for good.

Fiona continued to come for counselling and, although she was distressed, she did not fall apart. In the first session after Martin had left, the counsellor asked Fiona how she was feeling. Fiona said that she felt liberated, 'I should have stood up to Martin years ago, and I find it hard to remember why I didn't – how scared I was.'

Out of Martin's shadow, and forced to fend for herself, Fiona found that she was able to take charge of her life. She started caring for the way she looked and then found herself a job. A symbolic turning point was when Fiona moved out of the marital bedroom into another room, which she then decorated precisely the way she wanted it. The counsellor says, 'The change was extraordinary – she became a radiant person.'

Not everyone is able to find the resources to cope as quickly as Fiona, though counselling at this time can help. Understanding why your confidence is low, and discovering ways to bolster it, however, is also possible on your own.

## What's holding you back?

Low self-esteem often has its roots in childhood, as the chapter *What Went Wrong?* has shown. The end of a relationship is also often experienced as a failure. Something so central to your life, in which you invested your hopes and your commitment, has gone wrong. No wonder you doubt whether you have what it takes to determine the course of your life in the future, or to steer yourself towards happiness. You are left with the fear of failure, and it seems safest not to try.

Developing confidence is a complex process. It can be compared to learning to cook. You don't read an entire cookery book before you attempt a meal. You read one recipe, try it out, and the experience of trying it teaches you a little more and makes you slightly more competent. Over a period of time, by reading other recipes, and putting what you read into practice, you reach a stage where you are secure in your ability to turn out a meal. It is similar with building confidence. At one level it is something you can do theoretically, by reading this and other books – but it goes hand in hand with taking small steps, minor risks and experimenting with new ways of behaving. You don't develop your confidence and *then* take action. You build up a small inner reserve of confidence, use it to give you courage to take on something you feared doing, and then find that your confidence grows as you succeed.

Being on your own again forces you to do this – and if you have been involved with a partner who took charge, you can be thrown in at the deep end.

This was the case with Rory, whose wife, Sandra, walked out leaving him with their two children. Until that point, Sandra had been the ruling force in the house. She looked after Rory, the children, and Rory's invalid father. Rory had been a gentle, ineffectual man, who had never made a decision in his life. He had no job, and Sandra earned the money for all of them while also caring for the children and the home. First bossed by his mother, Rory was content to let Sandra take charge of everything. Finally, Sandra apparently grew tired of the responsibility. She disappeared one day, and Rory never heard from her again.

Rory arrived for counselling distraught. He was a thin, shy man who looked ill. He brought his two children with him, and he wept while his solemn six-year-old son patted his back. His little girl sat on the floor and played with some toys. 'I'm no good,' Rory told the counsellor. 'I've never been any good, and I don't know how I'll manage.'

Rory came for counselling for many months, drawing on it for support to keep going. In the beginning, simply looking after the children was too much for him. He had never been involved in their care before, and he was terrified they would be taken away from him. 'Women are incredible. I don't know how they cope,' he said to the counsellor ruefully. Gradually, however, he learned to be father and mother combined, and discovered he was a good parent.

Then the counsellor encouraged him to seek work. But he was unskilled, so he signed on for a course. The increased confidence that parenting his children well gave him spilled over into his studies. He did well, and got some qualifications that enabled him to find work that fitted in with the children's needs.

He left counselling after a year, with his life completely turned around. Six months later he popped in to see the counsellor, bringing his two children with him. They were all looking brown and healthy after a summer holiday in Spain. The counsellor said, 'Rory looked very different. He'd put on weight and was tougher and stronger altogether. He wanted to show the children off to me – he was enormously proud of them. He had been promoted, and had also found time to decorate his house. I felt proud of him, too.'

The point of this story is that Rory changed from a person who thought he was no good, into an exceptionally able and motivated human being. He had no idea of the potential that was inside him until the crisis in his marriage forced him to reassess. Before it happened he would have been the last person to believe that he had what it took to effect such a transformation in himself. His confidence grew as he revealed his abilities to himself.

When your confidence is low it is because your abilities are similarly hidden from your own view. You think you know who you are and what you can and can't achieve, but the likelihood is that you are under-estimating yourself. Building your confidence is often a matter of bringing your hidden potential into the light and giving yourself a chance.

The first thing to ask yourself is whether you truly know who you are.

## Who are you?

Knowing yourself is not a straightforward business, and you can never truly know yourself completely. Sometimes an ordeal can reveal strengths you didn't know you had (as in the previous examples) or can reveal fears and weaknesses that have been buried. In the same way, unknown aspects of yourself can also be revealed by exciting or joyful events.

There is the public aspect of yourself – what you know about yourself and choose to show to other people. There are also the things about yourself that you don't like, and seek to hide from others. Other people see you as the person you present yourself to be – but they also often see things in you that you don't see in yourself.

| | |
|---|---|
| This is what you show to the world – what you know about yourself, and what others see in you.<br><br>(A) | This is what you don't like about yourself and hide from everyone else.<br><br>(B) |
| This is what others see in you but you don't know about yourself.<br><br>(C) | This is the part of yourself that you don't know about – and neither does anyone else – hidden potentials and failings.<br><br>(D) |

For more of 'yourself' to emerge (A), a number of things need to happen. You can choose to show more of yourself to other people (B), and you can learn about other aspects of yourself (C) by listening to other people. Trying new ways of living and behaving will also cause some of the hidden aspects of yourself (D) to emerge, as will events and circumstances in your life, though some will always remain hidden.

The more confident you are, the more open you will feel able to be, and you will become more truly 'you'.

Meanwhile, how do you see yourself? If you are like most people, one of the ways you define yourself is through your relationships with other people. You are a child to your parents, a colleague at work, a friend socially, and so on. These relationships call up different aspects of yourself – you behave differently, or use different abilities according to the role you are playing. It can be useful to look at your different roles, by doing the following task.

! ———————————————— *Task* ————————————————

### Who am I?

Draw a small circle and put your name inside it. Draw lines radiating out from the circle, like the rays of the sun. Label each one with the title of the role you play in relation to the people in your life. For instance, a woman might have a range that includes 'daughter', 'mother', 'housekeeper', 'secretary', 'aunt', 'friend', 'committee-member' and so on.

Under each heading write sentences or adjectives to sum up what you bring to each role. Under 'friend', for instance, the woman might write, 'good listener, warm, someone to have a laugh with'. Under 'committee-member' she might write, 'conscientious, reliable, nervous about putting point of view', and so on.

When you have finished, consider which role is most 'you'. In which role would you like to change your behaviour? You can also add a line to represent a role you would like to play, and list underneath the qualities you would like to bring to it.                    !

These roles either call on your best qualities, or cause you to behave in ways that you cannot like, or reveal to you aspects of yourself that you would rather change. As you become more confident, you are likely to find that making changes becomes easier for you. Keep this diagram and look back on it from time to time. You can choose to redraw it substituting new descriptive words or sentences if you feel that your behaviour has changed in the context of any of these roles.

Looking closely at 'who you are' and how you behave might seem a pointless thing to do. But part of becoming more confident and developing self-esteem involves weighing up what there is to value in yourself. It also means coming to terms with the side of yourself with which you are least comfortable, or deciding how to strengthen and improve those areas.

● **My good points.** When your confidence is low, you are likely to gloss over the aspects of yourself that are admirable, and to consider ordinary the abilities that you have. Instead, you over-value the things that other people can do that you can't, or the qualities that others have that you don't.

If you have been brought up to believe that modesty is essential or you have been put down for a long time, then starting to think about what is good and admirable in you might seem wrong or impossible. But recognising what you have to offer is not 'immodest', it is simply realistic. Acknowledging to yourself that you have strengths does not mean that you shout it from the rooftops, or patronise other people because of them. What it does mean, however, is that you can use your inner certainty about your qualities to develop and use them. When you can draw confidence from your abilities, and the admirable aspects of your character, you start to behave differently. You are more assured, less likely to worry what other people think of you, and more able to withstand anybody who tries to put you down.

**!** ——————————— *Task* ———————————

## I am ...

Write ten sentences, each starting 'I am ...'. Finish the sentences to describe aspects of yourself that are positive. For instance, 'I am kind-hearted', 'I am efficient', 'I am creative', 'I am hard-working', 'I am a good friend' and so on.

**!**

The very act of writing this list opens up a new way of thinking. If you are in the habit of castigating yourself for your failings, you need to remember these other aspects of yourself. You should develop the habit of mentally adding a 'But ...' when you dwell on negative things about yourself, by reminding yourself of one or more of the good points in your character.

The same thing should be done with your skills. If you are low in confidence then you are likely to believe that a 'skill' is something that other people have, and what you can do is unimportant. You are a good driver? You probably find it easy to forget the work and practice that led to you becoming a good driver, and the continuing good judgement and co-ordination that keeps you good. You are a good cook? You are likely to think that 'anyone' could be so, forgetting the experience, creativity and flair that makes the difference between a good meal and an average one.

The same goes for 'human' skills. You are a good listener? If people feel drawn to tell you things, secure that they will get a sympathetic hearing from you, it is easy to under-estimate the compassion and forbearance in your own nature which makes this possible.

Once you recognise your skills for what they are, you can take quiet pride in yourself. By recognising that they *are* skills, particularly if they have been nurtured and hard-won, you are also forced to recognise that you have the ability to do something well. This inevitably means you have the ability to do other things well, too, when you let yourself try.

---

**!** ============================ *Task* ============================

## My skills

Look back at the diagram of roles you drew for the task 'WHO AM I?' On another piece of paper write the role headings again, leaving space underneath to write the skills you associate with each role. Divide the skills into two types, practical and human. For example:

### SECRETARY

| PRACTICAL | HUMAN |
|---|---|
| Good typing speeds | Helpful colleague |
| Good telephone manner | Good at carrying out instructions |
| Good at creating systems | Good at setting priorities |
| Good time-keeping | etc. |
| etc. | |

Include a heading JUST FOR ME, under which you list skills that don't fall into the categories of your roles. On the practical side, these might be hobbies or activities such as gardening or sewing, on the human side this can include coping skills, such as the ability to find humour in a difficult situation, and so on.

**!**

You will inevitably discover that, almost without realising it, you have developed skills in a number of areas of your life, which you overlook or discount. You need to start to value them – and also to realise that they can have wider applications. For instance, the practical and human skills that you develop as a mother and housewife are similar to those used by managers in business. If you have developed skills in one area of your life, you can develop them in others. This also means that you have the ability to reach your goal or 'dream'.

One further exercise can help you see this for yourself.

---

**!** ================= *Task* =================

### What is a skill?

Take four of your practical skills from anywhere in your lists, and analyse what are the elements that make them skilful. For instance,

● MAKING CLOTHES

precision

ability to understand technical information

good hand/eye co-ordination

patience

  etc.

● PLAYING FOOTBALL

physical co-ordination

strength

speed

ability to work in a team

  etc.

Now think of other activities or roles in which the skills you have developed could be put to practical use.

**!**

---

● **Learning to value yourself.** Lack of confidence is reinforced by the bad habit of putting yourself down. Developing confidence means reversing the habit, learning to value yourself. When you do, you feel better, and become more relaxed generally.

When Felicity came for counselling after the break-up of her marriage, no one would know to look at her that she lacked confidence. She was very smart and well-dressed, with her hair and make-up done as carefully as if she were going for an interview. But her self-esteem was very low. One of the first things she said to the counsellor was, 'I really am a pretty awful person, and you will think so, too.'

Over a period of time the counsellor helped Felicity work on her self-esteem. She started by making lists, like the ones in the tasks. At first Felicity found it very hard to make any positive statements about herself. The best she could do at the beginning was quote other people: 'My friends say I'm. . .', and 'My mother thinks I'm...'. Gradually, Felicity was able to allow herself to believe these statements, and genuinely to be able to recognise qualities for herself. She was helped by the counsellor's acceptance of her, and the way the counsellor was able to draw her attention to strengths and qualities that she was ignoring in herself. By the end of the counselling, Felicity was much more confident.

The counsellor says, 'An interesting consequence was that as Felicity felt good about herself, she felt less need to dress to impress. Towards the end she would come to see me in quite casual clothes. It was as if she were saying, "I can be myself, because that's a good thing to be."'

Good friends and close family members can sometimes help in the way a counsellor can – by showing that they accept you the way you are. Listen to them when they tell you what they admire or love in you. When your confidence is low, seek out people like this who can help you feel good about yourself.

The quiz on the facing page can be used as a framework to help you talk about these issues with a good friend, who you know likes and respects you.

You won't change your valuation of yourself overnight, but as you become used to thinking about yourself in more helpful ways, your confidence will increase. You are also likely to find that others respond to you more positively as this happens. People who don't know you well are likely to take you at your own valuation, and if that is low it can be hard for them to treat you with respect.

● **My 'weak' points.** No human being is perfect. We all have a side to ourselves that we would rather not acknowledge – bad habits, ugly moods, unkind thoughts or frailties that make us behave in ways of which we are ashamed in certain situations.

Becoming confident and developing your self-esteem does not mean ignoring this side of yourself. Indeed, the people who are best at hiding or denying their 'bad' side are often quite fearful. They suspect

**?** ——————————————— **Quiz** ———————————————

### You're my friend

Take it in turns with a good friend to fill in the quiz, according to the way you see each other.

3 = very, 2 = moderately, 1 = slightly, 0 = neither.

| Kind | 3 | 2 | 1 | 0 | 1 | 2 | 3 | Spiteful |
|------|---|---|---|---|---|---|---|----------|
| Helpful | 3 | 2 | 1 | 0 | 1 | 2 | 3 | Unhelpful |
| Easy-going | 3 | 2 | 1 | 0 | 1 | 2 | 3 | Critical |
| Contented | 3 | 2 | 1 | 0 | 1 | 2 | 3 | Discontented |
| Pleasant | 3 | 2 | 1 | 0 | 1 | 2 | 3 | Unpleasant |
| Interesting | 3 | 2 | 1 | 0 | 1 | 2 | 3 | Dull |
| Friendly | 3 | 2 | 1 | 0 | 1 | 2 | 3 | Unfriendly |
| Shy | 3 | 2 | 1 | 0 | 1 | 2 | 3 | Outgoing |
| Trustworthy | 3 | 2 | 1 | 0 | 1 | 2 | 3 | Irresponsible |
| Loyal | 3 | 2 | 1 | 0 | 1 | 2 | 3 | Disloyal |
| Conscientious | 3 | 2 | 1 | 0 | 1 | 2 | 3 | Lazy |
| Honest | 3 | 2 | 1 | 0 | 1 | 2 | 3 | Dishonest |
| Fun | 3 | 2 | 1 | 0 | 1 | 2 | 3 | Serious |
| Gentle | 3 | 2 | 1 | 0 | 1 | 2 | 3 | Dominant |
| Easy to talk to | 3 | 2 | 1 | 0 | 1 | 2 | 3 | Hard to talk to |

Afterwards, talk about your perceptions of each other, and anything the quiz has left out. What do you like most in each other, and why?

——————————————————————————————— **?**

that if they didn't work hard at suppressing these characteristics they would take over, and everyone would know the 'truth' about them. Some people who think like this become excessively withdrawn and timid, frightened of anyone knowing what they are really like. Other people hide their fears behind an arrogant attitude (which can be mistaken for confidence) and are likely to be intolerant of others, particularly those who have the very characteristics they hate in themselves.

Truly confident people recognise their own imperfections. They are not proud of them, but they manage them in a number of ways. Some they try to transform, others they work around, and the rest they tolerate – as they forgive and tolerate the imperfections in those they love.

For instance, Marion was ashamed of the envy she felt towards friends who achieved something that she hadn't. She felt that it showed she had a mean spirit, and she was usually such a loving and kind person. She discovered that she could transform her feeling in two ways. One was to become involved in her friend's achievements by offering a helping hand when she could, which gave her a warm glow that took the edge off the envy. When this was not possible, she found it helped to acknowledge the emotion to her friends – to say, 'I'm so envious! I wish I could have done that!' Openly admitting the feeling meant that it didn't fester, and also made her feel less mean-spirited.

Another example is Gerry, who despised himself for being lazy. When he had something he ought to be getting on with, he would often slump in front of the television. He eventually worked around this by 'awarding' himself rest periods, when he would tell himself that he must not do anything but lie down, so that he could enjoy those moments rather than feel guilty about them. He also discovered that he worked best in the morning, so he arranged matters so that important or difficult activities were scheduled for early in the day.

Joy was someone who learned to accept what she saw as her major failing: her difficulty being at ease with people socially. In a gathering she would be tongue-tied while people around her seemed to find it easy to make small-talk. She learned to 'forgive' herself this difficulty, acknowledging to herself that for her to feel at ease in company the gathering needed to be small, and she needed to know the others well. She accepted that socialising was likely to continue to be difficult for her, but she stopped giving herself a hard time because of it.

Duncan found that things changed for him when he recognised that he was extremely jealous about his girlfriends. Before he realised that the jealous feelings were in himself, he used to blame the women for *making* him feel bad. His partners only had to look at other men, or appear to enjoy talking to them, or to be friendly with male colleagues, for Duncan to throw a jealous rage at their flirtatiousness, accuse them of infidelity or, indeed, break up with them. When Duncan could see that *he* was jealous, not that his partners' behaviour was at fault, he could look at ways of managing his feelings, and was able to be more realistic about his relationships.

All these examples show that facing up to your 'weak' or 'bad' points has a positive side. Coming to terms with all aspects of yourself frees you to behave more openly and honestly, and adds to your confidence, rather than sapping it.

● **Re-assessing weaknesses.** When you can learn to accept and tolerate the aspects of yourself you regard as failings, there is often a surprising result. You can begin to realise that certain of your 'failings' are no such thing – sometimes they can even be strengths in disguise.

! ───────────────── *Task* ═════════════════

**I am ...**

Write five sentences, each starting 'I am ...'. Finish the sentences to describe aspects of yourself that you do not like. For instance, 'I am selfish', 'I am fearful', 'I am bad-tempered', and so on.

Decide which you would like to transform, which you can work around, and which you will learn to accept in yourself.

!

For instance, some people struggle to contain or deny certain emotions because they think they are bad, destructive or inappropriate.

Hannah was brought up to believe that women should be gentle, kind and well-behaved. As a child she was punished for temper tantrums, and grew up in fear of her own angry feelings. Most of the time she had them under control, but every so often they would burst out. When she felt angry, she also felt nasty, frightening and unloveable. When she was being counselled through a separation from the man she had lived with for eight years, Hannah was often brought face-to-face with her unbridled rage.

With the counsellor's steadfast support Hannah began to see that there was nothing wrong with feeling angry – it was natural and human. What mattered was how she handled her anger and expressed it. In the past, because she had bottled it up for so long, when it burst out she would become violently abusive, sometimes throw things or hit people. When she contained the anger she sometimes had panic attacks, stomach pains, or felt depressed. What she learned through counselling was that anger acknowledged and 'cleanly' expressed when it was felt had a positive side. It didn't fester, it could be handled, and sometimes a solution could be found to reduce the anger by tackling the causes. Hannah eventually learned to 'respect' her anger and appreciate it as she did the rest of her range of emotions.

Another example is Owen, who had the opposite problem. He had been a quiet, sensitive boy who was mocked and bullied at school and subject to a tussle between his over-protective mother and scornful father. All the contempt he had received from other boys and his father lodged inside him. He grew up describing himself as 'lily-livered', 'babyish' and 'weedy'. He was so suspicious of his own sensitive nature that he worked to make himself uncaring. By the time his second marriage ended he was out of touch with almost all his feelings. What had emerged, instead, was an unpleasant bullying side to his nature. Owen seemed drawn to people who were weak and unsure, and he would lose no opportunity to put them down, seeming to have a knack for finding their most vulnerable points. This was one of the main reasons his marriages had broken down.

For Owen, counselling was a revelation. One day he broke down and wept during a session – a painful and frightening experience for him, because he said, 'It makes me feel as if I have a river of tears inside that will never stop – all the tears I haven't shed since I was a boy.'

Of course, Owen's tears did eventually end, and he began to glimpse value in the sensitivity he scorned. He could see that his sensitivity made him alert to other people's feelings. When he was suppressing his gentler feelings, he used his ability to pick up on other people's frailties as a weapon. But, he realised, when he allowed himself to feel deeply, and respect his capacity to do so, he was able to turn this talent outwards into a compassion and empathy for others. Getting in touch with his sensitivity eventually released him to make more rewarding relationships.

A final example is Tony, who was shocked and disgusted by his powerful sexual feelings. His upbringing had caused him to believe that sex was a dirty and necessary evil for producing children and little else. When he became unable to make love to his wife after their family was complete they sought help from a sex therapist. Through the therapy Tony learned that there was nothing wrong with his high sex drive. He became able to release the sexual energy he had been suppressing in himself – and discovered that using his sexuality in a loving relationship with his wife was positive and life-enhancing.

These examples show that it is quite possible that what you have considered to be a 'failing' can be looked at in another way. Coming to terms with aspects of yourself, even those with which you are uncomfortable, allows you to find value in your true self.

Nevertheless, certain failings *are* failings. These are usually misplaced fears that halt your development. Through lack of confidence you shrink away from certain things – taking responsibility, developing your potentials, standing up for yourself, allowing yourself to love, and so on. However, when you compare your own shortcomings to the strengths of people you love or admire – and it makes you feel bad – you have already started the process of change.

The desire to 'own' a quality that someone else possesses has an energy that you can use to find that quality in yourself. For the truth is that the yearning to possess a quality is usually a sign that it is there within you, buried. All you need to do is find the way to develop it and bring it out into the open.

● **Developing your hidden qualities.** What happens when some of your qualities lie hidden and undeveloped? The most usual response is an unconscious desire to 'get' the qualities by matching up with someone else who appears to have them. If you find it difficult making up your mind, for instance, you are drawn to someone who is decisive. Or if you find it difficult to show your feelings you might be attracted to someone who is more emotionally open, and so on. This can be true in friendships and, particularly, in loving relationships.

What this unconscious matching up can do, however, is stop both partners feeling the need to develop the qualities the other partner has. The indecisive partner, therefore, never develops the capacity to make a decision, while the decision-maker feels obliged to be decisive at all times, and never learns to tolerate or explore uncertainty or ambivalent feelings. The emotionally contained person continues to hold on to feelings, and the emotionally open partner does not develop the ability to know when it is appropriate to control emotional excess. Dividing up qualities like this is the main cause of the unbalanced relationship patterns explored in *What Went Wrong?*.

When you are on your own again, you can often feel most painfully inadequate in the areas that your partner 'controlled'. To feel better and whole you often need to develop in yourself the qualities that your partner used to bring to the relationship.

This was the case with Alison, who asked her husband, Jeremy, to leave after twelve years of marriage. She had been unhappy for many years, and when she discovered that he was having an affair she decided that the marriage was at an end. She was thirty-three, and faced with bringing up their two children on her own.

Asking Jeremy to leave had been an act of courage that left Alison drained and frightened. Her main problem was doubting whether she would be able to cope. She had never taken responsibility for anything in her life. Her parents had brought her up to believe that she wasn't good for much, and she had never believed she would be able to run her own life. When she married Jeremy, part of the attraction was that he took control of everything for her. Although this was a comfort, Jeremy treated her as an idiot and she accepted this as her due.

When Jeremy first left, Alison panicked. She didn't want him back, but how was she going to manage? In the beginning she kept ringing him up – to ask what to do about minor matters, or to beg him to come over and fix something or to control the children. During counselling Alison came to realise that at some point she had to start doing things her way and managing alone.

The first major test came with the mortgage. Alison could not manage the repayments on the money Jeremy was giving her. She did not have a job herself and feared that the house would be repossessed. The counsellor suggested that Alison contact the building society and explain the position to the manager.

It had never occurred to Alison that she could do anything about the situation except wait for the axe to fall. She was terrified at the thought of talking to the manager at the building society, and of what he would do. At the next session, Alison told the counsellor with great excitement that she had explained matters to the manager, who was very understanding and had arranged a new payment plan for her. Alison was thrilled – not just that the worry was taken from her, but because she had organised it for herself. This was just the first boost to her confidence.

Soon after this Alison found herself a job. This increased her confidence further. She discovered that she was good at the job. She was expected to cope, and she did. She said that for the first time in years she felt that she could be herself – by which she meant a person who could stand on her own two feet.

From that point on Alison found that she could manage all the elements of her life – home, children and work, and that she could cope quite easily with most of it.

The counsellor says, 'Her confidence had been brewing underneath without her knowing it. She was ready to take responsibility – that was probably why she was able to initiate the separation.'

Alison's major achievement was to discover that the qualities she envied and admired in Jeremy and others also existed inside herself – and she had simply brought them to the surface.

Developing your own hidden qualities has two main effects. One is to make you more confident and independent. The other is to break the pattern of past relationships. When you are able to find in yourself qualities that you used to try to bring in from the outside by finding a partner who had them, relationships you make in the future will be different. The more 'whole' you are, and the more confident you become, the more likely you are to choose a partner with whom you can develop a more healthy, flexible relationship.

When you do the task on the facing page you sometimes find that your list includes characteristics that seem to belong to the other sex. A man might have identified that he was attracted to women who were 'soft and gentle', for instance. Surprising though this may seem, it usually means he would feel better if he allowed himself to become more comfortable with the gentler side of himself. Doing this won't make him 'effeminate' or 'homosexual' – you don't become less strong just because you also allow yourself to be tender and kind. It is quite the reverse, the *fear* of showing gentleness makes you less strong

! ============= *Task* =============

## It attracted me!

Make a list of the qualities and personality traits that attracted you to ex-partners. Don't worry if these were the things that you eventually grew to dislike, or which created difficulties. Just concentrate on the beginning of the relationship, and what you thought then. Anything goes: it could be your partners' 'strength', 'creativity', 'devil-may-care manner', 'emotional toughness', 'emotional sensitivity' and so on.

You are likely to find that some of these are qualities you think you lack, or daren't reveal. These are the ones you should seek to develop in yourself, to feel more positive, 'whole' and confident.

!

because you believe it will. It is only by experiencing the softer feelings and displaying them that you become secure in the certainty that your strong side is unimpaired.

In a similar way, a woman might identify to her dismay that she was attracted to her partner because of 'horrible' sides to his character – that he was brutal or cold or unreliable, for instance. Does this mean that she has to start behaving violently, or stop behaving lovingly, or start letting people down? Luckily, it does not. What it does show, however, are impulses or resentments she is repressing. It shows that she fears discovering a darker side to herself and is therefore drawn to be near someone who openly displays these unwanted characteristics.

If this is so in your case, therefore, what you should do is see what you can learn about yourself by examining the implications behind your attraction to these qualities.

Suppose your partners have been brutal. You should explore the way you handle your anger. For instance, have you let people put you down and avoided confrontations, feeling resentful and unhappy meanwhile? The attraction to someone brutal can show you that you need to develop the ability to stand up for yourself. It is not necessary to be violent to do so. When you are able to express your feelings and stop allowing yourself to be victimised, you are likely to find that you are no longer attracted to brutal people, because you have discovered a better way of handling the issue than by violent means.

Similarly, if you have always been attracted to people who are cold and distant, you should examine whether you have felt compelled always to be kind, loving and accommodating, even when you don't feel like it. This could show, for instance, that you need to be more honest about your feelings – not freezing other people out, but letting them know when you are tired, irritable, or in need of attention yourself.

If you have been attracted to unreliable characters, it is worth examining whether you have taken your responsibilities so seriously that you never give yourself a break to do things that are frivolous, self-centred or impulsive.

In this way, you can look at all the qualities – good and bad – that have attracted you in other people and see what you can learn from them, or how you can adapt them in the most positive way for yourself.

**!** ——————————— *Task* ———————————

### I'll do It myself!

Look at the list of qualities that attracted you to your partner. Turn them into a new list of qualities that you would like to develop in yourself. If one of the qualities is a 'negative' one, see if you can express it as a more desirable quality in yourself. Add anything else that you would like to develop in yourself – such as qualities that belong to people you admire.

**!**

Sometimes while making your list you might realise that your 'hidden' qualities are not completely hidden. You are able to use them in one area of your life, but not in another. This was the case with Maureen, who came for counselling with her husband, Gordon, after they had been married for thirty years. They had two children and a number of grandchildren. Maureen had been wanting to divorce Gordon for many years. She often threatened to do so, but backed down at the last moment. Gordon had been violent towards her, and was an unstable and unreliable man. He didn't get on with their children, and didn't like having the grandchildren around, which was intensely upsetting for Maureen. For the last five years he had been ill, which made it even harder for Maureen to end the marriage. Gordon wanted to remain married, but he saw no reason to change, or to treat Maureen any better. He was convinced that she would never leave him.

Gordon saw no sense in the counselling and soon dropped out. Maureen continued, trying to discover the strength to leave the relationship, and the source of her inability to assert herself within it.

The counsellor learned that there were two sides to Maureen. There was the mouse at home – the woman who had been used to being controlled all her life, first by her parents, and then by Gordon.

She had grown up believing that she had to be good – to do whatever she was told. This she continued to do in her personal life, even when it made her unhappy and even when she felt it to be wrong.

The other side of Maureen was the professional woman. She was branch manager in a bank, and was excellent at her job. She had no trouble delegating, giving orders, sorting out right from wrong, and asserting herself whenever necessary.

The counsellor helped Maureen looks at ways she could borrow the skills from her job to help in her marriage and her personal life. The counsellor asked Maureen to talk her through how she managed personnel problems at the bank: how did she work out priorities? What approach did she use when people were difficult? How did she assert herself when making unpopular decisions, and how did she implement them? They then looked at ways Maureen could use the same approach at home with Gordon.

She knew that she had to look at her options within her marriage as clearly as she did at work. What would happen if she left? How should she behave if she stayed? How was she going to manage to stand up for herself if she chose to remain in the marriage?

Maureen left counselling with a clear plan. She was going to give the marriage another try, holding more firmly to her views about what needed to change for her to remain with Gordon. She would behave more as she did at work – making clear her boundaries, and not letting herself be pushed around. If the changes in her did not effect corresponding changes in Gordon, then she would make a final decision to divorce him.

Identifying which qualities you want to develop is the first step. The next is to try them out for yourself – to act 'as if' they were natural to you. Developing these qualities involves behaving in new ways. As you do so, eventually they do become 'you', as many of the examples so far have shown. Just as Alison, on meeting the manager of the building society to discuss her mortgage, acted as if she were a responsible and decisive person, although inside she was frightened and unsure. Her success in this situation meant she was prepared to try this behaviour in other situations, rather than reverting to her old habit of looking for someone else to take charge for her. Eventually she *became* responsible and decisive: she was no longer pretending.

It was similar with Simon, whose wife had made all the practical decisions in the home. When he had to set up on his own, he found it impossible to make decisions about what to buy. On one occasion, he had to buy a new cooker. When he arrived for his counselling session he was in a terrible state, because he had been to every shop in town, and still didn't know which one to buy. The counsellor helped him to see what a decisive person would do in those circumstances. He or she would select a maximum of two or three shops, look at prices and performance of the various cookers, evaluate those and then make a choice. Simon acted on this. He set himself limits before making decisions of this kind, until it became natural to him.

Acting 'as if' you felt a certain way has another effect. When you behave differently, other people act towards you in a different way – which, in turn, builds your confidence. For instance, you might have had difficulty showing affection for fear you might be rejected. By consciously making the effort to find warm words or make a friendly gesture you will discover that people are warmer to you in return. It then becomes easier to show warm feelings. If you have feared showing vulnerability, then making an effort to explain that your feelings can be hurt will often result in people being more considerate, and so on.

**!** ═══════════════ *Task* ═══════════════

### Acting 'as if'

Pick one of the qualities you have identified as being one you wish to develop. Imagine yourself in a situation that would cause you to need this quality, or remember a situation in the past where you acted in a way that you wish to change.

Decide how you can act 'as if' you have the quality in this imagined situation, and determine to try out this behaviour in the future.

**!**

It takes time to bring out your hidden qualities. It can be compared to building up muscle. The repeated actions of lifting weights gradually develops the muscle until it is strong and you can lift heavier weights. In time, the repeated actions you take to develop a hidden quality results in an inner strength.

Other ways of dealing with some of these issues are looked at in Chapter Six, *Challenging Patterns*.

## USING YOUR CONFIDENCE

The most obvious result of confidence is a change in the way you relate to other people. Lack of confidence manifests in two main ways in your interaction with others: either it makes you anxious or diffident about standing up for yourself so that you are easily pushed around, or it makes you arrogant and bullying, getting your way at the expense of others.

Confident people, on the other hand, are able to steer a middle course quite pleasantly and reasonably. They are able to stand up for themselves when they need to, and see that they are not taken advantage of – but they are also able to accommodate the needs and desires of other people, because they know they are doing so freely and generously. The respect confident people feel for themselves is matched by the respect they feel for others.

Confidence in action can also be described as assertiveness, but this term is sometimes misunderstood. People equate it with aggressiveness – getting your own way at any cost, and without taking other people's needs and feelings into account. So by calling it 'confidence in action' confusion can be avoided.

When you have confidence you find it easy to tap into what you are feeling. Therefore you can be quite clear when too much is being asked of you and you need to say no. Similarly you recognise when you need to ask something of other people, and you are able to do so without awkwardness. Because you feel free to make your own needs and desires felt, you also find it easier to think of other people, and put their needs first when the occasion arises. These aspects of confidence in action are now looked at more closely.

## *The power to say 'no'*

Babies are born with an instinctive sense of their own needs: turning away from the breast when they have had enough milk, or registering their disapproval of rough handling with loud cries. Saying no is one of the first things children learn – before being able to ask for something or say 'please'. It is a sign that children have discovered their separate identity and with it their power to stand up for themselves.

But, as children, we also learn that we can't always say no: we must eat our greens, or go to bed when we want to stay up. We gradually learn about politeness, consideration, and being 'good'. What can happen along the way is that some people gain the idea that there is something wrong with saying no altogether: that they should always go along with what other people want, and stifle their own feelings.

But this is neither right, nor healthy. When you can't say no to other people you lose the ability to live your life the correct way for you. On a practical level you become over-burdened with things to do, so that your own priorities get lost amongst other people's demands. On an emotional level you feel resentful, stressed and unhappy. Within relationships, always giving in to other people backfires – hostility and misery build up inside you, which sours the good feelings.

A common pattern is to give in to other people until you are so harrassed and miserable that you finally put your foot down – usually accompanied by an outburst of angry justifications. It is often only when you have finally had enough that you realise that resentment has been building up inside you for a very long time.

When you are confident, however, you don't let things get this far. You are able to say no pleasantly and firmly at an earlier stage to any requests that are unreasonable or disturbing, or which would create difficulties for you.

Before you are confident, you can believe that saying no is selfish. You think that people will dislike you or become cross with you or that a nasty situation will develop. The reverse is usually true, however. In most cases, your refusal will be accepted in a matter-of-fact way. Sometimes people will feel an increased respect for you, because you know your mind and value your time.

It can, at times, be harder than this, however. Sometimes people will be annoyed, but you have to recognise that their annoyance carries no more weight than your own. Why should you always be the one to be over-burdened? Why is their distress more important than your own? Occasionally a person can give you a hard time – if it is not someone you know well then you can walk away from the situation. Handling their feelings is not your problem, but theirs. It could, however, be someone closer to you, who has been used to you always giving in, and who becomes angry when you no longer do so. It can be difficult for people to accept changes in you. But they will be able to do so if you continue to act with consistent, pleasant firmness. On the whole, people will tend to press, nag and try to coerce with anger or manipulation only when they sense that you are *not* firm, and that your no could be changed to yes.

If pleasant firmness does not work over a period of time, however, you need to think about your value to this person, and the value of the relationship to you. If it depends entirely on you giving in to the other person's demands, then as you grow more confident it might not suit you any longer.

Learning to say no is a three-stage process.

● **Identify what you are feeling.** When someone asks something of you, deciding how you feel about it is the first step. If you are used to saying yes to everything, it can also be quite difficult to know there and then what you feel. It is often only later, when you have committed yourself, and when the warm glow of the 'thank you' has worn off, that you realise that you feel resentful and that you have been taken advantage of.

If this is so for you, don't jump in with an answer immediately. To break the pattern, take time to consult your feelings. If necessary, delay before you give an answer, so that you have time to decide how you feel about it. Where necessary ask for clarification about what it involves. If you are still not sure, ask for time: 'Give me half an hour to think about it' or 'I'll tell you in the morning'. If you are told that there isn't any time to consider, you can say regretfully, 'Then I'll have to say no'.

Remember, when someone says, 'May I ask you to do a favour for me?' don't respond, 'Yes, of course!'. Instead, say, 'It depends what it is', or 'I will if I can'.

● **Saying no.** Say no pleasantly, but firmly and briefly. 'No, I'm afraid I can't look after your children on Wednesday.' Don't offer lots of explanations or false apologies, or you open the way for the other person to come up with 'solutions' that back you into a corner and make you reverse your answer. For instance, it's fair enough to say, 'I'm sorry you have a problem about Wednesday, but I'm afraid it is inconvenient for me to have the children'. But if you say, 'I'd really *love* to have your children, but my mother is coming over', you invite a comeback such as, 'They will really be no trouble. I'm sure your mother won't mind – and they do adore you!'

Similarly, if you refuse an invitation because you don't want to go somewhere, it is best just to say 'No, I'm sorry, I'm not free'. If you embroider this by saying, 'There's a programme I must watch on television', or 'I have to catch up with ironing', you might get responses such as 'You can video the programme, or watch it with us', and 'Leave the ironing till another night!'

In all cases, the truth is best. Softening your no with excuses makes you sound less sure. If the truth is unpalatable – you don't like the person or you don't want to help – then keep your no very brief without explanations.

● **Standing firm.** If someone tries to cajole or force you into changing your mind, repeat your no calmly and firmly again. Don't be drawn into giving unnecessary explanations. Just repeat, 'I'm afraid it's inconvenient', or 'It's not possible right now' or 'I really don't want to' or 'I'm sorry, but that's how it is'.

You can offer alternatives where appropriate, and when you genuinely want to: 'Wednesday is impossible, but perhaps one day next week', or 'I'm too busy right now, but I'll give you a call when things are easier', or 'I'm sorry I haven't been able to help this time, but please ask me again'.

It takes time and practice to get to the point where you feel natural saying no when you need to. Sometimes it is easiest at the beginning with people you don't know well or care deeply for. Gradually it becomes easier with friends, family and your own children.

Even though it can occasionally be hard to say no, over time the benefits far outweigh the drawbacks. The main benefit is that you feel so much better in yourself that you become a pleasanter person to be around. It also means that when you say yes, you do so wholeheartedly because you have exercised freedom of choice. Others will value the yes more when they know that you also say no. When they know they are taking advantage of you or that you are unwilling, they are likely to feel guilty, and that causes them to feel almost as resentful towards you as you feel towards them.

Ultimately, when you can use what you have learned in an intimate relationship with a future partner, you will find it enhances the interaction between you. Much imbalance in relationships comes from the partners' inability to make their needs clearly known – and not saying no is one symptom of this.

**!** ══════════════ *Task* ══════════════

### Trouble saying no?

If you are not sure whether you have trouble saying no, ask yourself one question, 'Do I often feel I have too much to do?'

If the answer is yes, then you do have trouble saying no. It usually means you also have trouble saying no to yourself. You probably drive yourself hard, and feel guilty when you are not busy.

In this case you have to learn to look at priorities. List the things you have to do in order of importance. If you find this hard, ask yourself two questions: 'How important is this to *me* (not anyone else)?' Those items go to the top of the list. The second question is, 'What is the worst thing that would happen if this didn't get done today/next week/at all?' Anything that has unimportant consequences should go to the bottom of your list – and those are the items you should say no to.

**!**

### The right to ask

Before you are confident, it can be even harder to ask for things than to say no. You are reluctant to ask people to help you, or to do something for you, or to show you consideration. There are a number of reasons for this. One is that you don't feel that you are as important as other people – that what you need doesn't count for much. Another reason is that you believe people should be able to know what you need without you asking them directly. If they don't, you think that it is a failure on their part, or that they are purposely upsetting you by ignoring your needs. You might also feel that asking for something is pushy, and people will like you less because of it, or, conversely, that asking betrays weakness – that people will know you are not self-sufficient and will take advantage of you. Finally, you might avoid asking for anything because you fear rejection – you don't want to handle them saying no to *you*.

As your confidence develops, however, it becomes easier to ask. You recognise that your needs are as important as other people's, and that it is reasonable, not pushy to make them known. You know that no one is self-sufficient, and just as you are prepared to give someone else a helping hand, so you know that others will be pleased to help you. Because you feel good in yourself, you recognise that if someone is ignoring your needs it is not out of spite, but because you have not explained them clearly enough. You become able to cope with a no because you can see that it is as reasonable to refuse as it is to ask, and you don't take it personally.

● **When to ask.** You should feel free to ask for something whenever you have identified what you feel and what you need. You will learn that reasonable requests, made simply, will often be granted.

Asking other people for help, for instance, can be hard before you are confident. Confidence means that you feel able to ask for help at an early stage, rather than wait till you are engulfed by problems. You know it is a sign of common sense rather than weakness. Fear of being thought weak can make people grab at straws rather than admit anything is wrong.

One counsellor talks of Sadie, who was very distressed after the break-up of her marriage, and desperately needed to talk about what she was going through. Sadie was able to talk to the counsellor because she was a 'professional' and because Sadie paid for the counselling sessions, but she was unable to unburden herself to friends. Sadie's confidence was starting to be rebuilt during the counselling but, the counsellor says, 'the turning point came when she turned up for a session with me on the wrong day by mistake. She had been saving all these things to say to me, and was so upset that I couldn't see her, that she did something she had never done before – she went straight to a friend's house and shared her feelings with her. To be able to show that she needed comfort – and receive it – helped her more than anything.'

● **The difference between asking and demanding.** Asking for something is a question, and like any question you cannot be sure of the answer. It could be yes, no or maybe. When you demand there is no question: you are asserting your right to something and your right to control another person. The difference is important because you have no right to control someone else, just as they have no right to control you. Getting your way by demanding takes away the other person's dignity and creates resentment.

Sometimes it is easier to see the difference when the issue is a favour. You want someone to do something for you, or lend you money, or let you leave work early. In these cases, you are likely to ask, rather than demand.

Where you might be demanding, however, is over issues to do with relating to other people, and how they treat you. You might demand someone talks to you, sees you when you want, telephones you when you want, agrees with you – or even loves you. Issues like these, which involve emotions and personal inclinations, as well as practical actions, can only be made as requests. You have the right to let the other person know that you need to talk, for instance, or that it would make you happy to see him or her. But the other person has needs and feelings, too, which might conflict with yours. That person has an equal right to express a need for quiet and silence, or time alone. When both of you are able to make clear what your individual needs and feelings are, you have a basis for negotiation – to adapt, compromise, or even for one of you to put your own needs on hold for a time.

Exercising power and control in your relationships – be it with friends, partner, or children – means that you make demands without considering the feelings and needs of the others. It is important to recognise when you are doing this, and not to confuse it with asking.

● **The difference between asking and nagging.** Asking is a request clearly put, so that the other person understands why it is important to you and what the consequences are if the request is refused. Nagging – repeating a request over and over again – is a sign that your message is not clear and, indeed, that the other person has stopped wanting to hear it. Both men and women nag, although men usually find another word to define what they are doing.

It is helpful to be clear about what is behind the nagging. It is usually a disguised demand: in other words, you make it over and over again until the other person is worn down and eventually does what you want (or continues to resist). For instance, you nag your children to tidy their rooms. The issue here is that their untidy rooms make you feel uncomfortable and irritable, and this conflicts with their own more tolerant attitude to the mess, or their desire to be doing something different.

Nagging can also be a disguised emotional demand. You nag about the fact that someone is reading the paper, for instance, when the real issue is that you are feeling unloved and ignored. A disguised emotional demand is a common reason for nagging. Asking outright for what you want, and explaining the emotional need behind it, makes you feel vulnerable. If the person were to say no to your emotional demand you would feel hurt and rejected. Instead, you concentrate on their behaviour, rather than your own feelings – showing your resentment and irritation but disguising the vulnerability.

By its very nature, therefore, it is clear that nagging is a form of asking that does not work and that is unfair. This is usually because you focus on what you want the other person to do, rather than explaining your own feelings and exploring theirs.

When you identify your feelings and explain them, and listen to the other person's, you are more likely to resolve matters than when you nag. For instance, if you say to your children, 'When your rooms are untidy I feel on edge and irritable – which puts me in a bad mood for the rest of the day', they know that the consequence of not tidying their rooms is your continued bad mood, which they will have to endure. If you listen to them, you might hear, 'I'm too tired this evening', or 'I really want to watch this programme', which gives you a basis for consideration and negotiation. Is your irritation more important than than their tiredness? Could you offer to help them tidy up? Could you suggest that they do so after the programme is over? You are now dealing with resolving a conflict of interest, rather than a battle of wills.

Similarly, it helps to identify when the issue you are nagging about conceals an emotional need of yours. For instance, if you say to the person reading the paper, 'When you read the paper, I feel that you are not interested in what I have to say. So I get upset and need reassurance', then the other person recognises that you are not making an attack but expressing a need. If that person then tells you, 'When I haven't read the paper properly I can't concentrate', or 'I need some quiet time reading the paper otherwise I feel harrassed and not in the mood for talking', then you can understand that the action of reading the paper is not intended as a slight on you. You are now able to weigh up your conflicting needs, and come to some arrangement without fighting.

When the other person is not prepared to do as you ask, even after you have clarified your feelings and the consequences that will follow, yet you keep on asking, then you must recognise that what you are now doing is demanding.

● **When not to ask.** There are certain situations in which you are obliged to tell someone to do something, whether they want to or not. If you find this difficult, you might frame it as a request, 'Would you mind . . . ?' or 'Could you manage to . . . ?' or even 'Would you like to . . . ?'

This is often a disguised order. You are the boss, for instance, and something needs to be done now. Or you are dealing with young children who need to be told firmly to do something against their wishes. Turning an order into a question, which apparently leaves the other person a choice can create misunderstanding and bad feeling. If they say no, you are in the difficult position of having to insist and reveal that it was an order. If they recognise they have no option and say yes, they can do so with bad grace, feeling they have been manouevred into pretending they want to do something when they would rather not.

In these cases it is better to be direct. To a colleague you might say, 'I know you are busy, but I'm afraid this takes priority', to a child you might say, 'I know you want to stay up, but it is bedtime now'.

Similarly, when you have identified that it is important to you that something should be done, you need to state this clearly and make your request in a way that does not suggest that it is a matter of choice for the other person. For instance, your neighbour is playing music too loud when you are trying to sleep, or you want your money back on a faulty purchase, or someone is treating you in an unacceptable way. In cases like these you need to express your request firmly but calmly: 'Please turn your music down, it is stopping me sleeping', 'The heel has come off this shoe, and I want my money back', 'I haven't finished what I am saying, would you please wait a minute', and so on.

In these cases, it is best not to be drawn into an argument, or be deflected from what you want by irrelevancies ('That's a fashion shoe, you can't expect it to stand up to ordinary wear') or by manipulation that makes you feel bad ('You're very pushy and sure of yourself, aren't you?'). Instead, repeat your request calmly and firmly again, perhaps choosing slightly different words or by adding, 'I don't think you heard me . . .', 'I haven't made myself clear . . .', 'But the point is . . .', 'That's not relevant to what I'm saying, which is . . .'. If the other person seems not to hear or understand, you can ask him or her, 'What do you think I'm saying?' or 'What do you understand my position to be?' If there is misunderstanding, you can clear it up and repeat your request again.

Sometimes requests are a disguised message about what you are feeling – which you hope the other will interpret to give you the response you want. For instance, you say, 'Would you like to go to the cinema?' when what you really mean is, 'I would like to go to the cinema', or 'Would you like to make me a cup of tea?' when what you mean is, 'I would appreciate it if you would make me a cup of tea'. Again, people can feel manouevred into expressing a desire that they do not feel by these requests. It is better to state your feelings directly in these cases, rather than as a question.

● **How to ask.** The way to ask is plainly and directly. This is easiest with a favour, concession or simple request: 'Would you help me move this piece of furniture?', 'Could I come in half an hour later tomorrow?' or 'Would you be free to come over on Saturday evening?' You can add an explanation where appropriate, so that the person you are asking has the full picture, but try to avoid adding pressure, or making the other person feel that it is impossible to refuse. Remember, if you are asking for something where a yes is essential, frame it as a statement, rather than a request. For instance, 'I have to come in half an hour later tomorrow, because I have a dentist's appointment.'

The essential thing is to be sure in yourself what you are asking and why. Is it purely practical, or is there more to it? It is especially important to recognise this when what you are asking has an emotional importance to you. In this case, it is helpful to state what that is; for instance, 'I am very upset and need to talk to you'.

Identifying what you are feeling, and stating it, is particularly important when what you are asking for is a change in behaviour, or when you are asking someone to do something they are not inclined to do.

For instance, if you want an older child to keep you informed about his or her movements, it is helpful to explain why. 'When you are late and you don't phone, I start imagining you have had an accident and I become terribly worried. Afterwards I get angry. Please just let me know where you are.' This is more likely to get the response you want than an angry demand, 'Where the hell have you been? You're so inconsiderate! You must phone when you are going to be late!'

When you have difficulty asking for something that has emotional importance to you, then it follows that you are sometimes unaware that you *need* to ask. Examine your own behaviour when you are feeling fed up or hard-done-by. Are you perhaps sulking and nursing your resentment? Are you becoming very irritated about minor matters that might not usually bother you? Are you withdrawing from the other person by ignoring or avoiding him or her? Are you changing your behaviour to be extra nice or accommodating, hoping for a similar response in return? These and similar ways of behaving usually indicate that you have an unspoken request. Ask yourself, first, what is it you really want from this person, and why? Then make your request clearly, and in doing so explain your feelings in the matter.

● **Dealing with no.** You are free to ask, but other people are also free to say no to you. When you can accept this, it is easier to accept the refusal in the spirit that you wish your own refusals to be accepted: with an acknowledgement that you have a right to say no to anything that is disturbing, inconvenient or against your wishes.

It is easier to accept someone else's refusal when you can also take responsibility for your own feelings and needs. If your well-being is too dependent on other people doing as you ask, then you are left powerless when they refuse. Have in your mind what you can do if they refuse, and, when relevant to the others, explain what this is.

It is essential for you to clarify to the other person how important the request is to you, by explaining your feelings. You call a friend and ask if you can come over immediately, for instance. Is it a spur of the moment decision, because you are at a loose end and fancy a chat? In this case, it might not matter too much to you, as you can flick through your address book and call someone else. Have you a difficult decision to make and you value your friend's advice above anyone else's? In this case it is more important to you, but perhaps it could wait until tomorrow if your friend has other plans. Or are you perhaps feeling despairing and suicidal, with nowhere else to turn? In this case it is of top priority in its importance to you.

When the importance of the request is acknowledged, then so is the importance of the refusal. If something is not very important, then you need to be philosophical about a refusal. Don't take it personally, and don't make a mountain out of a molehill. Recognise that the other person's own needs or wishes have simply clashed with yours. When it is more important, you have to ask yourself whether you succeeded in making its importance known to the other person. If not, they are not at fault. If you are sure that you have, you must evaluate what has happened. Are you perhaps ignoring the importance of the other person's circumstances or what he or she is feeling? Or is the other person truly demonstrating a lack of consideration or respect for you?

You need also to remember that if what you are asking has emotional implications for someone else, or requires a change in behaviour or a change in circumstances, then you must consider what you are offering, as well as what you are asking. When you ask someone to do something for you, such as pay you attention, share responsibilities, spend more time with you, promote you, and so on, it is helpful to clarify what you are prepared to do in return.

In complicated matters such as these, what starts as you making a simple request must also involve you listening to the other person's point of view, and seeing whether this includes a request of you. Then you have a basis for negotiation, which can result in the most positive outcome.

● **Thinking of others.** When you are able to say no, and ask for what you want and need, it becomes easier to act towards other people with genuine consideration.

Before you are confident, you might routinely put other people's needs before your own. But you can do this out of fear or a sense of powerlessness, which breeds resentment, becomes manipulative, and loses the quality of being an unselfish, generous act.

When you are confident, and therefore able to take action to ensure that your own needs are met more often, it becomes natural to take other people's feelings into account. You also become more able to put your own needs on hold from time to time, when someone else's needs clash with your own, because you know that this is a concession freely made, and that you can attend to your own needs at a later date.

Being able to say no, being able to ask, and knowing how to show consideration for others are the fundamental nuts and bolts of any relationship. You can practise them in any situation – out shopping, at work, among friends and in your family. As you become able to express yourself honestly in ordinary situations, and deal with the reactions of other people, these ways of behaving eventually become second nature to you. When this is the case, your confidence and well-being increase.

This means that when you eventually find a new partner you are well-equipped to deal with the sensitive negotiations that make intimate and loving relationships so difficult – and so rewarding.

## INDEPENDENCE

When you have started to take control of your happiness, and you are working on building your confidence, you also gain independence.

Independence means that you can function alone, and that you do not have to rely on others to support you practically or emotionally. It does not mean that you don't need or want other people or close relationships, but it does mean that they are not essential to your survival.

Surprisingly, this often makes you more open towards others, and more willing to become intimate. When you are no longer over-vulnerable and concerned to protect yourself, you enter relationships with less fear. With increased self-esteem, however, you are more likely to make relationships that are healthy and good for you. When you have your independence you can be more choosy because being alone does not hold the same worries for you. The loving partnerships you make therefore become more equal.

Independence based on a higher level of happiness and inner strength is also very attractive to others. It becomes easier to make new friends, and for one of those friendships to turn into an important relationship.

# 6

# CHALLENGING PATTERNS

Before you start another relationship, it is helpful to have a
fresh look at the patterns that have dominated your relationships in the past. It is easier to challenge these patterns when
you are single, and before you become engulfed in the strong emotions
of love and passion that usually accompany the start of a relationship.

The patterns include long-held beliefs about men, women and relationships, as well as behaviour you believe to be appropriate, when perhaps it is not. They also include the way you usually respond when
emotions are highly charged – specifically when you are angry.

Challenging these patterns means working out where they have
come from, and deciding whether you think they are valid. If not, you
can start the process of changing them. Although changing is easier
said than done, putting change in motion while you are single gives
you the best chance of starting well in a new relationship.

## 'MESSAGES' FROM THE PAST

As has been shown in earlier chapters, many of the ideas we have
about relationships are developed very early on – when we are children
and watch how our parents get on together. This gives us ideas about
how men and women are likely to behave in relationships, and we can
grow up expecting our partners to behave in similar ways, and adopt-
ing some of the ways ourselves. We also receive more direct messages.
Perhaps a girl is told that 'all men are bastards' or 'men are only after
one thing' or a boy learns that 'a woman's place is in the home' or
'women never know their own minds'.

The trouble with these messages is that although they might be
true for a certain man, or some men, and a particular woman and some
others, they are only generalisations. Watching how your parents
behave, similarly, shows you how one couple handle a relationship, not
how every couple does – or should do.

Many of these ideas are so deeply rooted in you that you are not even
aware that you hold them. Or you are so convinced that they are true
that it never occurs to you that other people might have different ideas.

But what these ideas do is create a pattern for a relationship, even before it starts properly. Rather than learning about the individuality of your partner, you often 'expect' certain behaviour and reactions. This can have a number of unfortunate results. You might ignore the aspects of your partner that do not fit in with your pre-conceived ideas. Or you might be disappointed or outraged when your partner behaves differently from what you expect. Or you might behave towards your partner *as if* he or she fulfils your expectations, even when that is not the case. Or, indeed, you treat your partner in such a way as to provoke the very behaviour that you expect. Another effect of your expectations is that you might find yourself choosing a partner who does, in fact, fit in with what you think – and behave as you expect – even when these ways of behaving cause you unhappiness.

Luckily, when you become aware of the unconscious ideas that you hold, you are more able to see that they are generalisations that don't necessarily fit the individual. You can also see that you are free to choose someone who behaves differently from your earlier expectations, so that a more rewarding relationship is possible. Working out why you have these ideas – because of your early observations, or because of what you were told – can also help you see when they are inappropriate.

The following tasks can help you identify your hidden expectations. First, 'Men and Women' on the facing page.

Although you are likely to recognise that what you write in this task *are* generalisations, and you might believe you don't apply them to all men and women, they uncover a broad set of beliefs that you hold which are very powerful. What this means is that you are likely to *notice* behaviour that fits these generalisations, and either *ignore, misinterpret* or *mistrust* behaviour that doesn't.

For instance, if, as a woman, you write 'men are unreliable', you are likely to be rather suspicious of men who seem to behave reliably, questioning whether they are *really* like that underneath. When a previously reliable man lets you down on one occasion, you are likely to think, 'I knew it! Now it's coming out!' You are therefore likely to react very strongly and perhaps out of all proportion to the event.

In the same way, if, as a man, you write 'women are less intelligent', you are likely to dismiss signs of intelligence in a woman, or believe she has 'got her ideas from someone else', and, indeed, feel that she has less right to talk or express an opinion.

These are examples of negative expectations, and of course you will have positive ones, too. Although these are more helpful – by expecting positive things you tend to draw them out of other people – it can also have its difficult side. Because you assume certain qualities

!————————— *Task* —————————

**Men and women**

Take a large sheet of paper and divide it into eight sections. Label each section in the following way:

Men are ...

Men think ...

Men want ...

Men usually ...

Women are ...

Women think ...

Women want ...

Women usually ...

Without pausing to think, fill in these sections with as many generalisations as come into your mind about what men and women think, want and how they usually behave.

!

are there, you can be unreasonably disappointed when you find you were wrong.

The next task, over the page, is similar, but broadens your expectations to include behaviour within relationships.

You might be surprised to find that some of your ideas about men and women are different when you think about them in the context of a steady relationship.

Again, the expectations often influence your own behaviour towards your partner, as well as your assumptions about how your partner will behave.

For instance, if, as a woman, you write, 'men want to be waited on hand and foot', you are likely to expect a man to leave all the household chores up to you. Even if you don't approve of this situation and wouldn't choose it, the fact is that you are more likely to find yourself putting up with it.

And if, as a man, you write, 'women usually nag', you are likely to interpret an ordinary request, reasonably put, as nagging. This can mean that you routinely ignore what a woman is saying – so she says it again, and the result is that she turns into the nag you were expecting.

—————— *Task* ——————

## Together

Take another large sheet of paper and divide it into eight sections. This time you are writing about how you think men and women behave in relationships. Label each section in the same way.

Men are ...

Men think ...

Men want ...

Men usually ...

Women are ...

Women think ...

Women want ...

Women usually ...

Without pausing to think, fill in these sections with as many generalisations as come into your mind about what men and women think, want and how they usually behave when they are married or living together.

You can also discover your hidden expectations of *yourself* within a relationship when writing this list, which might be different from your conscious intentions.

For instance, if, as a woman, you write, 'women usually take all responsibility for the children', it can point to the way you expect your future to go. You might say now that you want a man who shares in the care of the children, but when it comes to it you take all the responsibility on yourself.

And if, as a man, you write, 'men usually take all the financial decisions', it can mean that you assume the burden even if you are not happy to, are not good at it, and even if your partner wants to help.

Of course, these *are* only generalisations, and you might well be able to see that you have not followed them slavishly in your attitude to other people, or in your relationships. But by bringing them all into your conscious mind when you write these lists, you can reveal to yourself if any of them have been motivating you in ways of which you were previously unaware.

! ———————————— *Task* ————————————

**Who started it?**

Look back at your lists, and see what your earliest memories were of a man or a woman thinking and behaving in the ways you have noted. Put the initials of the person by the description – or the initials of the person who told you that this was how men and women are.

!

This task shows you that your ideas originated somewhere. The earlier your impression the stronger it is. It is important to acknowledge to yourself by doing this that these people *formed* your ideas, and made you sensitive to these ways of behaving. As a result, you might meet people who conform to these ideas, but your own hidden expectations contribute to helping you 'recognise' them, or even to be attracted to them.

While making these lists will not transform your basic ideas, you can start to work with them – to challenge them. Which of these generalisations do you disagree with, or wish were not true? How many exceptions can you think of to these 'rules' – among people you know, or among famous people? Can you see ways in which these assumptions have affected your behaviour in relationships in the past?

Becoming aware of how these generalisations might have affected how you responded to partners, or chose them in the past, can also help you in the future. You can be alert to the process and start looking at potential partners in a different way.

## ———— 'MESSAGES' ABOUT BEHAVIOUR ————

As you grow up you also acquire ideas about how the world functions, and what is acceptable behaviour. Many of these lessons are valuable and helpful, some only partially so. Certain messages are unhelpful and cause you to act in ways that make life and relationships less easy or pleasant for you. Some common messages are looked at here – and the way they can be helpful or not is examined, too.

### Message: 'You shouldn't be selfish. Think of others first'

You learn that your needs are less important than other people's, and that thinking of yourself first is a selfish act.

● **Unhelpful effect.** You lose the sense of what you want and need, and only think about other people. This leads to unbalanced relationships, with bad feeling on both sides.

● **Helpful response.** You recognise that your needs are as important as other people's, and that by looking after your own needs you become more able to do things for others effectively.

## Message: 'It's a dog-eat-dog world – if you don't get them first, they'll get you'

You believe that the world is a hostile place, and that other people are motivated by cruel impulses and desires.

● **Unhelpful effect.** By acting aggressively or suspiciously towards other people, you attract aggression and hostility in return – thereby confirming your ideas.

● **Helpful response.** You recognise that you must stand up for yourself at appropriate times, but that other people aren't out to 'get' you. By treating them with the trust and respect you would like for yourself, you discover that you receive good treatment in return.

## Message: 'Be sensitive to other people's feelings. Never hurt other people'

You believe that other people's well-being and happiness lie in your hands – therefore, you must be constantly alert to what they are feeling, and do things to make them feel better.

● **Unhelpful effect.** You interfere inappropriately to help other people at times when nothing anyone else can say or do is useful. You hesitate to express any thoughts or wishes that might upset someone else – even when not doing so leaves *you* upset or angry.

● **Helpful response.** You recognise that someone else's thoughts and feelings are their own, and that you can't always change them just because you want to – though you are prepared to help if they ask.

You also recognise that it is impossible to go through life without ever hurting someone else. This can be because your desires or needs conflict with theirs. Also, some people are unusually sensitive, and even with the best intentions you might upset them. You also see that certain others use their 'hurt' to manipulate you if they know that you become too involved with their feelings. If you accidentally hurt someone, you are prepared to say sorry.

## Message: 'If you care too much you get hurt – it's best not to get close to people'

You believe that allowing yourself to love people and care for them makes you vulnerable and open to hurt, so you make an effort to distance yourself.

● **Unhelpful effect.** By distancing yourself from other people and learning not to care for them, you invite them to be less loving and caring towards you. Consequently, their actions and behaviour do hurt you. You miss the shared *joys* of closeness, while concentrating on the possible *pain*.

● **Helpful response.** By recognising vulnerability in yourself you realise that relationships have to be handled carefully. You act towards partners with respect and consideration, which they then show you in return. Because of this, you are able to build trust, open up, and become more loving.

## Message: 'I must make people like me, and approve of me'

You believe your value can be measured by how much people like you, and how much they approve of what you do and who you are.

● **Unhelpful effect.** You act in ways to make people like you – even if it goes against how you feel or want to be. If someone doesn't like you, or disapproves of you in some way, you believe it is proof that there is something wrong with you, which must change.

● **Helpful response.** You appreciate and welcome the people who like you and approve of you, while recognising that it is impossible to be liked by everyone. You try to be true to yourself, and what you think is right, knowing that other people usually respond positively to this. When someone doesn't like or approve of you, then you accept that this sometimes happens – and that it is more a reflection of them and their feelings than an accurate evaluation of yourself.

*Message: 'You're either a lucky person or you're not. If not, there's nothing you can do about it'*

You believe that when things are not going your way it proves that you have bad luck. When you look at other people who are happy or successful, you deduce that they are luckier than you.

● **Unhelpful effect.** When difficulties occur in your life or your relationships, you bemoan your fate, assuming that it is not your fault, and there is nothing to be done about it. Seeing other people, for whom things are going well, makes you feel bitter and resentful, because you believe they have had luck that is denied to you.

● **Helpful response.** You recognise that there is a certain amount of random luck, both good and bad, but this is only one factor in life. You also know that most people 'make' their own luck, by taking responsibility and being prepared. When things go wrong, you look for ways to improve matters. When you see other people who are living well, you analyse what it is, other than luck, that has contributed – and this spurs you on to make similar things happen in your own life.

!————————— *Task* —————————

### Life messages

Write down any statements about life and behaviour that you recognise as being part of your thinking. These can either be ideas that you have formulated for yourself, or that were told to you as you were growing up.

Examine them to see how they have contributed to the happiness or unhappiness of your relationships, and the way you live your life.

Can you modify the basic principles in such a way as to make sure they have a positive effect in the future?

!

Again, bringing these hidden ideas to the surface helps you challenge them. Changing them can be difficult, because they have formed your basic habits of behaviour. But if you can see that any of them have contributed to making you unhappy, by affecting the way you relate to other people, then you have started the process of change. Acting 'as if' you were motivated by different ideas (as explained on page 165 in the last chapter) can also help. Practising new ways of behaving can prepare you for more healthy emotional relationships in the future.

## _ CHALLENGING YOUR RESPONSE TO ANGER _

An intimate relationships calls on your very deepest feelings. Although you can feel great love for children, parents and friends, the experience of loving a partner touches emotional nerves that no other love reaches. In life things happen to make you angry – but no one can ever make you quite as angry as a partner with whom you live.

Of course, you don't just feel angry or loving in a relationship – there is a host of other emotions that you feel and express. But how you handle those two – anger and love – can determine the success of your relationship.

The way you show and receive love in an intimate, loving partnership is different from loving in any other kind of relationship. If, while reading earlier chapters, you have identified that you have found difficulties in doing this, you might well want to challenge and change the way you do so. However, this is something you can't 'practise' while single – it needs to be actively addressed when you are in a relationship. The way to do this is looked at in Chapter Eight, *Starting Well*.

It is different with anger, however. Although the degree or depth of anger you might feel can be different in a partnership, the way you handle your anger can be consistent, whatever the situation or provocation. Challenging your usual responses, and learning to subsitute more helpful ones, is possible even when you are not in a relationship.

Angry feelings were looked at in Chapter Three, *What Went Wrong?* (page 60) when you were asked to trace the way you handled anger with a previous partner back to your experiences in your family as a child. You are likely to have recognised that the way you handled angry feelings contributed to some extent to the way your relationships evolved, and sometimes to their breakdown.

Changing the way you handle your anger, so that it is constructive and cleanly expressed, can make a lot of difference in future relationships. And, as anger is a feature of life, you can start to practise new ways of handling your own when you are not in an intimate relationship. It benefits your day-to-day existence, and your relationships with people who are not particularly close to you, as well as the ones who are.

First of all it helps to identify what makes you angry, and what happens when you are angry, or when confronted by other people who are angry.

● **Your own anger.** Anger is like fire – it needs fuel to be activated. Although when you are angry you are mainly aware of the heat of your emotion, what has fuelled it can be any number of other emotions. It is useful to discover which are the underlying emotions that are most likely to make you angry.

The following task, which can help you do so, is adapted from a task in *The RELATE Guide to Better Relationships*.

! ——————————————— *Task* ———————————————

### The hit list

Keep a diary of your angry moments. Note down the incidents that triggered them off. Underneath, write down what else you were feeling at the same time. This can include physical feelings, such as tiredness, headache or other pain, but it is even more important to note other emotions. These are some common underlying feelings, but you can add your own to the list:

| | | | |
|---|---|---|---|
| sadness | envy | nervousness | depression |
| fear | jealousy | hurt pride | self-dislike |
| guilt | insecurity | grief | protectiveness |
| contempt | boredom | frustration | irritation |

Once you have a better idea of the feelings involved you can start to sort out what you need to do to acknowledge these other feelings and deal with them, without suppressing them or going on the attack.

When you have kept your diary for a while, make a checklist for yourself under the following headings:

– The situations that make me angry are . . .

– People make me angry when . . .
!

This task is useful for a number of reasons. If you have difficulty expressing your anger, then you usually find it quite hard to recognise its first stirrings. Because you don't like feeling angry, or are uncomfortable when you do, you ignore the early stages of anger in the hope that it will go away. Part of handling anger effectively involves knowing when you start to be angry – so that you can deal with the causes before your anger level rises. By keeping your diary, you develop the habit of asking yourself if you have felt angry, and why.

It is also useful if you are a more openly angry person, who flares up quite quickly. Although you have less trouble getting in touch with your anger, you might not have identified what triggers it before. When you know what situations or people make you angry, you can begin to question whether you are putting yourself in a position to be made angry, by the people you associate with, or in choosing to enter certain situations.

In either case, the most important element in the task is identifying the feelings that underlie the anger. Expressing your anger – but not revealing the feelings underneath – means that the causes remain. It is the same with suppressing your anger – the feelings that have caused it remain unsatisfied.

These are the two main unhelpful responses to anger. Either expressing it without inhibition, in an attacking way that doesn't address the real issues, or holding it in – controlling your feelings and living with the misery that results.

Ask yourself the questions in the following short quiz.

**?** ———————— **Quiz** ————————

## Better or worse?

After you have expressed your anger do you feel

a) better   b) worse   c) the same?

When you suppress your anger do you feel

a) better   b) worse   c) the same?

————————————————————————— **?**

If you feel worse, or even the same, after you have allowed yourself to express your anger, or after you have successfully held it in, then you are not handling your anger in the right way.

You can feel better at the moment of expressing your anger, because of the release of tension, but if you have provoked anger in return, or you have frightened or humiliated the person you confronted, or nothing has changed in the situation, or perhaps it has worsened, then the good feelings soon fade.

Similarly, you can feel good when you manage to hold your anger in – because you feel you are exercising control. But if the cause of your anger has not been addressed you are likely to feel the same, or worse.

It is possible to feel better when anger is handled correctly, even if you don't get the response you have hoped for.

## Dealing with your own anger

You have a right to your angry feelings. If you express them at the time they first occur then they won't build up until you explode with rage. But expressing anger needs to be done with care.

● **Identify what is making you angry.** When you feel yourself becoming angry, work out why this is. Sometimes it might be a situation out of your control: you are waiting for a bus that is late. In this case, there is nothing you can to do to remove the cause of your anger, you just have to put up with it.

But is it something that someone is doing or not doing that is making you angry? If this is so, then you have identified that you need to let that person know what it is. Explaining that something is making you angry can help to soothe your feelings, even if nothing changes in the situation.

Ask yourself *why* it is making you angry; in other words, what are the feelings underneath that have resulted in anger. Has it upset you? Are you feeling jealous? Or has it perhaps triggered off a feeling of shame or guilt in you? Knowing what the underlying feelings are, so that you can explain them clearly, often contributes more towards clearing the air than a simple statement of anger or a request for someone to change his or her behaviour.

● **Express your anger cleanly.** This means explaining how you are feeling, and, perhaps, making a simple request to someone to do or not to do whatever has angered you.

This is what most people find hard. When you are angry you are not feeling reasonable. The impulse can be to attack or blame – or, if you don't like showing your feelings, to withdraw, sulk or become depressed.

When you are angry because your feelings have been hurt in some way, it is also natural to protect yourself further by not admitting that you have been wounded. Instead, you become angry about a minor detail, or something that has nothing to do with the real cause of your anger at all. None of these ways are effective.

Directly explaining your feelings is the most positive way. You can say simply, 'I am angry' (or 'very angry' or even 'furious'). But it is even more important to state your other feelings: 'because I am upset', 'I feel hurt', 'I feel humiliated'. Explain the specific action that has made you feel like this. For instance, 'When you walk out of the room when I am in the middle of talking to you I feel upset. Then I become angry.'

These clear statements, which concentrate on your own feelings, allow you both to focus on the issue. If, instead, you criticise or blame, the other person will not care what you are feeling, because he or she becomes more concerned with his or her own hurt feelings. Any statement of yours that starts 'you make me . . .' or 'you always . . .' or 'you're so . . .' will make the other person defensive, and not prepared to listen to you.

But what if you are angry because of feelings in yourself that have nothing to do with the other person? For instance, you have finally arrived home soaked after waiting in the rain for that bus for an hour. Or your boss has picked on you, or you have had a warning letter from the bank. The frustration and irritation you feel can bring your angry feelings closer to the surface, so that any small annoyance is likely to trigger them off – including things that wouldn't normally bother you. In these cases, it is helpful to warn other people how you are feeling. 'I'm feeling very angry because . . .' or 'I'm in a bad mood because . . .'. The other person then knows the situation and that you are likely to over-react, and is less likely to take things personally – or, indeed, might even be more considerate. This also helps you to avoid a situation where your anger spirals, and you feel you must justify your over-reaction by blaming the other person further. It also makes it easier for you to apologise if you do pick on someone as a scapegoat.

It is hardest to deal cleanly with anger that arises from deep vulnerability, or when you feel bad about yourself. For instance, you feel jealous, which activates your most sensitive feelings of insecurity, or it has been pointed out to you that you have done something wrong, and you are feeling ashamed or guilty. These are the times when you are most likely to go into the attack, because that feels more comfortable than facing your painful feelings about yourself.

In these cases it is vital to recognise that it is not the other person's fault. On these occasions it is most appropriate to control your anger if you can. It is best if you can manage to explain your other feelings, if only briefly: 'I'm rather upset', 'I feel very shaken'. Perhaps you need to remove yourself from the other person's presence if you feel the urge to be unpleasant or critical, until you are clearer in your mind what your real feelings are. If you find yourself attacking or blaming unjustifiably in a moment of anger, then it is best to apologise swiftly, rather than compound the injustice by getting drawn into a row. You can say, 'I'm sorry, that was unfair', or 'I'm really angry with myself, I shouldn't be taking this out on you', or 'I didn't really mean that, I'm just upset'.

● **Knowing when to stop.** When your anger is a justifiable response
to the way someone is behaving, it can be tempting to go on about the
issue – particularly if they are not changing in the way you wish.
However, once your argument starts going round in circles, and
becomes a full-blown row, then it is not achieving anything. If the other
person becomes angry too, you will both be protecting your own positions and will not get anywhere. You must be prepared to close the
issue – perhaps bringing it up again at another time when you are both
cooler.

Other ways of handling this are also explained on page 170, 'The
right to ask'.

## Other people's anger

There are two typical responses to someone else's anger. One is to fire
up and become immediately angry yourself. You feel attacked, so you
go into the attack. The other main response is to be frightened – to
avoid the confrontation, or immediately back down or try to placate the
other person. Neither of these responses is most helpful.

---

! ================= *Task* =================

**Other people's anger**

List your thoughts and reactions under the following headings.

When someone is angry with me I feel . . .

When someone is angry with me I think . . .

What I do when someone is angry with me is . . .

================================================= !

---

## Dealing with other people's anger

Once you can recognise that when *you* are angry you need to have your
feelings, and the cause for them, acknowledged, it is easier to see that
this is also true of someone else. With other people you must continue
to bear in mind that the anger you see is the top surface of their emotions, and underneath are likely to be any number of different feelings.

In some instances, however, the feelings and the cause are likely to
be clear-cut – you have pushed in front of someone in a queue, for
instance, or have damaged something that you have borrowed. In these
and similar cases, the most helpful response is an apology, and an

attempt to sort the matter out. Or you might have a brush with a stranger, who is clearly angry generally – someone picks a fight with you in a pub, or a driver threatens you when you overtake the car, or a shop assistant is rude to you for no apparent reason. In these sort of cases, it is best not to be drawn into the other person's anger by an aggressive response. Either remove yourself from the situation or ignore it where appropriate, or remain calm and reasonable yourself.

However, when it is a person you know well, the situation is likely to be more complex. The angry feelings need to be explored in more detail, and handled with care.

● **Acknowledge the emotion.** Anger often builds when you feel that the other person is not paying attention to your feelings. People are sometimes driven to explode with rage as the only way they know to show you that they are suffering. When someone is angry, therefore, it can help them to show that you have recognised this before it comes to the point of explosion. Sometimes a simple statement such as, 'I can see you're very angry', or 'I'm obviously irritating you', releases them to explain their feelings directly, rather than in an angry, attacking way.

It might surprise you how often this defuses the situation. The other person can then feel released to tell you if you are causing the anger, or if there is some other reason behind it ('You're right, I am angry – I've had a terrible day').

● **Try to identify the feelings behind it.** If the angry person is not too enraged, and is receptive to the idea of talking further, you can try to help in exposing the other feelings behind the anger. You can ask, 'Is anything else the matter?', 'Do you want to talk about it?', 'Is it something I'm doing?' Often a sympathetic response and an acknowledgement that there might be more to the feelings helps an angry person focus on the real cause.

When the anger has little to do with you, but you are simply bearing the brunt of it, this is often enough to cool the other person's anger. However, if it has been caused by something that you are doing or not doing, then that cause must be addressed, too.

● **Deal with the cause.** Occasionally it is possible for you to change what you have been doing to provoke the anger, without causing difficulties for yourself. In this case the solution is clear to you.

At other times, however, it is inconvenient, impossible, or distressing for you to do so. For instance, a child might be angry because she wanted you to take her out when you have to stay in, or a colleague might be angry because you are taking leave that means extra work for him, or a friend might be angry because she wants you to support and listen to her when you are feeling drained and in need of care yourself.

In these cases, when you might feel that the other person's anger is a violation of your own feelings, it is all too easy to become angry yourself. Don't be drawn into an argument, however. It is more helpful to repeat your acknowledgement of the other person's feelings, and his or her right to feel that way, by saying, 'I can see this has made you angry, and I'm sorry that is the case'. You can then go on state the situation, 'But there's nothing I can do about it, I'm afraid' (to your child or colleague), or 'But I'm not up to it at the moment' (to your friend).

It can also be appropriate to make your own feelings clear: 'This upsets me too', or 'When you say that I feel angry as well', and so on.

When you are sympathetic in your acknowledgement of the other person's feelings, and clear about your own feelings and position, the anger is often taken out of the situation, even when it can't be resolved to everyone's satisfaction.

● **Dealing with rage.** Trying to tackle the situation calmly and reasonably can be impossible if the other person has become intensely angry and enraged. If you have tried your best to sort matters out to no avail, then you need to say something like, 'I can see there is nothing helpful I can do at the moment.' When possible, it is best to remove yourself from the other person, to avoid being drawn into an argument and becoming very angry yourself. However, if you can't resolve things at the time, you should come back to the issue at a later time or another day when the other person has cooled down. It can then be possible to look freshly at what made that person angry, and tackle the causes in a less heated manner.

Do remember, however, that there is always a period between the anger starting and the rage exploding. If you can acknowledge the anger at an earlier stage, without becoming angry yourself, then you can usually stop the anger spiralling out of control.

Practising these ways of dealing with anger in situations that are not emotionally over-charged can help you start to change your instinctive response to your own and other people's anger. Seeing that these new ways work also helps you establish a different automatic response that is more helpful. It then becomes easier for you to use these new ways of reacting when you become involved in an intimate relationship.

# Part Three
# STARTING AGAIN

# 7

# A NEW SOCIAL LIFE

Starting again on your own has implications for your social life. It will almost certainly go through changes, which can give you the opportunity to develop it in the way that suits you best.

An enjoyable social life is more than an added extra. It helps to put problems in perspective and gives a respite from emotional and practical problems for a few hours. When you are single again you have the chance to re-assess how you spend your spare time. You can discover which friends are important to you, make new friends – and perhaps enlarge your range of activities in a way that wasn't possible when you were part of a couple.

This chapter looks at these issues – and also the issue of new relationships. The idea of 'dating' again can be exciting or terrifying, as can the idea of sex with someone new. The question of knowing when you are ready to form a serious relationship is important – and the implications of rebound relationships are examined in detail.

## What happens to your social life after a break-up

In emotional terms, everyone who has suffered a separation will find that their social life is affected in some way. Grieving saps your energy. You might shun your friends, or feel exceptionally needy and want their company more than ever. You might lose interest in activities that usually excite you, or feel the need to fill up the spaces in your life with increased activity.

For some people a break-up hardly affects their social life in practical ways at all. This is most likely to be the case if you were not married, and were only together for a relatively short time, particularly if you also retained as friends people you knew from before the start of your relationship.

The longer you were together as a couple, however, the more likely it is that your separation will have an impact on your social life. You probably saw more of other couples in a similar situation to yours, who became joint friends – and less of individual friends. Perhaps you felt there was little reason to maintain a social life, or were unable to because of family or financial reasons, so most of your free time was spent at home together.

When you have been together for a long time you can find that friends feel awkward when you split up. Perhaps they take sides, and you find that some of them drop you. If your socialising has been with other couples it can happen that you aren't included in the usual get-togethers, even when you remain friendly. Perhaps you are invited as the only guest, or to family suppers, or not at all. This is not only upsetting, it also makes you feel insecure about your value at a time when your self-esteem is likely to be low anyway. If you saw a fair amount of your partner's family, you can also find that this changes now that you are apart – leaving another hole in your usual social pattern.

It can also be difficult to go to the places you used to go as a couple – cinemas, clubs, pubs, restaurants and so on. It can seem that breaking up with your partner has turned your familiar haunts into no-go areas. These are a few of the difficulties reported by both men and women coping with a separation. However, some of the problems are different according to whether you are a man or woman, so they are looked at separately here.

● **Problems facing men.** In some ways men have it easier socially. A 'spare' man is often sought after, and might even find that couples continue to invite him to formal occasions to 'look after' him or 'feed him up' – or even to set him up with someone else. It can sometimes be easier for a man to go to places on his own without feeling awkward or standing out.

Your problem as a man is that most people ignore your emotional distress during this time. They expect you to be coping fairly well emotionally, and become embarrassed if you aren't. Other men, particularly those in established relationships, might even envy you being 'on the loose', so that you feel unable to talk about what you are going through.

This was the case with Glen, who came for counselling when his wife Sally decided that their marriage was over. They had three children, and their marriage had been good for many years. But two years previously Glen had been made redundant, and went from being the strong partner to a depressed and needy man who wanted Sally to take care of him. Sally found the change in Glen too frightening and she couldn't cope with his demands on her, so she asked him to leave.

Glen came for counselling for some months. This rejection on top of the redundancy had depleted all that was left of his self-esteem. The only friend he saw was an ex-colleague who had been made redundant at the same time as he had.

Whenever Glen met his mate they would get drunk and swap jokes. Glen would listen to his friend's anecdotes about how good his life was now, and Glen would offer stories of his own that suggested that he too was having a good time. Glen's friend would make leering innuendos about what Glen must be getting up to now that he had 'got Sally off his back'. Glen went along with this, winking at his friend, and implying by his manner that he was quite right. To the counsellor, however, Glen reported how lonely and misunderstood these evenings left him feeling. He also felt worse about himself afterwards – what sort of man was he that he wasn't getting a lot of women into bed? In the state he was in, he couldn't believe that any woman would be interested in the 'wreck of a man' he had become.

Glen's turning point came, the counsellor said, when he met his friend one evening when he was feeling so low that he could not shift his mood into pretending that everything was all right. To his horror, he found himself pouring out his sorrows and feelings of inadequacy instead. To his surprise and wonderment, instead of laughing at him and despising him, Glen's friend admitted that he was unhappy as well, and went on to tell Glen about the difficulties in his own life.

From this point on, Glen began to feel better. When he knew that he wasn't the only man suffering – and that he could talk about what he was going through with a friend as well as the counsellor, he began to feel that life wasn't so grim. He began to notice the world around him again; he once reported to the counsellor that a waitress had flirted with him: it must mean he wasn't so hopeless after all. He also started to think about what he was going to do with his life – how he would search for work, take up fresh interests, see more friends.

While some men welcome the chance to live a single life, many men miss the comfortable routine of being part of a couple. This is often what drives men to jump too quickly into a new, serious relationship, before they have properly got over the last one.

● **Problems facing women.** Women are much more likely to be able to draw on emotional support from close friends after a break-up, and to feel able to express what they feel.

Your problem as a woman often has more to do with the formal aspects of your social life. Many women feel they have lost 'status' as a single woman, particularly if they were married. Whereas a man on his own can be seen to be 'playing the field' a woman on her own is often supposed to be unable to find a man. Although this is ridiculous, it is hurtful – even worse if you are recently separated and it is something you find yourself believing.

You are more likely to be excluded from gatherings of couples than a man is. Sometimes it is because you are regarded as a threat by the other women, who worry that you are going to be interested in their men – or, indeed, that their men might look at you differently. More subtly, it is because the break-up of an established couple threatens the security of other couples. The women can worry that it is somehow 'catching', that their own relationships could be under threat. They believe that the sight of you, a single woman, might lead their men to speculate about what your man is up to and how he is using his freedom. It is slightly different when a lone man joins the group: this signals that his life is not substantially different, just diminished by the loss of his partner, making his situation less enviable to the other men.

## Rebuilding your social life

In the early days of a break-up you are probably most concerned to see close and sympathetic friends who can give you emotional support. You probably feel most comfortable seeing people one-to-one, in a situation where you do not have to make too much effort. At some point, however, you will want more than this – and that is when you look at the state of your current social life, and how you want it to be in the future.

Forcible changes in your social life might not be pleasant, but they do allow you to rebuild it again in a way that suits you better. The meaning of this will obviously vary for individuals. There are some general considerations, however, which are looked at here.

● **Dealing with other couples.** If your social life to date has revolved around activities with other couples, you are likely to find that this has dropped off somewhat since your separation. Looked at from their point of view, this is often because they are feeling awkward about the situation. They might not know whether you want to be included in their activities, or if you are ready. They might not know what to say to you. Just as many people avoid someone who has suffered a bereavement because they don't know how to behave, so some people suffer similar embarrassment after a relationships breaks up.

It is wise, therefore, to give your friends the benefit of the doubt. If they are not calling you or inviting you to join them, don't immediately assume that it is because they don't want to. Instead, make the first move yourself. Telephone for a chat and let them know how you are feeling generally. You can dispel their awkwardness simply by talking about your situation. It is also worth being quite straightforward about your attitude to being invited over by them. You can say, 'I'm not ready to start entertaining yet, but I do miss you and hope that you will remember to include me in what you are doing.' You can also add,

'Please don't feel you have to match me up with someone. I don't mind about odd numbers, if you don't.'

You are likely to find that some of your friends respond well to this, and some don't. There will inevitably be people who are not comfortable continuing the friendship in the changed circumstances, particularly if the separation has been acrimonious and they remain friendly with your partner. In retrospect you are likely to recognise that they were never very good friends, and therefore no real loss.

You are likely to find, as time goes on, however, that you don't miss these couples' gatherings in the same way. It is human nature to gravitate to people in similar circumstances to yourself, because of the things you share in common. Couples are drawn to other couples, parents are drawn to others with children of the same age, and so on. While you are single you are likely to find yourself more interested in the company of people who are also single, and more socially flexible.

● **Your single friends.** If you have kept in touch with single friends, you will often find them a great help after a separation. Many people only realise after a break-up, however, that they have let some of their friendships with single people lapse because of the reasons already mentioned. When they were still with their partners they had more in common with couples than with their single friends.

If this is the case with you, therefore, you might feel hesitant about getting in touch again. However, most friends are usually forgiving, and will be delighted at the opportunity to revive an old friendship. You can learn the lesson that friends are valuable and should be treated with care. If you drop them when you find a new partner, though, you will find that they become less happy to pick up the friendship if you find yourself on your own again at a future date.

Your new situation might make you determined to make room for all your different categories of friends when rebuilding your social life – not just now, when things are changing, but later, when you have established yourself again and are feeling happier.

● **New activities and new friends.** The greatest opportunities lie in expanding your social life to include new activities and friends. Were there interests and hobbies you were unable to pursue when you were part of a couple? Or have you discovered a desire in yourself to try things that you have never tried before? When thinking about these issues, you should look again at 'Towards Happiness' (page 134) in Chapter Five. Specifically think again about the sections 'Treating yourself', 'Giving space to happiness', 'My dreams', and the tasks within those sections. These reveal to you activities that give you pleasure, and goals towards which you want to aim. Contained in these are usually clues to how you might expand your social life.

If sport gives you pleasure, for instance, then taking up the sport of your choice introduces you to like-minded people. Or if you want to make a contribution to society, finding appropriate voluntary work puts you among committed people with similar aims. Choosing an activity that gives you pleasure or is important to you is a more sure way of making new friends than choosing an activity simply because it is a way of meeting people. If the activity itself is satisfying then making new friends becomes a pleasant bonus, rather than the main reason for doing it.

## DATING AGAIN

Sooner or later you are likely to be thinking about forming a new relationship. The longer you have been part of an established couple, the more nervous you are likely to be about 'dating' – seeing someone with a view to deciding whether he or she is a possible potential partner. The last time you did this might well have been when you were a teenager or in your early twenties, and many years might have passed since then. Even if less time has passed, and you have had a series of relationships since reaching maturity, it can still be a difficult and nerve-wracking time. You have been bruised by the break-up of one or more relationships, and are consequently likely to be less optimistic, more nervous, less sure of your ability to choose well or to attract someone new.

It is outside the scope of this book to look at ways of meeting potential new partners – it could be through introductions by friends, clubs, new activities you are involved in, dating agencies or advertisements, and so on. But it is relevant to look briefly at the issues raised when you start dating again.

### The etiquette of dating

Many people are bewildered about the 'rules' of dating when they are mature, sexually experienced, and perhaps have children. As a teenager it was often quite clear: who did the asking, who paid, how much physical contact was allowed when, and so on.

There are no such clear rules for mature adults. The only real rule is to consult your own feelings and inclinations and do what feels right for you. Although this sounds easy, it is only possible to do this when you are feeling confident and happy with yourself; if you start dating too soon after a break-up, your confidence is likely to be low, and consequently it is harder to believe that your feelings are important. If you are dating mainly as a way of making yourself feel good about yourself and your attractiveness, you are more likely to let the other person dictate the progress of the relationship. These are some other considerations:

● **Asking someone out.** It is perfectly acceptable for either the woman or the man to ask the other out. As a woman you might find this hard to do, particularly if you have never done so before. It can be challenging to find the courage to do so, and if you are feeling vulnerable then a refusal can come as a real blow.

Whether you are a man or a woman, it is kindest to yourself (and easier for the other person) if you ask in such a way as to make the invitation casual, so that it is neither too difficult to refuse, nor too upsetting for you if you are refused. For instance, suggesting a drink that evening, or a visit to the cinema that perhaps includes other people is fairly safe. It is legitimate not to be free on the day asked, or not to wish to see a particular film, and you open up the possibility of the other person suggesting an alternative night or activity.

● **Who pays?** It is probably best if you both pay your own way when you start dating. If you continue to see each other, there might be a case for the one who has more money paying more, or picking up the bill more often. There are usually ways of making the balance more even if you wish: the one with more money pays for a good meal, the other pays for the cinema tickets, or arranges a low-cost outing in return, and so on. This is sensible and logical, and should have no bearing on the rest of your relationship. In other words, the one who pays more does not buy the right to call the shots in the relationship: the other does not have to 'pay back' with sex, or in any other way. If you find this concept difficult, look again at the section starting on page 167, 'The power to say no' and 'Right to ask' in Chapter Five.

● **Sex.** When to sleep with someone, or if to sleep with someone is often a major preoccupation. How soon should you sleep with someone – and is it wrong not to?

Again, the most important element is how you feel about it – but this can be more complicated than the other considerations. If you don't feel ready to embark on a sexual relationship, then you shouldn't. Any pressure to make you do so is wrong. Your right to decide what to do with your own body is unquestionable, and you should resist suggestions that it is 'about time', or that you owe this new person a debt of gratitude. If you are worried about losing the new relationship, you can explain your unreadiness and reasons for not wanting sex. Anyone who continues to push, or is not willing to see you without sex, is not right for you at this time in your life.

But perhaps you are missing the regularity of your sex life and feel that you need to be sexual again, or you find yourself very sexually attracted to the new person. In these cases you might feel that it is right to embark on a sexual relationship. Whether it is right or not, however, depends as much as anything on your attitude to sex and your vulnerability at the moment.

If you are quite detached and casual about sex then it is possible for you to have a sexual relationship even with someone to whom you are not close. However, for many people – particularly women – the start of a sexual relationship heralds a deepening of the relationship. What starts off as purely sexual can lead you to attach more importance to the relationship than it has in reality. If your new partner does not share your feelings then you risk feeling bad about yourself if the relationship does not continue. You have to weigh up the relative merits of satisfying your sexual desire, against the possible consequences of an emotional involvement that might not be reciprocated.

For instance, Amy started seeing a new man only six weeks after she had broken up with her husband. She found him very attractive, but was frightened of having sex with him because she knew that she was feeling vulnerable. She managed to convince him that they shouldn't sleep together for the first month that she saw him – but during that time he piled on the pressure.

'Eventually I told him that I would sleep with him, but I explained how I was feeling, and said that it was a big step for me. The sex was enjoyable, but he didn't call me for ten days afterwards.' Amy felt terribly crushed by this. She thought that it meant that she wasn't attractive enough or 'good enough' in bed to interest him. In the event, when he did ring up she was so relieved that she saw him again and went to bed with him again. Despite the fact that she explained how bad she had felt the time before, the same thing happened again. This time he took two weeks to call her back. She continued to see him for two more months, hoping that things would change, feeling worse and worse about herself during that time. She said, 'Whenever I saw him he appeared so nice and concerned, and I was convinced that the relationship would become more serious. I eventually realised that I was just convenient for him, which made me feel cheap and used.'

The experience so upset Amy that, when she went for counselling some months later, she reported that she was scared of dating men, and her self-esteem had plummeted further than when she had broken up with her husband. The counsellor helped her see that the timing had been wrong for her. She needed to cope with her feelings about her ex-husband first. Next time, she also needed to build a secure relationship with someone before she had sex with him.

Some people go on a whirl of one-night stands after a separation. This is of limited benefit – it can prove that you still have 'pulling power', but it can be lonely. Whereas some men can justify these as conquests to themselves and others, even if they had been hoping for more, women tend to feel rejected and not attractive enough to merit more of a relationship. Even people who feel that it proves they are sexually successful find that the novelty palls and they start to wish for something more permanent.

● **Parents with children at home.** Trying to re-start or maintain your social life when you are left with the children has difficulties all its own. For a start, children often need you more in the early days of a separation, and can feel abandoned if you are out a lot. You need to be sensitive to their need for you, as well as your own needs as an individual.

Dating is especially difficult. Children can feel threatened by both your excitement and your nerves. Older children can be shocked or disapproving when they see you dressing up, and by your obvious concern to look attractive or young. They are also affected by the way your attention becomes focused on a new adult, and will be especially attuned to any distress you feel when a promising relationship ends or goes wrong.

Again, it is better for all concerned if you delay dating until normality has returned to the children's life to a certain extent, and you are feeling better and stronger in yourself. On the whole it is also best to keep your dates away from the family home, and not to introduce a new partner unless the relationship is showing signs of becoming stable and important to you. Younger children, especially, will have a tendency to become attached to adults who are around a lot, and it is damaging for them if the people they are attached to keep disappearing – as, after all, one of their parents did. It makes it even harder for them to make consistent love relationships when they become adults themselves.

It is best not to have sexual partners to stay the night for similar reasons. If you are sexually active, and have a number of partners, or they change frequently, it is confusing and disturbing for your children to be exposed to this. It is doubly important, for their sakes, to test the strength of a relationship before introducing a new partner into the home and into your bed.

Nevertheless, your children must also come to understand eventually that you need friendships of your own, and – if this is the case – to know that you hope one day to make a new relationship. Children must not feel that they have the power to dictate your life and your friendships. If you treat their feelings and opinions with respect and consideration, they will eventually learn to do the same with yours.

## REBOUND RELATIONSHIPS

A rebound relationship is one that you make before you have finished grieving for your old relationship, and worked through the angry and sad feelings. It is the process of doing this that helps you learn what went wrong before, and what needs to happen for a new relationship to be successful. In addition, a relationship might also be classified as 'rebound' if you haven't reconciled yourself to being on your own – by rebuilding your life in such a way that you find value or pleasure in it. Entering a relationship when you feel sad or angry, or because life on your own is unbearable, is a poor start. The new relationship is inevitably affected by these feelings. Either your heightened emotions spill over into the new relationship, or you put up with something that is less than good for you because it is better than being on your own.

Whatever your own inclinations, you might find yourself being subtly or openly pressured by other people to start a new relationship. Sometimes your family or your friends urge you to look for someone new. One counsellor talked about Judy, who was left with two young children when she broke up with her husband. Previously they had been in counselling, but they had made no progress. Judy worked very hard to try to improve her marriage, but her husband was uncooperative. It eventually emerged that he was having an affair which he had no intention of ending, and had had many affairs since they were first married.

The counsellor continued to see Judy on her own after the separation, as she struggled to come to terms with it. Judy reported she had a number of friends who, in a misguided attempt to make her feel better, kept telling her how attractive she was, and urging her to find someone new. The counsellor says that she was able to support Judy in resisting these friends. Judy herself knew that she was feeling too scarred to jump into a new relationship. She continued counselling for many months, and during that time the counsellor saw great changes in her. 'Originally she seemed almost too fragile to survive, but she gained great strength. I admire her, and know that a relationship she makes in the future stands a much better chance than any she might have made at that early stage.'

## Transitional relationships

Many people do embark on new relationships before they are really ready. Indeed, some people embark on a relationship before they leave their partners – in these cases, the 'affair' is actually a way of giving themselves the courage to make the break. Although these relationships might not technically be rebound relationships, they carry the same problems. There is emotional unfinished business from the previous relationship, and you have not had time on your own to assess what you really want from a new relationship. Indeed, these relationships are often transitional: eventually you discover that they have served their purpose in helping you over a bad patch, but that they are no longer what you need.

An example of this is Sophie and Oliver, who had been married for fifteen years. Oliver had an affair that broke up his marriage when Sophie found out about it. He went immediately to live with the other woman. Although the affair had been going on for two years, when Oliver made the break and moved in with his lover it only lasted a further two months.

At the time, Oliver believed that he wanted to return to Sophie – but she was adamant that she didn't want him back. The affair had been with a friend of hers, and she felt too humiliated to want to mend the marriage. In fact, with counselling, Oliver came to understand that he had wanted to leave Sophie for a long time, and he had 'allowed' her to find out about the affair. He had believed he loved the other woman, but their relationship became so changed when he moved in with her that he realised that the 'love' had been dependent on the circumstances rather than anything they shared between them. His initial desire to return to Sophie had been provoked by fear of being on his own. He knew that their relationship was unhappy, and he wasn't prepared to work at it.

Another example of the effect of transitional relationships is what happened to Brian, after he left Nicola, his wife. Their relationship had lasted seventeen years, and they had three children. The relationship had never been very satisfying for either of them – they had married young, when Nicola became pregnant with their first child, but for the last four years things had been become very bad between them. They had grown apart. Brian had had a couple of secret affairs, and Nicola had become increasingly wrapped up in her work for an animal rights organisation. Brian felt that he was Nicola's last priority, a long way after the children and her work.

The counsellor continued to see both Brian and Nicola after the separation. Nicola, who initially felt that she couldn't cope, soon found that her work with the animal rights organisation acted as her solace, just as it had acted as the catalyst to break up the relationship.

Brian complained that in Nicola he had found a mother rather than a partner, and he felt that life must offer more. However, he was so depressed after the divorce that he lost his job, and was at an all-time low. During this time he met another woman. She was slightly older than him, and was a widow with two children. The counsellor remarked that he seemed to have found another mother figure, but Brian said she was just what he needed, and indeed, she seemed to be. Soon afterwards he told the counsellor that he was ready to leave counselling.

Some months later he got back in touch with the counsellor to say that he was moving to another city. He had finished the relationship with his older woman and was planning to start a new life. The woman had served her purpose in helping him cope through a difficult time, and he was now ready to look for a real partner, rather than another mother.

While transitional relationships can serve a certain purpose, they can leave you with a sense of failure when they end, following so close to the end of another relationship.

## Problems with rebound relationships

There are a number of problems with rebound relationships. For a start, you are still so close to your last relationship that you might not see that you are making the same mistakes. This truth is obscured by the fact that you are still suffering emotionally from the break-up, as well as being caught up in the excitement of the new.

This was the case with Emma, who finally found the courage to leave her dominating husband, Stephen, after fourteen years of marriage, during which time he physically abused and terrified her. They had been coming for counselling for some months, and there was no change for the better in the relationship. Emma finally decided that the only way she could manage to end the marriage was to leave the country. She arranged to go and live with her sister, who was married and living in Australia.

By this time she had forged a good relationship with her counsellor, and so she kept in touch after she had left. She soon wrote to say that she was ecstatically happy – she had met another man and had moved in with him.

Only a few months later, Emma wrote again. This time to confess how disastrous the relationship was. The new man had turned out to be a carbon-copy of Stephen – bullying and repressive. This time, however, Emma said she felt that she had learned her lesson. Counselling had opened her eyes to the process, but the intoxication of falling in love had temporarily misled her into believing that everything would be all right. She wrote, 'I'm learning to be an adult now, and I want to be on my own for a while. That's what I need. I want an equal relationship next time, and I won't get that until I sort myself out.'

Another reason rebound relationships have a poor chance of success is that the suffering caused by a separation means that your new partner is not getting to know the 'real you'. What the new person sees is someone emotionally distressed and needy. You are likely, therefore, to form an unbalanced relationship on the lines of one of the patterns outlined in Chapter Three, *What Went Wrong?* As time goes by, and you get over the last relationship, you are likely to change substantially. As you become less needy, the 'fit' between you and your new partner works less well – you have to learn about each other all over again and make adjustments. Sometimes the pattern has become so fixed that you find this difficult to do, or the other person resists your attempts to become 'whole' and well. This can lead to all kinds of problems, including the breakdown of the relationship.

The repeat of an old pattern, or the establishment of one of the other less healthy patterns, also becomes more likely because of your vulnerability and neediness at this time. Fear of losing the new partner, and lack of confidence in yourself, leads you into the subterfuge and 'games' of an unbalanced relationship. You try to manipulate your new partner emotionally, or adjust your behaviour in ways to suit the new relationship, hiding aspects of yourself that you fear are unloveable or unattractive. This means that the relationship is built on a falsehood – lacking the openness and intimacy of a truly healthy relationship. All these things mean that problems are more likely further down the line.

## How do you know if you're on the rebound?

In the drive to get on with your life after a relationship has finished, you want to believe that you are over it as soon as possible. Some people are angry at the suggestion that a new relationship has been formed on the rebound. So how can you tell whether you are ready to think about a serious relationship again?

There is no normal time limit after which everyone is heartfree again – it varies from person to person. But you should bear in mind that the grieving period for a serious relationship lasts at least a year, and two years or more is typical. These are some of the matters you should consider when weighing up your readiness:

● **Are you still angry or suffering?** If you are still very angry at your ex-partner in a way that leads you to think about your relationship a lot, or are still obviously upset, then you have not got over it yet. What this means is that you are still emotionally connected to your ex-partner, and do not have space in your heart to welcome a new relationship. If you are still feeling vengeful, the danger is that you will unconsciously transfer your desire for revenge on to your new partner, wanting to make him or her suffer instead of the person who originally made you so unhappy.

● **Do you feel that your life is empty without a partner?** This means that you haven't adjusted to life outside a couple. Wanting a relationship is one thing – feeling that life is purposeless without it is another. If you start a relationship because you hate being alone you risk developing a relationship along the lines of one of the less healthy dependency patterns, which is not a good start. Waiting until you have expanded your life to become meaningful and satisfying allows you to choose a partner for the best reasons – because you like and love him or her, not out of need or fear.

● **Do you idealise the past relationship and want to re-create it?** This means that you haven't come to terms with what went wrong in the relationship, and why it didn't work. If you want to re-create it, then you have not distanced yourself realistically from it. The danger is that you do not see potential partners as individuals, but as replacements – therefore you are not prepared to work at creating a unique relationship between the two of you. You expect your new partner to slot into your vision. Either you do choose someone very similar – and so the same problems occur again, or you behave to your new partner as if he or she were the same as the last one, which creates a different set of problems.

This was the case with Ian, whose marriage had broken up when his son was three. He was desperate to find a replacement family: not just a woman he could love, but one who had a small boy, so that his life could continue on the same lines as before. He pursued women with children, without any concern for what the individual woman was like. His attitude was, 'Ah well, she might do.' He never thought about whether he was right for the other person, or what he would offer to a relationship.

The counsellor who tried unsuccessfully to help him change his attitude says, 'In an extreme way he was demonstrating what some other people I see do – trying to re-create the ideal of being married – but without thinking that being married has anything to do with you as a person. Marriage, they believe, is something that you "have" or "do".'

## Falling in love on the rebound

While it is sensible to wait before forming a serious relationship, it is true, unfortunately, that love is not sensible! You might find yourself falling in love with someone when you are well aware that you are not really ready. Relationships formed on the rebound can work if you are aware of the problems, as outlined in this chapter, and are prepared to address them. Although the next chapter is aimed at couples who have waited until they were properly over their past relationships to start new ones, the advice contained within it can also help you if you have fallen in love on the rebound.

# 8

# STARTING WELL

There comes a moment in a new relationship when you know that it is going to be serious. For some people this happens very quickly, for others it dawns more slowly, perhaps over months. This is usually the time when you are talking about moving in together, or getting married.

It is at this point that you can lay the foundations for a relationship that has lasting power, and which will be a healthy and positive experience for both of you. This partly means looking at what you both want for the future, and in doing so finding ways to deal with differences of opinion and expectations which might otherwise create problems between you later.

The best time to confront potential difficulties is when you are in love, and feeling very good about yourselves and each other. What most people do at this stage, however, is enjoy the good feelings and the passion, ignoring anything that might get in the way of the sheer intoxication and bliss of having found someone to love. Later, when some of this ecstasy wears off, the reality of living together can reveal difficulties. Even then, some people continue to ignore irritations and disappointments, in the hope that they will go away. It is the experience of counsellors, however, that when a relationship reaches crisis point – sometimes years after the couple first met – the causes can often be traced to ignored and unresolved problems that were apparent from the very beginning.

This is the case with all relationships. When it is a second (or third or subsequent) serious relationship, it becomes particularly important to look at these issues, to save yourself the heartbreak and disappointment that will follow if they are ignored once again.

One counsellor, representing the views of many colleagues, says, 'I wish couples would come to see us and say, "We are having this relationship and we want to get together, but we recognise that because there have been problems in earlier relationships we know we need to sort ourselves out." Instead people seem to think, "Second relationship! It's going to be fine!" They leap into it, and perhaps we see them five years down the line, when the problems have emerged and become entrenched, and there is a lot of unhappiness to unravel.'

Counsellors are seeing more and more people who are on a second marriage or subsequent serious relationship, which has encountered difficulties; only then have they realised that they are repeating patterns and problems from the past.

When the first major relationship goes wrong you can think that it was bad luck, or perhaps the other person's fault. The counsellor says, 'When couples come who have been involved seriously before, I ask whether they had counselling during earlier relationships. They usually say no. When we begin to work on the problems they often say with surprise, "That was an issue in my first marriage, too!" Instead of trying to sort it out the first time they've hoped that it won't happen again. So, as a counsellor, you've got a double dose – you're not only trying to sort out the hurt and disappointment in the current relationship, you're also dealing with resolving the problems in earlier ones.'

So what is it that counselling can do at the start of a relationship – and can you do it yourself?

A counsellor would prompt you both to talk fully about yourselves – your past relationships and, even further back, your childhood. You would both hear each other explain the experiences that have formed you to date, and thereby learn what your expectations are, where you are especially vulnerable, and what aspects of being in a relationship you find difficult. This process requires honesty and is painful at times, but it brings you close in a very special way. You can learn things about each other that you never knew, sometimes even things you wished to hide, but in doing so you create an intimate understanding and are able to build a picture of what difficulties you are likely to encounter together, and decide on strategies for coping with them.

It is possible to attempt to do this for yourself. If it becomes difficult or painful, then it is wise to consider continuing the process with a counsellor.

## Getting to know you

Many of the quizzes and tasks in this book are good starting points for getting to know each other in more depth than would otherwise be the case. Even if you have already done them for yourself, it is worth redoing them with your new partner, and discussing the issues that are raised. The most helpful ones for this process are the quiz *Growing Up* (page 56) and the tasks *It stopped being funny* (page 57), *Showing love* (page 60), *Cross purposes* (page 63), *The dark side* (page 65), all in Chapter Three, and the section on 'asking' in the same chapter – *The plate of biscuits* (page 66). Also in Chapter Three, you should both look again at the relationship patterns (starting page 69), and discuss which ones correspond most closely to your own experiences. In Chapter Five, the best tasks to do together are *My life* (page 141), and *Who am I?* (page 152). Useful tasks in Chapter Six include *Men and women* (page 181), *Together* (page 182), and *Who started it?* (page 183). You should look at the section *Messages about behaviour* (page 183) in the same chapter, and do the tasks *Life messages* (page 186), *The Hit list* (page 188), and *Other people's anger* (page 192).

The conversations that these tasks open up for you can be very illuminating, and doing them at the start of your relationship can make you feel very close and sympathetic to each other. The tasks in Chapter Six, especially, are likely to reveal where your expectations of your roles in a relationship are likely to differ. This can stop misunderstandings developing later. It can also help you understand how you each cope with anger, which will help when problems arise in the future.

Another task, which was included in *The RELATE Guide to Better Relationships*, is more open-ended, but it can have exceptional results. It is adapted here:

## Task

### I want to know who you are

Make a date to talk to your partner for one hour specifically about yourselves and your feelings. Toss a coin to see who begins. Take half an hour each to talk about yourselves: what you think, feel, like or don't like, what you have been doing this week, and how it has affected you – almost as if you were talking to someone who doesn't know you at all. While each person talks, the other must be silent and listen with full attention. On the half-hour you switch roles.

During this time you should not talk about your partner or your relationship, though you can talk about your past. At the end of the hour stop the conversation and don't discuss what has been said. If you want to talk about it, make a date to do so, but not for a few days.

You might be surprised at how difficult this is – particularly to listen to your partner without interruption. You will start to feel closer if you do this regularly.

A strict rule is that you must never 'use' or twist what you have heard in these sessions during an argument. If you do so you risk losing trust and closing down communication between you.

This task sounds very straightforward, and simply reading about it gives you little idea of how intimate and liberating it is. 'Normal' conversations involve a lot of interrupting and challenging of ideas and views. Talking without interruption in this way, and listening attentively, is a completely different experience. The person doing the talking finds there is something very special about being able to expand on feelings and ideas without worrying about the other person's response. It releases you to say very personal things, and is particularly helpful for people who are not in the habit of talking about themselves. Listening with care to your partner is exciting and informative – it gives you a unique insight into your partner's individuality and separateness, but in doing so makes you feel very close.

Talking in these ways tells your partner about you and what you need and expect in a relationship – as well as what problems you have faced in the past. It also highlights areas of potential difficulties. What it also does, of course, is show you the same about your partner. While you might have developed a clear idea about your own feelings and needs, you have to take your partner's into account, or a promising relationship can fail.

This was the case with Gail. She came for counselling with her husband, John, after they had been married for three years. As far as Gail was concerned, the relationship had very suddenly gone sour. She had been happy, but John had recently closed up and she didn't know what the matter was.

Gail was thirty-eight and John was twenty-nine. It was a first marriage for both of them, but Gail had had two serious relationships before meeting John. Those relationships had taught her what she did and didn't want in marriage, and John had appeared to fulfil all her requirements.

During their first session, Gail took charge. She told the counsellor all about their 'ideal' relationship, while John sat silently, and apparently seemed to agree with everything she said. The counsellor tried to draw him out, but he shook his head shyly, and let Gail do the talking.

In the middle of the next session, as Gail was telling the counsellor what 'we' liked and didn't like, there was an extraordinary change. John suddenly put his head in his hands and started crying. He said he was feeling suffocated and controlled. Appalled, Gail just looked at him. She didn't know what she'd done to provoke the outburst. Then John got up and said, 'That's it! I've had enough. I'm never coming back to you!' Then he walked out.

John had not just walked out of the session, he also walked out of Gail's life. She came for counselling for two months after that, heartbroken about what had happened. Gail spent most of the sessions crying, she desperately wanted John back but, strangely enough, she was no longer puzzled about why he had left. The moment John had walked out, she had seen clearly what had gone wrong.

As Gail explained to the counsellor, John was a gentle, undemanding man. He was easy-going, and Gail had found it simple to mould him to her ways. This had been fine when they were newly in love, and she took care to consult his wishes. But she realised that at a certain point she had stopped considering John's thoughts and feelings and just assumed that he would do whatever she wanted. 'I never asked him how he felt about anything – just said we are doing this or that. He complied, and I expected him to.' It wasn't just their life together that Gail controlled. She told John what to wear, insisted he joined a gym to build his body, and told him to get rid of certain friends she thought were beneath him.

Gail realised that at some point there had been a subtle change in John. He became more grown-up, more confident, and occasionally he mildly remonstrated with her when she told him what to do. She ignored this. There were signs that John was feeling angry, but he never showed it openly. Nevertheless he switched to an aggressive martial art against her wishes. She even tried to 'ban' him from taking part, but he carried on anyway.

All this Gail saw, with little help or prompting from the counsellor. She felt sad and guilty, and wished she could turn the clock back. 'I created my ideal relationship, but I never stopped to think whether it was right for John as well.'

The case of Alan, which has a happier ending, shows how preliminary talking, and gaining insights into each other at an early stage, can create a strong foundation.

Alan had the good fortune to come for counselling when his marriage to Ros was breaking up. Although it did not seem fortunate at the time, what it did was help him later when he met Lauren and wanted to marry her.

Alan and Ros had been married for twenty-five years. They came for counselling because their sexual relationship had ceased and they wanted to do something about it. Alan was a defeated-looking man, who attempted a cheeky bravado to cover up his feelings of inadequacy. Ros was a domineering and forceful woman, who had ruled the roost from the start of their marriage. Alan was clearly frightened of her, and she treated him with contempt.

Although they wanted sex therapy, the counsellor thought that their general relationship needed work before they were ready. During that time, they looked closely at their childhoods and the progress of their relationship. Alan found it illuminating to connect the way he had been ignored and put down when he was a boy to the way Ros treated him – which, therefore, had seemed so natural and right. As the counselling progressed, Alan wanted to make changes in the balance of their relationship, but Ros resisted. She didn't want to continue the counselling, but Alan did. Ros said it was making him 'horrible'; he countered that it was allowing him to become more confident and less happy to put up with being tyrannised. In the end Ros gave him an ultimatum: he stopped counselling or he moved out.

Alan called Ros's bluff. He said he would continue with the counselling, and would move out if she wished. Ros crumbled at this. For a while she behaved lovingly, and was careful how she treated him. The relationship improved so much that they stopped coming for counselling.

A few months later Alan made an appointment with the counsellor. He was shrunken and crestfallen. He told her that within two weeks of counselling ending, Ros had gone back to her old ways. She had refused to re-enter counselling. He felt that if he stayed with her he would be completely crushed, and he wanted to start a life on his own. He had glimpsed his own possibilities during counselling, and he felt that, at forty-seven, this was his last chance. It took all his courage, but Alan made the break.

Alan moved away, and the counsellor heard no more for two years. Then suddenly he made an appointment again, having moved back into the area. When he arrived, he had Lauren with him. She was a widow, the same age as himself, whom he had met some months previously. Since leaving Ros and moving to another city he had been seeing another counsellor, and working on his confidence and self-esteem. Alan looked a different man. He seemed to have grown taller, he was less brash but more forceful. He and Lauren were hoping to marry.

The counsellor says, 'Alan was keen for me to meet Lauren. I felt quite touched, particularly when he told me how carefully he had set about developing this relationship.'

Alan had learned from his long period of counselling. He had gained insights into himself, and into how relationships worked. He had not wanted to go rushing blindly into something. Although he and Lauren had been instantly attracted to each other, he had set a slow pace to the progress of their relationship, so that they could work out what they each wanted. With his other counsellor Alan had made lists of his expectations, assumptions and needs in a relationship. He had drawn a diagram of two figures coming together, showing what they are bringing to a marriage and how they have to negotiate before they can make a success of it. When his relationship with Lauren showed signs of becoming serious he had shared these lists and diagrams with her, and she had responded by working on her own set.

The counsellor says, 'It was not coldly done. It was loving and fun, but in an organised kind of way. They had sorted a lot of issues out, and looked set to make a good relationship. She saw in him the person he had always been underneath. They were lovely together.'

It is inevitable that sometimes these conversations reveal that it would not be right for you to build a permanent relationship. Louise and Mark came for counselling when they were engaged to be married. They had both been married before, and were wary of taking the plunge. Problems had already arisen between them, so they were concerned to discover whether these were issues that they could successfully sort out. In fact, in the course of the conversations they had with the counsellor, they decided that some of their differences were too basic and irreconcilable for them to be able to make a success of their relationship, and they decided not to marry. They did, however, continue counselling as a couple for a while afterwards, and parted as friends.

The counsellor says, 'Although this was not the outcome they had originally hoped for, they both realised that it was better to recognise their mistake now, than to have married and lived together unhappily.'

## What about the children?

If either or both of you have children, then an important part of your discussions will involve what implications this has for your relationship. There are a number of practical and emotional details that need sorting, and these are examined in the next chapter.

## ___ BUILDING A HEALTHY RELATIONSHIP ___

If, after your discussions, you decide that your relationship does have potential, then you will want to ensure that it is healthy and satisfying for you both. The elements of a healthy relationship were looked at in Chapter Three: 'a healthy relationship is mutually sustaining'; 'a healthy relationship is healing'; 'in a healthy relationship you are both free to grow'. Now we can look at what this means in practical terms – and how you can hope to achieve a healthy relationship for yourself.

### A healthy relationship is mutually sustaining

This means that you can depend on each other, because you offer each other steadfast love. This is different from passion or sentiment – it is a love that is made up of kindness and generosity, as well as pleasure in each other's company and sexual compatibility. With this kind of love, life's difficulties are easier to bear, because you can rely on your partner for support and encouragement. When a relationship is mutually sustaining it also means that when you have problems, either of your own, or between you, you can count on each other for the commitment to work at solutions in the interests of the greater good of the relationship.

These are fine words. But, as we have seen over and over again in the cases described, many people have difficulty with intimacy – showing and receiving love – and that it is typical to avoid problems or not deal with them effectively. So what can you do about it?

## Showing and receiving love

There are a number of common difficulties in this area, which can overlap. One is that you have difficulty showing love to your partner in ordinary affectionate ways, with hugs, kisses, kind words and loving comments. This does not necessarily mean you can't be affectionate to children, other family members or friends. Neither does it mean you can't be sexual, or say 'I love you' when you are feeling passionate towards your partner, but outside those moments you are more inhibited.

Another common problem is that you find it difficult to accept love that is shown to you, or to believe that you are loved, so that you either demand constant displays of affection from your partner, or conversely, you distrust or actively discourage them.

A further common problem is that when you feel deeply for someone it frightens you. It makes you vulnerable and needy – so you fear love, and try to harden yourself against loving someone or opening yourself up to someone's love.

The reasons for these difficulties were looked at throughout Chapter Three, specifically in 'Your feelings about yourself' (page 55) and 'Love and affection' (page 58), as well as in the discussion of relationship patterns, and what causes them. It is worth reminding yourself by looking back over these sections. To restate briefly, however, it is usually the case that as a child you did not feel loved enough for one reason or another, and did not learn how to be loving.

The talking point on the next page is adapted from *The RELATE Guide to Better Relationships*. It can highlight quite quickly any problems that you have in talking about intimate feelings. It also allows you to explore the possible problems that might arise because of this.

An example of how this issue can cause problems, even when there are good, positive feelings in a relationship, is the case of Jean and Terry, a couple in their thirties, who had been married for two years.

Both of them had been married before, and Jean brought her five-year-old daughter into the marriage, to join Terry and his two teenage sons.

---
**❝** ——————————— *Talking point* ———————————

**Love is . . .**

Spend half an hour talking about love together. For five minutes one of you describe why you love the other; then it is the other's turn. After this, take it in turns to describe for five minutes what a loving relationship should be like. For the last ten minutes discuss what you both have said, and any difficulties that you can see with this.

---

When they came for counselling they were having constant terrible rows, followed by sex, when they would make up. They had a number of problems. Terry was very jealous. He would not let Jean do anything without him knowing, because he feared she might run off, as his first wife had done. He monitored her during the day at work, and would collect her each evening. Jean was finding it very difficult learning to be a mother to teenage boys, when her only experience had been looking after her little daughter. Terry had abdicated all their care to her ('Jean is your mother now') and gave her little support with them.

These were problems that could be resolved, and they both desperately wanted to resolve them. They declared that they loved each other very much. The main difficulty was that Terry's jealousy was symptomatic of his problem with showing and receiving love. From the age of seven he had been pushed to be a 'little man' and had received little affection. He supposed he wasn't loveable, and therefore constantly feared that Jean would leave him. He couldn't show affection to Jean or his children, because he had no memories of being treated lovingly as a child.

The only time Terry was able to show his feelings for Jean was when they made love, particularly after a fight. The counsellor was able to draw their attention to the fact that perhaps this was why they argued rather than tried to resolve their problems. Terry was also able to tell the counsellor that he loved Jean very much, but found it harder to tell her to her face. The counsellor set them tasks to show each other affection more often. She also helped Jean see that her habit of threatening to leave Terry when she was upset or angry was the worst thing she could possibly do. She never meant it, but it made him even more insecure and jealous.

By the end of the counselling their relationship had improved, and they could see that there was a way of living together without so many rows. They were talking more about their problems, and Terry was beginning to develop the habit of seeking and showing affection at all times, rather than only through sex.

The tasks that Terry and Jean were set were uniquely tailored to their personalities and their relationship. But some of them would have boiled down to developing new habits of behaviour – making time to sit together and cuddle without expecting it to lead on to sex, for instance, or making sure that they kissed and showed affection when saying goodbye and hello. They might have been asked to make a point of saying loving and kind things when it occurred to them, to hold hands and so on. These relatively simple actions can make a lot of difference to the general atmosphere of a relationship. People like Terry, who might find them awkward at first, eventually find them more natural, and appreciate the way they feel more secure when love is more open. Their partners' pleasure in the changes, and the resulting warmth, also help them to keep up the new habits.

If your relationship misses these elements because you are unused to showing love, you can make a pact to try these new ways of behaving with your partner. This talking point, below, from *The RELATE Guide to Better Relationships* can also help you to focus on the issue.

❛ ——————— *Talking point* ———————

## Your relationship bank account

It is useful to think about your relationship as a bank account, into which you pay in and take out. When things are going well for you and you are acting towards each other in ways that are loving, you are making 'deposits' that keep the account healthy. When matters are going wrong or you are rowing a lot you are drawing on the good feelings that are there. When the account is empty you begin to run into real trouble.

But, as with a bank account, you can make the effort to 'pay in' when things are not easy for you. Any little loving gestures or words you use with your loved one can help to build up the account, even during bad times. Making a positive effort to make time to talk, listen, have fun together, or to do something kind or generous for each other keeps something in the account to tide you over rocky patches. Discuss this with your partner – how can you do this for each other?

❜

Another example of difficulties with showing and receiving love – and how two people can create problems for themselves because their needs are different – is the case of Rebecca and Gavin, a couple in their fifties. They had both been married before, and had grown-up children from their first marriages. Rebecca taught infant-school children, and Gavin was a solicitor. When they came for counselling they had been married for five years, and felt themselves to be drifting apart. They were encouraged to talk more together about their feelings, which Gavin found hard initially, but he soon discovered it had great benefits for him. They were much closer together by the time they finished their six sessions of counselling.

However, three months later Rebecca returned on her own. They had continued to talk, and things were much better, but she was frustrated. She said, 'I'm asking for hugs and laughs and all he wants to do is talk it out.' She felt that there was a 'child' inside her who was not being satisfied by the relationship.

The counsellor helped Rebecca go back in her mind to childhood, and explore the feelings of the real child she was then. It turned out that Rebecca had been a 'mistake'. Her mother was in her forties when Rebecca was born, and through the early part of Rebecca's childhood went through a difficult menopause. Her older brother and sisters had received all their mother's love and had much happier childhoods.

While she was talking about this Rebecca became very angry. The counsellor said, 'You must be very resentful of the older ones having all the fun.' 'Yes!' Rebecca said, 'There's so much I resent!' The counsellor suggested that Rebecca make a list of everything she resented about the past. It was very long. She resented not being allowed to have a pet (as the others did); she resented never being read bedtime stories; she resented being told to go out and play when there was no one to play with, and so on.

The miraculous thing from Rebecca's point of view (though unsurprising to the counsellor) was that writing the list made a substantial change in her feelings. She was able to say, 'That was then! I'm not a child anymore, and I'm not deprived!' She realised that unconsciously she was putting her resentments from the past on to Gavin, as if he could somehow make up for what she had missed as a child. She had demanded affection from him angrily and sulkily, and he had been bewildered and put off by this. The exercise helped her express her needs more clearly to Gavin – to explain why she needed the hugs and the laughs – and he was able to respond in the way she wanted because he now understood what it was all about. Rebecca was, in turn, able to be sympathetic to Gavin's need to sort things out by talking about them.

The task on page 223, from *The RELATE Guide to Better*

*Relationships*, can help if you find yourself in a similar situation to Gavin and Rebecca – when you are 'missing' each other's individual preferences when it comes to showing love.

---

**!** ================ *Task* ================

### It makes me feel loved

Which actions or words make you feel loved and special to your partner? They can be things that your partner does, used to do, or you would like your partner to do.

Make a list of these. Give your lists to each other and discuss which you will find easy and which difficult. Keep each other's lists and try to find occasions to do what your partner would like. **!**

---

For some people the trauma of unhappy childhoods makes it hard for them to recover completely, or truly become at ease with loving intimacy. Recognising that this is so, however, is helpful in itself, and you can find ways of dealing with it.

This was the case with Kate and Robert. They arrived for counselling wanting to split up, but felt that they should give themselves one last chance for the sake of their daughter. They were cold to each other, and had many unpleasant rows. Robert had been married before, but it was a first marriage for Kate.

The counselling was slow and difficult. Both had had a very difficult time as children, and were reluctant to talk about it. Kate had been brought up to feel rotten and useless, and she carried a burden of guilt about all the 'sins' she was supposed to have committed as a child. She thought it was quite right that she hadn't been loved. She was a very attractive woman, but she didn't believe it. Robert certainly never told her that she was, and her feelings about herself meant that she had gone off sex – she couldn't bear Robert to see her naked.

Robert was similarly scarred by his childhood. If anything, he felt worse about himself than Kate did about herself. He had no idea how to relate to a woman.

Counselling was the first time that they were able to talk about the misery and deprivations they had suffered as children. They both came to understand how needy they were – they wanted love, but didn't know how to show it. The cause of their rows, which often seemed inexplicable, was a deep disappointment that they were not getting the love they had never known, but yearned for.

Slowly their relationship began to improve with these insights, and they decided to stay together. They learned to offer each other more support and say nice things to each other, and they built up to becoming more affectionate generally, but, the counsellor says, 'With that level of childhood misery it is rather as if their capacity to love has become frozen in a huge block of ice – it can take many, many years to thaw.'

Kate and Robert, in fact, found this thought reassuring and helpful. They were able to recognise when their anger at being unloved in the past was turned against each other. They developed a joke, 'That's my frozen need speaking!' And were able to stop getting themselves into unproductive rows.

They also found that sometimes one or other of them felt too tired or vulnerable to offer the affection that the other needed. In these cases they learned to say, 'I can't manage this at the moment, let me off for a while, will you?' This was a marked improvement on their old habit of picking a fight when they had felt like this in the past.

Although Kate and Robert's case was severe, it does show that it is possible to create a more loving relationship, even when you find it very difficult. The following task, from *The RELATE Guide to Better Relationships* is one way of dealing with issues like this.

! ━━━━━━━━━━━━━ *Task* ━━━━━━━━━━━━

## Do it for me

Make a pact whereby every day you take it in turns to ask your partner to do something for you that you would like. It must not be something that your partner would be unwilling to do. It can be very simple: allow you to choose the evening viewing on television, do the washing up, give you some time alone, or bring you a drink in bed. It can also be something to do together: go swimming or for a walk, or weed the garden. It could be very personal, such as giving you a massage, washing your hair for you, or perhaps something sexual that you both enjoy.                                    !

This works because it helps you focus on what you want or need from your partner *now*, and because you both understand that this can also include recognition that you need looking after, or time alone. Because you both get a chance to ask for something, and have agreed that you will both honour this within certain limits, the trust and warmth between you grows.

There will always be some people who have been too damaged by past experiences to find any of these tasks or new ways of behaving helpful, however. In these cases individual counselling or therapy can be useful, and can help you learn ways to come to terms with what you have been through.

## Dealing with problems

All relationships meet problems, and when one or both of you has been involved before, problems might crop up that are connected to past relationships, as well as issues between you as a couple.

Recognising this from the beginning is a helpful start. Dealing with problems as they arise, rather than trying to pretend that they don't exist, will also help towards keeping your relationship mutually sustaining.

It is the fear that problems mean that the relationship is on the rocks that stops some people from facing them. This fear can be particularly acute when you have already suffered the painful end of one or more serious relationships.

This was the case with Mary and Alec, both of whom had been married before. They had been married for four years, and lived with Mary's son from her first marriage. Alec's children lived with his former wife. When they sought help, they were arguing a lot. They felt pulled apart, and intensely frightened that it meant they were failing at their marriage, and that they should never have married.

It quickly became clear to the counsellor that they were under great pressure. Alec's business had recently failed, and he had managed to get a low-paying job below his capabilities. He was committed to paying his ex-wife substantial maintenance, and he and Mary had to sell their house and move into a smaller one. Mary was resentful because she had put up much of the capital to buy the house in the first place. Now they were slipping behind with the mortgage payments for the new house. There were a number of other more minor irritations, to do with everyday living, the children and the division of housework; although these were less important, they were the ones they rowed about. Life was fraught, and they felt that they were losing control of everything, especially their relationship.

What counselling enabled them to see was that although they had many problems, the important ones were *external* issues, outside their relationship. But instead of tackling the problems together they were fighting each other on the minor matters – thereby not only making themselves unhappy, but weakening their otherwise good marriage.

Once they recognised this, they spent very little time in counselling looking at the state of their relationship, or further back at earlier relationships and childhood. Instead they talked about tackling the problems. Money was a problem, so they asked themselves what they were going to do about it. They drew up an action plan and became a partnership again. They learned to talk through all their problems, and take responsibility for their own feelings rather than blaming each other.

Once they were focused on the big issues that were causing them so much strain, they were able to put the smaller issues into perspective. For instance, they had argued a lot because Mary was on a diet and only bought low-fat products. Alec said he felt deprived – he wasn't on a diet, why couldn't he have the food he wanted? As their relationship improved this ceased to be an issue, and Alec was able to see that he could buy himself any food he wanted, but keep it away from Mary in deference to her diet. Similarly, Mary would become irritated when Alec would be a 'know-all' about something, keeping on about it until he had her agreement, which she would often withhold because he angered her. She became able to understand that Alec's confidence was suffering since his business went bust, and it was one way of making himself feel better. Once it stopped bothering Mary, Alec seemed to have less need to prove that he was right.

These are normal tensions in a relationship, and Mary and Alec were able to deal with them because they had stopped ignoring the larger problems that were overshadowing their life together.

If problems are ignored they are likely to become more serious, even those that started out as minor irritations. Chapter One offers some advice for problems in relationships that have reached crisis point, and it is worth looking back at this to see ways of handling the emotions and the issues raised. For a more comprehensive look at dealing with all the normal problems that arise over time in relationships it is best to read *The RELATE Guide to Better Relationships*.

## A healthy relationship is healing

When a relationship is healing, on one level it means that through loving each other you feel better about yourselves. Because your partner values you – and shows you that this is so – you experience yourself differently and are able to gain confidence. This allows you to be more honest and open about yourself, not fearing that your partner will be put off by aspects of yourself that you wish were different. This trust is built over time, a result of behaving towards each other with consideration and respect, and showing that you *like* each other, as well as love each other.

On another level, which is particularly relevant to second or subsequent relationships, the 'healing' involves soothing wounds from past relationships. Through a loving understanding of what happened in the past, you can learn to do things differently in your own relationship, and also take into account difficulties that either of you might have in doing this.

Being prepared to look at past relationships together is essential if you want this relationship to be healthy. If you don't, then unresolved issues and old hurts from the past can start to affect your current relationship – without you understanding why.

Some people are very resistant to looking back. They don't want to open old wounds by re-living past mistakes and misery. But avoiding doing this doesn't blank out the past. As one counsellor says, 'People mentally shut the door on a past relationship and lock it. But they can't move on in the new relationship by blocking off the past. They can only move forward by working through the old stuff. All the old emotions come bubbling underneath that door, anyway.'

Another reason for avoiding talking about past relationships, or the more distant past of childhood, is that some people believe that nothing will ever change. Because something traumatic or difficult happened, they believe that their behaviour will be forever marked by it, and there is nothing to be done about it. Fortunately this is not true either. Talking about the past doesn't change what happened, but it can help you formulate ways to act differently in the future, and it also gives your partner the insight and understanding to help you do so.

An example of a couple whose relationship was handicapped by issues from the past is the case of Michelle and Frank. They were both divorced when they met. Michelle had been on her own for four years, successfully bringing up her two sons. Her first marriage had been disastrous, and she had left her husband.

Frank's marriage had ended acrimoniously. It had been tempestuous and painful, and it still hurt him to think about it. He never talked about what went on, but focused on his anger at the way his wife was bringing up their two daughters, and felt that she was turning them against him.

Michelle and Frank were having a lot of problems, most of which were connected to these past relationships. Because Frank had blocked his own marriage out of his mind, he wanted Michelle to do the same with her first marriage. He couldn't bear her ex-husband's name to be mentioned and wanted Michelle to get rid of every stick of furniture and memento of the past. Understandably these strictures made Michelle angry. She needed to talk about their father to her children, and her old things meant a lot to her. Frank said, 'If you love me you will do as I say.' Michelle saw this as unreasonable. She felt that she showed him in every other way that she loved him, but he seemed to discount this.

Their pattern was for the tension to build up until they had huge rows. Frank would threaten to leave, and then Michelle would weep and beg him not to go. Her tears made it worse and he would leave for a few days.

During counselling they looked at why all this was happening albeit very reluctantly. Neither of them wanted to confront the past, but it was clear that their problems would continue to escalate until they did.

One of the things they uncovered was that Frank's first wife had used tears as a weapon, and as a way of manipulating him. Consequently, whenever Michelle cried he became angry and defensive and backed away from her. Michelle was an emotional woman, who had always released her emotions with a burst of tears. What she needed was to be held and reassured, and then she would feel better. Frank's reaction frightened her and made her feel unloved. Once they both understood their different reactions, however, things improved. Frank knew that Michelle was not 'being like his ex-wife', and became able to hold her hand and show some support when she cried. Michelle understood Frank's difficulty with her tears, and didn't take it so personally that he couldn't cuddle and baby her in the way she wished. Michelle also learned that she could control her tears. When they had a row, she saw that it made things worse when she cried. Instead of begging him not to leave when he threatened to do so, Michelle found that it was more helpful to say, 'I don't want you to go, but I will understand if you decide to.' When she said this, Frank, in fact, would stay.

Because Michelle was encouraged to talk about her relationship with her ex-husband in counselling – which Frank had never allowed her to do – he also came to see that she was not yearning for the past. Her attachment to her furniture and other things was because she liked them – not because they reminded her of her first marriage. He stopped asking her to sell them, and they compromised for the time being by putting them into storage, with the commitment to think about them again at a later date.

The counsellor says, 'They are both fiery people, and they will probably always have a stormy relationship, yet there is a lot of love and commitment there. Counselling helped them see where the past was inappropriately intruding, and they understood each other better. Now when they have disagreements they are not fighting the ghosts of their ex-partners.'

Bad experiences in the past can lead you to transfer fears and negative expectations on to your new partner – and they can also lead you to ignore whatever good there was in previous relationships, which could be usefully imported into the new one.

Counselling helped Sylvia and Phil with both these issues. Sylvia came on her own for counselling at first. She was attracted to Phil, and their relationship was promising, but she did not know whether she should marry him. Part of the problem was that she had been sexually abused as a child, and all her previous relationships had been with powerful and violent men whom she had feared, but with whom she had had good sexual relationships. Phil seemed very different. He was quiet and kind, but she didn't know whether she could trust him – weren't all men the same at heart? He was also quite inexperienced sexually, and their love-making, which he took charge of, was disappointing and unimaginative.

The counsellor helped Sylvia work through her grief and anger over the sexual abuse, and to see that she was feeling guilty about it needlessly. They also worked through her anger towards the men she had been involved with in the past. Consequently, Sylvia's confidence and self-esteem rose. At that point Phil was invited to join counselling.

The counsellor encouraged Sylvia to tell Phil about what had happened in the past. Sylvia had expected him to be appalled. Instead, she was delighted at the understanding and support that he gave her. In the interests of hiding her past, Sylvia had also hidden her greater sexual knowledge, because she thought it made her seem cheap. Liberated by the new openness between them, Sylvia became able to tell Phil what she did and didn't like sexually. She took the lead, and began to teach Phil how their love-making could be improved for both of them. Sylvia was so much 'healed' that they went on to marry, and kept in touch with the counsellor, telling her when they had their first baby.

These cases show how helpful it can be for your new relationship to confront the past, and how healing it can be. You can talk to your partner in an informal way about earlier relationships – perhaps not all in one go, but in a conversation that continues over time. If you would like to do so in a more structured way, the talking point over the page can be helpful.

These conversations can help you home in on the aspects of past relationships that caused you problems, and therefore point to where you are most likely to be sensitive in the future. You can continue by discussing how you are both going to deal with similar situations in your current relationship.

If you find these conversations too difficult or painful – because it upsets you to think about the past, or you become angry and jealous when talking about your partner's earlier relationships – it is worth considering counselling. With a counsellor present it can be easier to

❛ ——————— *Talking point* ———————

**Healing the past**

Take it in turns to discuss your past relationships in the following categories:

● What upset me most in past relationships. You can talk about incidents or ways of behaving.

● How I reacted to this. Explain how you coped with your feelings, and how you behaved in response.

● What frightened me most in past relationships. You can talk about things that happened, or fears you harboured unconnected to events (such as your partner leaving you or dying).

● How I reacted to this. How did your fears lead you to behave – was it helpful or not?

● What made me most angry in past relationships. Talk about events or behaviour patterns that made you angry.

● How I reacted to this. How did you handle your anger – did you show it or hold it in?

❜

talk about anything distressing, and the counsellor will help you deal with the emotions that arise.

*In a healthy relationship you are both free to grow*

A consequence of doing the tasks suggested in this chapter is that they not only make you feel closer and more intimate, they also highlight your differences. You learn about your different experiences, your different ways of coping with things, and the fact that you might view things differently, and feel differently about various issues. When you can see and respect the individuality of your partner, you are well-placed to understand that your very differences and separateness can be a source of strength for your relationship in the future.

Being 'free to grow' means that you both recognise that you will change over time, and both have a need to develop within the safety of your loving relationship. This makes for a flexible relationship, and it is flexibility that helps a relationship survive even difficult patches. These are some considerations to bear in mind for the future:

● **Keep talking.** There never comes a time when you know your partner completely – although many people act as if this is the case. They might talk intensely and openly at the beginning of a relationship, but after a while they don't bother. Conversations become limited to the practical side of life, and virtually cease in any more important way.

Making time for each other continues to be essential. If you don't keep in touch with your partner's changing feelings, ideas and needs, there comes a point when you are not relating to the real person but to a memory. Couples with the strongest relationships know each other intimately because they continue to talk. This gives the relationship flexibility because they are automatically making little shifts and changes in the way they relate, to accommodate the subtle changes in each other. When you don't talk, there is likely to come a point, years down the line, when a crisis brings home to you that fact that your partner has been changing, unnoticed by you, and your relationship no longer fits with the new people you have become.

● **Be prepared to support and be supported.** One of the striking features of the unbalanced relationships, as described in Chapter Three, is that they are rarely mutually supportive. One person takes charge, or looks after the other – but the favour is not returned. However, in life we all have our vulnerable moments – times of crisis and change when we are no longer able to cope as well as we might have previously. These times often herald a period of growth, when we learn new things about ourselves, and develop differently.

A flexible relationship supports this growth, because the partners take it in turns to look after each other at difficult moments. You take on the caring, 'parental' role when your partner is having a hard time, secure in the knowledge that he or she will be there for you in the future when you have difficulties. Sometimes, of course, you have to weather a crisis together. You are both suffering and have to make difficult decisions, being both loving and supportive when you both feel low. Although this is hard, it is easier for people who have learned that sometimes they can cope and sometimes they can't. You become able to share the load, rather than fight because one of you wants the other to take charge.

● **Respect separate interests and friends.** You are two different people, and this means that there might well be activities and friends that one of you likes more than the other. A relationship can be enriched by these separate interests.

Some people feel threatened by the knowledge that their partners can find satisfaction in things outside the relationship, such as hobbies, interests and other friends. Either they try to stop their partners from doing these things and seeing other people, or they behave jealously and sulkily when they won't.

Both of these ways of behaving are counter-productive. They cause bad feelings, and the underlying message is that you feel you 'own' your partner, who must only behave in ways acceptable to you.

Being generous in your appreciation of your partner's separate needs instead promotes greater warmth and intimacy – even when doing this means time spent apart. Similarly, paying attention to your own separate interests and friends can make you feel closer to your partner – because you do not feel the fear that accompanies believing that you have to rely on him or her for all your pleasures.

Talking together about your separate lives keeps the relationship fresh and stimulating. As each of you grows you have more to offer each other.

● **Balance time together and time apart.** All of these elements require a delicate balancing act, and an understanding of each other's needs and moods as they change. Sometimes you might need to spend more time together, at other times you are happy to pursue more separate lives. This requires the flexiblity and sensitivity which become second nature to you as you continue to talk and learn about each other over the years.

# 9

# THE FAMILY NETWORK

When either of you already have children it adds an extra dimension to your new relationship. You have to consider the impact the children will have on your relationship, and also how it will affect them. There are dozens of practical and emotional issues that arise, which need to be thought about and negotiated. However strong, loving and healthy the relationship between you is, whether it will be successful or not often depends on how you handle these issues.

There is no such thing as a typical step-family. The possible combinations are endless. At its simplest, you might be a part-time step-family – one of you has a child from a previous relationship who lives with the other parent, and who comes to stay with you for arranged visits. Contrast this with another possibility: both of you have children from a previous relationship; both of your ex-partners are married again to people who also have children, making three inter-related couples with children and step-children, and all of you have added to your families with children from the new union! The practical, financial and logistical problems are daunting; for instance, which children are staying with whom, when? There could be six sets of grandparents in this situation, all vying for some time over Christmas. An added complication is that these relationships might not survive, so new partners can be added to the growing family network over the years.

Entire books have been written on the subject. This chapter can only hope to give an overview – point out matters to consider, and offer some advice. You should read it in conjunction with Chapter Four, *Your Children*, as much of that advice is relevant here. At the back of the book there are suggested publications and organisations that can give further help.

## THE STEP-FAMILY

A step-family is an instant family, but that does not mean it instantly works. When a couple without children get together there is a period of adjustment to each other's ways. When you add children to the equation this is less easy. *All* of you are adjusting to each other, and it is not surprising that this causes tension.

Learning to live together takes time. It is estimated that it takes at least two years for a step-family to work out ways of living together and settle into feeling like a united family. Some relationships don't survive this two-year settling-in period. The difficulties that arise can break up a relationship, even one that was good and loving.

A fairly typical case is that of Anne and Mike, who came for counselling after they had been married for eighteen months. Anne brought four daughters from her first marriage, and Mike had the custody of his two sons. His children were having trouble accepting Anne as a mother-figure, and were feeling hurt because their own mother had a new boyfriend and didn't want to see them as much.

Mike was grappling with learning how to be a father to girls, when his only previous experience was as a father to boys, and they were having to deal with the hostility of Anne's first husband, who resented another man seeing more of his children than he did. The counsellor says, 'It really wasn't working. They hadn't thought about what it would mean. They had fallen in love and thought that would be enough to see them through any difficulty.'

Even the nicest children in the world are going to have problems when they are confused and unhappy about what is happening to them. They are not only having to adjust to a new parent in the home, they are also maintaining their relationship with their absent, natural parent, and dealing with conflicting loyalties and loss. If the children are not happy, it is hard for you, as a couple, to be happy.

One thing that helps is to have someone to talk to who is not intimately involved. Ideally, it should be a close friend or a counsellor. Of course you will also need to talk to your partner. But on occasions when you are angry and upset and just want to let off steam, your partner is not necessarily the best person. When the issue is children the adults involved usually feel very torn.

## Discussing the implications of the step-family

Before you decide to marry or move in together, you should discuss together how the children are going to affect your relationship, and how you are going to cope with the practical concerns. One way to do this is to read this chapter together, and discuss it section by section, relating it to your own situation.

Don't ignore the issues that disturb you when doing this. It is better to sort them out before you take an important step, rather than hope that they will sort themselves out later.

You should agree from the start what the step-parent's role is going to be. This might change over time, but it should be clearly defined at the beginning. For instance, how intimately concerned is he or she going to be in the care and disciplining of the children? If the step-parent has no children of his or her own, this will be somewhat theoretical, because he or she won't have the practical experience to know what is involved.

This role needs to be discussed to avoid different assumptions about what will happen. For instance, Clarissa eventually decided not to marry Gus because of this very issue. She had no children of her own, and had moved in to live with Gus prior to their marriage.

Gus's two children, aged nine and five, came to stay with them every weekend, and Gus automatically expected Clarissa to be their 'mum'. In fact, he used to leave her alone with them for much of the time while he went off with his mates to play football and go to the pub.

Clarissa was not only completely inexperienced when it came to looking after children, she also found herself facing two hostile little ones, who resented her and played up. When Gus returned to find Clarissa furious and upset, he would take the children's side.

The counsellor, from whom Clarissa sought help when she was wondering whether to marry Gus, says, 'They never negotiated what the situation would be. Gus's expectations were unreasonable in the circumstances, though if they'd talked about it before, Clarissa might not have felt so bad.'

In the event, it had created such bad feeling between them that Clarissa decided not to marry Gus, and moved out.

● **Financial responsibilities.** This is also the stage to look at the financial implications of the children. The step-parent needs to know how much financial responsibility he or she will have to bear – for instance, in contributing to the household where the children live with the other parent, or in paying for their care at home. He or she also needs to know whether this responsibility also includes a say in how the money is spent.

## Making introductions

Ideally, the step-parent should meet the children regularly before you move in together, so that there is a gradual, getting-to-know-you period.

Don't be over-concerned that the children should like the step-parent at this stage. It is better to behave normally and in a pleasantly friendly way rather than to 'buy' the children's affection with special attention and treats. Let the children become used to the new person as they would any other adult.

Older children and teenagers are likely to be very wary of the new partner, and will prefer not to be rushed into a special relationship. They need to be allowed to make up their minds in their own time. It is best for children of all ages if they have had time to become accustomed to the new partner before he or she becomes an official step-parent.

When you know that your relationship is going to become permanent, it is worth talking to the children about what this means. The natural parent can reassure the children that the love between them is not going to change. The step-parent can let the children know that he or she is not planning to 'steal' the natural parent by saying, for example, 'I appreciate that your relationship with your father is important, and so is mine.'

## When you marry or move in together

This signals that the relationship is serious. Whether the children live with you or not, they are likely to regard the situation and the step-parent in a new way.

When your relationship becomes serious it often brings home to the children that the relationship between their parents is truly over. You might have thought that they had come to terms with this before, but they have often been secretly hoping that you would get back together. Consequently, they are likely to be uspet and angry all over again. This also sometimes means that they take against a step-parent whom they had previously liked.

You should prepare yourself, therefore, for a difficult period with the children as they make this new adjustment. Don't be down-hearted if your children now feel less positive about your partner. If they previously had a good relationship, then it will improve again when everyone settles down.

If the step-parent moves in with you and the children, life is likely to be even more fraught for a while. You, of course, are gaining a new and much loved partner, but it is not quite such a happy occasion for the children. A new adult is in the home, taking your attention. They have to put up with this new adult whether they like it or not, and older children particularly might not be sure they like it at all.

One of the difficulties is that when the step-parent was a visitor, he or she probably had little say over the children's behaviour. Now that the step-parent is a fixture in the home this is likely to change – and the children can resent this. That is why house rules and a clear line on discipline is important (see page 240).

It is useful to have fresh discussions with the children and with your partner during this time. The step-parent, used to having you on your own when you were dating, might now feel pushed out by the children. Your children can worry that your new preoccupation with your partner is leaving less love left over for them. Both sides need reassuring that they are no threat to each other, and occupy different places in your heart.

On the plus side, if you are happier and your home life has become more stable and pleasant because of your new relationship, the children will benefit, too. It is good for your children to see that you are loved and valued by your new partner, particularly if their other parent treated you badly. If you were a single parent previously you might be more financially secure, which is also better for the children.

## Who lives where?

As the family network changes, and new families are formed, one of the most important decisions is to do with where the children live, and how much time they spend with the absent parent. Access issues were looked at in Chapter Four, *Your Children*. Apart from saying that it is important for the children to continue to see both natural parents, there are no hard-and-fast rules about how best to organise living arrangements. Each family network has to work out what suits the adults and children concerned best, and sometimes arrangements are changed over the years.

Ideally, children should be able to see both parents freely, and spend plenty of time with the absent parent. In practice this can be more difficult: the natural parents live far apart, or the non-custodial parent does not have room to put the children up for very long, or the children's own social life and arrangements conflict with what the adults have decided. You have to juggle as best you can, and be sensitive to the changing needs of the adults and children in question.

● **Juggling two homes.** One home is likely to be the children's main base, and sorting out the living arrangements will be a priority. It is often less well sorted out in the household that the children visit.

If the children are going to feel secure and welcome, however, then attention should be paid to this. If space permits, they should have their own rooms, so that they feel at home. If not, you should try to make a corner that they know is their own: a toy box that no one else touches, and their own drawer with spare sets of clothes and nightwear. Similarly, their own mug, and their toothbrush in the bathroom, helps them feel they have a stake in this household.

When they arrive for their visit they should be allowed to settle in at their own pace, rather than be bombarded with questions and attention. Children are more relaxed when they are treated normally, and not as special visitors.

When lots of children are involved, it can become more difficult to balance the arrangements. When the sets of families are seriously at war, the arrival and departure of the children can be very emotional and a major upheaval. If the difficulties created are too great, then you sometimes need to think again.

For instance, Debbie and Tim had five children from their previous marriages. Both their partners had married again, and it was agreed that the children's time was to be split evenly between the families. The children spent half the week with each natural parent, and alternate weekends with one family or another. Because there were two different sets of children they always seemed to be going in different directions at different times. The constant adapting to different ways of living was putting a strain on the children, and they were often disruptive when they arrived back.

Debbie and Tim found it so stressful that they felt they couldn't go on with the arrangement. They never felt that they had time to settle down as a family. They called a conference with the other parents and said that they thought the children should choose to live at one place or the other. Once they had decided, the children could go to the other parent for a holiday, but otherwise would stay put. The other two couples agreed, and so did the children: three elected to stay with Debbie and Tim, and the other two chose to stay with their other natural parent. What Debbie and Tim were left with was a unit that considered itself a family, and they felt that decisions and ways of behaving were not going to be interfered with by anyone else.

## Being a step-parent

Being a step-parent is difficult. You haven't chosen the children. You have fallen in love with your partner, but you do not necessarily feel so positively about the children, or they about you. If you haven't had children of your own, it can be bewildering to step into a family and to learn how to cope with children of different ages. If you have children of your own, and are parted from them, you can feel torn about the fact that your daily contact is with children who are not yours. If you also have your own children with you, then it can be difficult playing fair by dividing attention and care between all the children – and extra children can make you feel harrassed. Whatever the situation, it is always hard fitting into a ready-made family at the same time as consolidating a new relationship.

Being a part-time step-parent also has its problems. You can feel that you don't have the chance to become part of the children's lives because they don't live with you all the time, while having to care for them when you do see them. If you and your partner work, you can feel annoyed that weekends are taken up with looking after step-children, when you would prefer to have time alone with your partner. Sometimes the children, too, will be reluctant to come to stay for one reason or another. You have to cope with your own resentment, at the same time as trying to make things pleasant for them. If you have your own children living with you, it can be disruptive when your step-children come to stay.

While these annoyances won't go away, it is helpful to be very clear about what is expected of everyone in this situation.

● **House rules.** It is worth agreeing on what the house rules are to be before you move in together. These can be modified later, as new things occur to you, and as the children grow older. But don't expect to muddle through without rules. If you try this, the situation is likely to arise in which the natural parent says one thing, contradicted by the step-parent who says another. Children are quick to spot this, and exploit it by playing you off against one another.

The rules should cover what is expected in daily living together. Bedtimes, mealtimes, standards of behaviour, acceptable noise-levels, discipline, how money is handled, and so on. You won't be able to cover all the issues before you start living together as a family, but you can draw up broad guidelines. Later, as issues crop up on which there are different opinions, you can discuss and agree how you are going to handle them.

Even young children can be included in some of these discussions, and all children tend to be more amenable when they have been involved in drawing up the rules and know why they have been made. This is particularly essential for the step-parent, who is likely to be unpopular with the children when he or she takes charge of discipline or has to tell a child off. When this is part of enforcing agreed rules of behaviour, the natural parent will offer appropriate back-up, and the two of you can stand united.

Even when the children grumble about rules – which might be different in one household to what they are in the other – ultimately they prefer to know where they stand and appreciate firmness. It is not good for you as a couple to fall out over ways of coping with the children, and it does them no good either. Children feel insecure when they know that they can manipulate the adults and set them against each other. Children who argue with the rules can be told simply, 'This is the way we live here.'

This is a continuing process. As the children grow older, rules need to be changed, and new rules added. Talking about it continues to be important. Small misunderstandings ('Dad said I could', 'Well, he didn't say that to me!') can grow into large, acrimonious issues if they are not addressed.

● **Discipline.** You also need to agree on how you discipline the children. It is usually best if the natural parent and the step-parent are equally responsible for discipline. If it is just left up to the natural parent the children are prompted to believe they can misbehave with the step-parent. Similarly, it is hard on everyone to expect the step-parent to take charge of all the disciplining from the beginning. The children will resent this, and the step-parent will feel uncomfortable if placed in the role of the 'bad' parent in the children's eyes.

You might prefer to agree on a limit to what the step-parent is allowed to do. For instance, you might decide that the step-parent does not smack the children. Be clear to each other about this. It is not a good idea to row about it in front of the children ('How dare you hit my child!').

Discipline will have to be reviewed from time to time. If new behaviour on the part of the children starts to annoy or upset the step-parent, then he or she should talk to the natural parent about how it should be handled.

Try to avoid a situation where discipline becomes a big issue. If anger is building between step-parent and step-children, the natural parent will be very torn – feeling that whichever way he or she turns will be wrong. This is another occasion when it is worth discussing as a family what can be done about it, and agreeing on acceptable ways of resolving the conflict in the interests of a happier home.

● **Decision-making with the absent parent.** When the other natural parent remains involved with the children many of the important decisions need to be arranged between the two natural parents, sometimes with suggestions from the step-parents, when there are financial or practical implications.

When the children live with you, you need to be clear about which decisions to do with the children are yours (the new couple), and which decisions are theirs (the natural parents). For instance, issues to do with education are the domain of the natural parents. Other issues that need to be sorted out include health care, diet, arranging holidays, attendance at school events, and so on. You also need to consult each other on discipline, bearing in mind the absent parent's wishes on the subject within reason. When problems arise with any of these issues, the natural parents should discuss them together if possible. You might disagree on something as fundamental as bedtimes, or the severity of discipline, which is confusing for the children. If no agreement can be reached then you might have to compromise by having separate house rules for each household, and the children should know that this is what you have decided.

There also needs to be agreement over large items of expenditure involving the children. What expensive things are allowed, and who is going to pay for them? Step-parents' feelings need to be taken into account, especially if buying something dear for the children means the step-parent going without something else that is needed.

● **Honesty.** Honesty is important in all relationships, and particularly for children who have had to deal with the break-up of their parents' relationship. There have probably been many secrets and mysteries surrounding the adults in their lives. With all the upheavals, and the new relationships being formed, children have a need and a right to know where they stand.

On one level this means respecting the children's feelings about what is happening in their lives and allowing them to express them. Some parents try to shut out the past ('This is our family now, we'll forget about the old one'.) The children need to be able to talk about things as they were, to love and talk about the absent parent, and to be quite clear about their relationship to the step-parent. It is tempting to tell children who are too young to remember that the step-parent is their 'real' mum or dad, but this is unwise. They will be shocked and upset when they find out the truth, as they eventually will. Children are quite capable of coping with the concept of natural parents and step-parents, and it won't affect their relationship with the step-parent.

It is also a good idea for the step-parent to talk frankly and openly about the difficulties of the step relationship, and encourage the children to do the same. It can be illuminating for the child to hear you say that you find it hard adjusting to the situation, and that if you are sometimes angry or upset it is because of this, not because you don't care. At an early stage in the relationship you can say, 'There will be times when we are both going to be angry with each other or jealous of each other, and that's perfectly normal.' It is a weight off the children's minds to know that you understand their mixed feelings, and that they don't have to feel guilty about them.

You should also be honest about the relationship between the two natural parents, and step-parent and the absent natural parent. You don't have to go into details of rights and wrongs, but it is perfectly acceptable to be frank and say, for example, 'Your mother and I aren't able to be friendly, but we both care about you.'

A sympathetic step-parent can play a helpful role here as the concerned adult whom children can turn to when they need to talk about issues to do with their natural parents.

● **Love.** There is often an unrealistic expectation that step-parents and step-children will love each other. Some do grow to love each other over time, but this is a bonus, and you should not think that anything is wrong if they can't love each other. Sometimes they might not even like each other very much, or go through phases when they like each other less than before.

Both step-parent and step-children need to know that loving each other is neither expected nor automatic. It's important that everyone understands that it's all right not to love or even like each other just because you are connected through the natural parent.

What you *can* expect – and should enforce – is that whatever the feelings between you all, you *behave* towards each other with consideration and respect. You don't have to like someone to be polite. Just as children are expected to behave well towards teachers, whatever their feelings for them – and, indeed, teachers are expected to treat children fairly and reasonably even if they don't like them – so step-parents and step-children need to take similar care with their own behaviour. The result of treating each other with consideration and respect can be the development of a good relationship – you like each other more, and love might follow.

Even if you and the children like each other a lot, and perhaps love each other, it is still different from the relationship between natural parents and children. What you can aim for is to be a good friend to the children – a different sort of parenting relationship than you would have with your own child. It can be valuable for the children to have a close relationship with an adult who has more of an emotional distance than parents have. Friendships like these develop over time. They can't be forced. They are built up by an accumulation of pleasant times together, honest conversations and mutual trust. Remember, it takes time for children to adjust to step-parents, and to learn that they are going to stay around and become a feature of their lives.

● **Feeling jealous of the children.** It is natural that you might also feel jealous of your partner's relationship with the children. As one counsellor, who also happens to be a step-mother says, 'There is a sense in which his children will always be more precious than you.' Parental love can be very deep and protective, and it can be hard to accept the importance of children in your partner's life.

While you can talk to your partner about this, and seek reassurance about your own importance in your partner's life, you should not set up in competition with the children, or take out your feelings of resentment on the children. This sort of behaviour backfires, as its main effect is to make your partner unhappy and thereby sours your own relationship.

This was the case with Christine and Isaac, who had only been married a year, but their marriage was being torn apart over this issue. Both had been married before. Christine was in her late forties. Her two older children had left home, but her twelve-year-old son was living with her and Isaac. Isaac, who was in his early fifties, had two grown-up children, both living independent lives.

Christine expected Isaac to accept her children, and be a father to her son. Isaac was willing to do this, and was putting the boy through private school. Christine, on the other hand, bitterly resented Isaac's children. When Isaac paid for his beloved daughter's wedding she went mad. From that moment on she wouldn't allow the young woman in the house, and she never lost an opportunity to say unpleasant things about her.

Counselling couldn't help them because Christine could see nothing wrong with her behaviour. The counsellor says, 'They gave up counselling quite quickly. They were going to stay together because Isaac didn't want to end his marriage and be on his own again at his age. Nevertheless, he was an unhappy and disappointed man who felt that he was losing his daughter.'

● **Coping with step-children's antagonism.** Some children show their anger and misery about their parents' break-up by being hostile towards the step-parent. Some children are hostile because they don't like the step-parent, or because they resent the way the step-parent is treating them, or the fact that the step-parent is so important to their natural parent. Some children get on well with the step-parent for a time, and then seem to turn against him or her. These are just some possibilities, and what lies behind the antagonism can be different in individual cases.

The first step, therefore, is to encourage the children to talk about what the matter is. If this is going to be effective, the children must know that they can say whatever their feelings are without anyone becoming angry or telling them they are wrong or bad to feel such things. Sometimes, when the children feel that you know and understand what they are feeling, it can be enough to stop the difficult behaviour, which had previously been their only way of showing you that something was the matter.

Talking won't necessarily make the feelings go away, but it is still important for the children to understand that their bad behaviour can't be allowed to continue. Again, respect their feelings. 'I don't expect you to like me and I know that you find this situation hard, but you must still be polite.' Your partner, of course, should back you up on this.

You can also say, 'We all have to live here, and this situation is making everyone unhappy, let's discuss what we can do to make it more bearable.' If the child's response is, 'It would be better if you went away!' you can say, 'That's not possible. Let's talk about things we can do.' You should be prepared, where appropriate, to modify aspects of your own behaviour, in return for the children doing the same.

If the children are playing you and your partner off against each other you also need to talk about this together. Talk first to your partner to get matters straight between you, and then include the children. If there are any genuine misunderstandings you can clear them up with everyone present. Ask the children to explain their understanding of rules or incidents that they are making difficulties about, and then clearly re-state what the real situation is. Check that they understand at the end of it.

Teenagers can present particular problems. If you are a new step-parent to teenage children they can be alarmed and disgusted at the recognition that their natural parent has a sex life. If they have offered their parent strong support over the years they can feel displaced by you. They are also at an age when they are likely to fight against any authority figures, and can resent your arrival as an extra authoritative adult. Sometimes, however, you have been a step-parent for many years before your step-children become teenagers, and you find to your horror that they are now being difficult and antagonistic.

What you must bear in mind is that *all* teenagers are difficult, and the problems that you are having are not unique to the step-parenting situation, even if that is what the teenagers concentrate on. Nevertheless, it is hard to cope with a sullen and hostile adolescent. Even natural parents find their sympathies strained, and may actively dislike their own children at such times! As one counsellor says, 'As a step-parent you have a a bit of emotional space because the children are not your own, but there are also times when you feel, "Why am I putting up with this from somebody else's child?"'

As with younger children, you should try to get to the bottom of the feelings of resentment and jealousy, and let the teenagers know that you understand their difficulties. Be frank about your own difficulties as well. Teenagers are so wrapped up in their own feelings that they often need reminding that adults suffer too. Again, after your conversations, be clear about what behaviour is acceptable in the house, and make sure that you and your partner agree on this.

   If you and your partner are experiencing great difficulties with this, and find it hard to agree on how you should handle the children, counselling can help you put it into perspective. If you do seek help, tell your children that you are doing so, and why. It is good for them to know that you are taking the problems seriously and want to sort them out. You can keep them informed while the counselling progresses.

● **Your relationship with your partner.** Thinking about your relationship with your partner can seem to be a luxury when there are step-children involved. But you will care for them better – and be happier – when you pay attention to your relationship as well. Some natural parents and step-parents become so bogged down in the details of family life that they never think of themselves, and everyone suffers as a consequence.

   This was the case with Norah and Dick, two busy social workers in their thirties, who lived together with their four children from their previous marriages and the child they had between them. As the counsellor says, 'To put it in a nutshell, they were missing each other the whole time.'

   Norah believed she must be perfect and do everything herself (as her mother, who had been a full-time housewife, had done). As well as looking after her own family, she also tended her ailing in-laws from her first marriage. She had no time for herself, and no time for Dick. On the occasions they were home at the same time, Norah would be getting on with the cleaning or involved with the children, and Dick would be catching up on DIY. They had had a brief few weeks of courting before they married, and were now entrenched in domesticity. They were both disappointed, and they took this out on each other by arguing over little things. The children were frightened by this, and the youngest one, who had been out of nappies, had now regressed to needing them again.

   Counselling was mainly centred around discussing how their unhappiness was having a bad effect on the family, and on giving them 'permission' to make time for themselves as individuals, and time as a couple. Norah, for instance, yearned for a good long soak in the bath, but, she told the counsellor, 'The moment I get in, there are two or three little bodies on the side wanting to talk, or begging to join me.' They made lists of activities they enjoyed, which they never had time for any more. They were ordinary things: for Norah it was shopping alone, or visiting an exhibition with a friend, *without* the children. She had also stopped drawing, which she used to love. Dick wanted to be able to play squash and have the occasional night out with the boys.

   They also realised that if their relationship was to improve they needed to make time for each other. The counsellor says, 'They hadn't fully appreciated how much stress it put on their relationship that they had no time together or private space. They felt guilty about leaving the children with a babysitter. I said, "If it makes you happier together and you are able to resolve your problems by talking alone and having more fun, then you have nothing to feel guilty about – it's *good* for the children."'

It wasn't easy for Norah and Dick to make more time, but once they saw that it was a priority rather than a self-indulgence, they found ways to do so by dropping other, less important things, which they used to put first. One decision they made was to hire a cleaner to visit twice a week, as they were both earning and could afford it.

Time together away from the children also gives you a chance to talk about how your new family is settling down. You can air any resentments and discuss difficulties that you are having, so that these feelings don't fester and cause greater problems.

Some couples also need 'permission' to show their love for each other in front of the children. Even children who might seem jealous and resentful of your relationship benefit from knowing that you love and value each other. It makes them feel secure. It is a sign that your relationship will last, and also shows them that adult couples can be happy and loving together. Having a cuddle, giving each other a kiss, or holding hands is all perfectly fine, so long as the children feel they get their share of loving attention, too, and so long as what you are doing in front of them is not overtly sexual.

● **Bad feeling between step-parent and absent natural parent.**
It is unsurprising that there is often a certain amount of bad feeling between the step-parent who has care of the children and the natural parent who is absent. Usually this is partly because there is bad feeling between the two natural parents.

But there are other issues, too. The natural parent is likely to feel jealous that another person is taking his or her place in looking after the children. The step-parent can feel resentful that while he or she has the daily care of the children, they still feel greater loyalty and love towards their absent natural parent. This is exacerbated by the fact that when children are involved, your partner's ex is a continuing presence in your life. It is a constant reminder that they used to love each other, and because the ex-partner continues to be involved, you are still exposed to the on-going resentments and bitternesses that result from the break-up.

All of these feelings are difficult to handle, but if you keep the welfare of the children uppermost in your mind, then you recognise that it is important to contain your resentments as far as possible.

As the step-parent this involves talking about the absent parent with respect in front of the children, even if you don't like or approve of him or her. You also need to bear in mind which issues are more appropriately dealt with by the absent parent, rather than trying to take his or her place. You have to be able to say, 'This is something that you and your mum [or dad] need to agree on.'

The absent natural parent needs to behave in similar ways. It is essential to remember that you increase your children's unhappiness if you say unpleasant things about the step-parent with whom they must live. If your child has complaints about the step-parent, similarly you can say, 'This is something you need to sort out with your step-parent and your mum [or dad].' Obviously, if an issue is important, you should be sure to discuss it with your ex-partner and the step-parent.

## WHEN BOTH PARTNERS HAVE CHILDREN

Many of the issues already covered are the same when both of you have children, though some of the problems can be magnified. From the children's point of view, this extra dimension can create different problems. For instance, a child used to being the eldest might now have a step-brother or sister who is older, and feel displaced. Similarly the baby might no longer be the youngest. An only child might find it difficult learning to share and be part of a larger family, and so on. While some children might welcome having more children around, others might dislike them, and find coping with their presence an added burden when they are already dealing with learning to live with a step-parent.

You need to be aware that these changes are likely to cause you some difficulty in adapting, and considerable upset. Respect the fact that the children might be disturbed, and give them some time to talk about it. Family conferences, in which everyone's grievances are aired, can be a useful way of bringing issues into the open and deciding on ways to tackle them.

● **Fairness and love.** When both of you have children the issue arises of how each is treated, and whether you show favouritism to your own children.

The fact is that you will almost certainly love your own children best. This is quite natural. It is also impossible to treat all children equally. Children are individuals, and even in families where the children have both natural parents living with them, the children receive different treatment according to their ages and differing personalities.

Nevertheless, you can strive to be fair in the way you treat the children, and you should be alert to one of the children feeling unhappy or hard-done-by because another child appears to be getting more treats and attention. You should aim for a situation in which the children get a turn to spend time on their own with their natural parent. You can usually incorporate this special time in ordinary daily living. For instance, one child can accompany a parent to the supermarket, and they can go on to a cafe together afterwards.

## Children between you

The time might well come when you decide to have a baby. This will have an impact on the children you share already, just as any new arrival in the family does. Some children will feel upset and displaced. The mother will naturally be less available and more tired than usual, and attention will be focused on the baby.

The problems of this situation are not very different from the problems that arise whenever older children have to deal with the arrival of a new sibling. They need to be reassured that they are still loved, yet be allowed to express their own feelings of resentment and know that they will be heard and understood. In some cases, particularly when the other children are much older, the new baby serves to unite the family. Children who feel less able to love a step-parent, can find no difficulty in loving a half-brother or sister.

If this is a first child for the step-parent, it can happen that he or she becomes less tolerant of the step-children. Perhaps the step-parent is worried about the impact of the step-children's behaviour on the new child, or is simply less prepared to give time and care to the other children. This needs careful handling. The natural parent of the first children might need to give them special time and attention – at a moment when time is at a premium, particularly if the natural parent is also the new mother! The step-parent needs to be reminded that the happiness of the household partly depends on the members within it being happy, and that includes the step-children. Everybody needs to talk together about the feelings that are connected to the arrival of the baby, and allowances should be made for how the various individuals involved feel.

## __ GRANDPARENTS AND OTHER RELATIVES __

As relationships break up and new relationships form, the wider family network of grandparents and other relatives grows. These relationships can be very important for the children, and sometimes they can be supportive and helpful for you. Undoubtedly there are also problems both practical and emotional.

It can be especially difficult and upsetting for grandparents when their children's relationships break down. They have no legal rights over their grandchildren, and cannot insist on access or continued contact, although under the Children Act they can apply for them. If you have custody of the children, and you didn't get on with your in-laws, you might see this as an opportunity to cut your ties with them. It is best for all concerned, however, if you let them continue to see their grandchildren. The children benefit from the continuity of these relationships when the rest of their life seems unstable. If the grandparents create difficulties, by talking badly about you and the step-parent in front of the children, for instance, it is best to talk to them about the problems this raises, rather than stop them seeing the children. You are in a good position to let them know what you expect, and most will abide by this in the interests of seeing their grandchildren.

Most similar problems can be dealt with by clearly explaining the situation, and by negotiation. When there are a number of people involved in the family network, for instance, someone will probably have to be disappointed about Christmas or other family occasions. Try to offer alternatives where possible – as a solution children won't mind if they celebrate Christmas more than once, for instance!

When extra children come along, and step-children are added to the family, grandparents might need reminding that in the interests of fairness these children should be remembered, too. It helps for family relations if step-children receive cards on special occasions, and token presents at Christmas. If money is limited, it is wiser for the grandparents to buy a joint family present, such as a game, so that all the children can participate.

The feelings of these other relatives need to be taken into consideration. They, too, are likely to be sad about the end of the first relationship, and fear that they will lose much by it. If you are sensitive to their feelings, you can also be firm about them being sensitive to yours, and respecting the new rules and changed circumstances of your family.

This has been a necessarily brief look at the issues that affect step-families. The problems have been emphasised, but there are joys, too. Most of the problems have solutions if you look for them, and there are always places you can turn to for help.

Second marriages, or subsequent relationships, with a number of children involved which survive are very strong. When you can work out ways of living together satisfactorily you have proved that you have the commitment and flexibility to make a good relationship, which will endure when the child-rearing years are over.

# FURTHER HELP

## ORGANISATIONS

*The British Association for Counselling,* 1 Regent Place, Rugby, CV21 2PJ. Tel 01788 578 328
An organisation that publishes a national directory of counselling services. Booklets detailing the services in your area can be obtained free from the BAC, or in your local library.

*Families Need Fathers,* 134 Curtain Road, London EC2. Tel. 020 7613 5060
Offers support for fathers separated from their children.

*Gingerbread,* 16-17 Clerkenwell Close, London EC1R 0AA. Tel. 020 7336 8183
A network of self-help groups for single parents, with a national office that offers advice on all issues affecting single parents.

*National Council for One-Parent Families,* 255 Kentish Town Road, London NW5 2LX. Tel. 020 7267 1361
Offers legal and practical advice to single parents.

*Parentline–Opus* (Organisation for Parents Under Stress), Endway House, The Endway, Hadleigh, Essex, SS7 2AN. Tel. 01702 554782
An organisation that helps parents under stress because of their children. OPUS encourages parents to help each other and gives them space to share worries and let off steam. Local Parentline–OPUS groups are run by trained parents and offer a befriending service and telephone helpline.

*Parent Network*, Room 2, Winchester House, 11 Cranmer Road, London SW9 6EJ. Tel. 020 7735 1214
A national charity that runs the Parent-Link programme, a support and education system for parents. It teaches parents to deal effectively with everyday problems such as untidiness, bad behaviour, bedtime problems, adolescence. and so on.

RELATE *National Marriage Guidance*, Herbert Gray College, Little Church Street, Rugby, CV21 3AP. Tel. 01788 573241 (for local address look in the telephone directory under 'relate' or 'Marriage Guidance')
Offers relationship and sexual counselling for couples and individuals.

*Step-Family* (National Step-Family Association), Chapel House, 18 Hatton Place, London EC1N 8RU. Tel. 020 7209 2460 (admin), 0990 168388 (telephone counselling)
An organisation that offers support to step-families.

# BOOKS

*Divorce: The Things You Never Thought You'd Need to Know* by Jill Black (paperfronts)
Jill Black explains the usual sequence of events and how things are set in motion. She translates the mumbo jumbo and officialese surrounding divorce into plain English.

*Divorce: Legal Procedures and Financial Facts* (The Consumer's association)
This covers legal advice, conciliation, legal aid and its drawbacks, the financial problems and the question of children.

*Helping Children Cope With Divorce* by Rosemary Wells (Sheldon Press)
Invaluable book for parents, grandparents or anyone else who wants to help a child through divorce.

*How it Feels When Parents Divorce* by Jill Krementz (Gollancz)
Children ranging from seven to sixteen years old discuss what their parents' divorce has meant to them. A book for young people of twelve and over to read.

*Mike's Lonely Summer: A Child's Guide Through Divorce*,  by Carolyn Nystrom (Lion)
A ten-year-old boy lives through his parents' divorce. Beautifully written and illustrated; from a religious book publisher. Ideal for young children up to the age of twleve.

*The Parent Book – Getting on Well With Our Children* by Ivan Sokolov and Deborah Hutton (Thorsons)
An excellent and practical book on communicating with children of any age, from babies to adolescents. It is helpful and reassuring, with plenty of experiences from other parents and practical exercises.

*Better Relationships* by Sarah Litvinoff (Vermilion)
The first RELATE guide, which deals comprehensively with relationship issues from first love to retirement, concentrating on communication, and using practical tasks to help couples cope with typical relationship problems.

*Sex in Loving Relationships* by Sarah Litvinoff (Vermilion)
A guide to improving the quality of your sex life by understanding your own and your partner's sexuality, using practical tasks from RELATE's sex therapists, and illustrated by dozens of real-life case histories.

*Step-parents and their Children* by Stephen Collins (Souvenir)
This practical and refreshing book presents a viewpoint that encourages a more relaxed and clear-sighted attitude to step-parenting.

*Note*: most of these books are available by post from the relate bookshop, Herbert Gray College, Little Church Street, Rugby, CV21 3AP.

# INDEX